IN THE ARENA

The NCAA's First Century

A physical space

THE ARENA is the tangible stage where athletics competition occurs: a manicured swath of grass, a rain-slicked quarter-mile oval, an island of polished hardwood in a sea of cheering fans. During the past century, student-athletes from all walks of life have competed against one another in venues equally as diverse. The characteristics of the physical arena may vary, but its essential purpose—providing a home for those driven to compete—remains constant.

A mental place

THE ARENA is a state of mind, a playing field where
the boundaries, hurdles and goals that most define athletic
competition are the ones not visible to the mere spectator.
For more than 100 years, the NCAA has championed the
intellectual growth that comes with participating in sports.
It is here, in the mental arena, that millions of student-athletes
confront their fears, realize their potential and achieve great
victories that no scoreboard could ever reflect.

FOOTBALL PIONEER WALTER CAMP IN 1880

IN THE ARENA

The NCAA's First Century

by JOSEPH N. CROWLEY

Staff for this book
THE NCAA
DAVID PICKLE, *Project manager*
MARTY BENSON, *Copy editor*
JACK COPELAND, *Editorial assistant*
ELLEN SUMMERS, *Librarian*
URSULA WALSH, *Researcher*

RICH CLARKSON AND ASSOCIATES, LLC
RICH CLARKSON, *Photography and design editor*
KATE GLASSNER BRAINERD, *Designer*
JENNIFER FINCH, *Photo editor*
JAMIE SCHWABEROW, STEPHEN NOWLAND
and CHRIS STEPPIG, *Photo research*

Published By The NCAA

Contents

PUBLISHED by THE NCAA
P.O. BOX 6222, INDIANAPOLIS, INDIANA 46202

FIRST PRINTING: January 2006
ISBN 0-9774-9460-9
Printed by AB HIRSCHFELD PRESS, Denver, Colorado

PREVIOUS SPREADS:
PAGE 2/3: HOUSTON'S MEN'S BASKETBALL TEAM DEFEATS UCLA
IN THE HOUSTON ASTRODOME BEFORE THE LARGEST CROWD
EVER RECORDED ON JANUARY 20, 1968.

PAGE 4/5: ON A WET DAY IN MAY, THE MOUNT UNION ANCHOR
OF THE 1,600-METER RELAY TEAM SMILES AS SHE CROSSES
THE FINISH LINE OF THE 1995 DIVISION III WOMEN'S OUTDOOR
TRACK AND FIELD CHAMPIONSHIPS.

SOME YEARS AGO, when I was serving a term as an NCAA officer, I suggested to the Association's executive director, Cedric Dempsey, that he consider commissioning an updated history of the organization. Jack Falla had written a book covering the Association's first 75 years, but much had happened since its publication in 1981. Reform had been an almost constant priority in the years that followed. Despite valiant and well-conceived efforts by the NCAA communications staff, the Association's leading role in reform was not well understood by the general public, which was conditioned to think of the organization as a regulatory monolith that functioned also as a defender of the status quo. The media often reported on the organization as though it were a distant, stony-hearted organization serving its own narrow bureaucratic interests instead of those of the members, somehow achieving this status even though the members had controlled it from the day it was born. From time to time, a member institution would offer a similar description, particularly if it had just been punished for violating rules it had participated in making. A better understanding was clearly needed. That is why I made the suggestion to Dempsey. He liked the idea and asked me if I would be interested in writing the book. I declined. I was an Association volunteer, but I also had a full-time job as president of the University of Nevada, Reno. There simply would not be enough time to do the work such a book would require.

The idea then took up residence on the proverbial back burner. Other matters demanded Dempsey's attention. He asked me again, five or six years later, after I left the campus presidency. Conversations ensued, but other priorities stood in the way. I still thought the book needed writing. If it was going to be done, however, someone else would have to be the author.

In spring 2003, David Pickle, the NCAA's managing director of publishing, called to tell me that the time for a new history was at hand. The Association Centennial would be celebrated in 2006. Would I be willing to consider the authorship of a Centennial history, Pickle asked. The third time proved to be the charm. We talked. I said I would need to have editorial freedom. It was readily granted. Thereupon, I swallowed hard and accepted the job.

Volunteers from the membership play important roles in the varied and complex operations of the NCAA. Over the years, thousands have served in a wide range of capacities — as officers, for example, and as members and chairs of the councils, boards, commissions, committees, cabinets and assorted ad hoc entities that make up the Association's governance structure. They are key decision-makers. The NCAA could not function without these volunteers. Indeed, for the organization's first 45 years, the Association was composed of nothing but volunteers because there was no staff. The volunteers — hundreds of them in any given year — still play a critical role. I have had the privilege of being one among the many since 1987, serving as member, chair or vice chair of this or that committee or council and spending a two-year term (1993-95) as Association president. This experience may help explain why I was asked to write the book. I thought I knew more than enough to do so. I was wrong. I still have much to learn.

One thing I did understand was the dedication of the NCAA staff. The Association is indisputably a creature of its membership. For 55 years, since the first staff member was appointed, service to the members has been the organization's primary responsibility. Walter Byers was the first staffer. He hired people who understood that responsibility. A number of them, Byers included, stayed with the NCAA for many years. Some still work there. Others went on to important positions on campuses, in conference offices and in other entities involved in intercollegiate athletics. I cannot name everyone, but I can propose that those listed here stand for all the others whose service has contributed so much to the NCAA's advancement.

Marjorie Fieber was Byers' first hire, and she remained with the Association for decades. Arthur Bergstrom, who came on board in 1956, was the NCAA's first full-time enforcement officer and later served as controller. Tom Jernstedt was part of an outstanding group of employees hired in the early to mid-1970s. He is now the Association's executive vice president and has been for years the individual primarily responsible for administering the Division I men's postseason basketball tournament. Wally Renfro belonged to the 1970s group and is now senior advisor to the NCAA president. David Berst, long-time head of enforcement, is currently vice president for Division I. Others who joined the staff during that decade and went on to serve in major positions include Dennis Cryder, a senior vice president; Tricia Bork; David Cawood; Steve Morgan; Louis Spry; Ron Stratten; and Ted Tow. Dennie Poppe, Lydia Sanchez, Fannie Vaughan, Jack Waters, Shirley Whitacre, Jim Wright and Pickle are others who have given long and valuable service to the Association.

Wayne Duke, the second person Byers appointed, was key to the NCAA's early development. He later became commissioner of the Big Ten Conference, establishing a pattern followed by Wiles Hallock (Pacific-10), Tom Hansen (also Pacific-10), Jim Delany (who followed Duke at the Big Ten) and Chuck Neinas, former Big Eight commissioner and subsequently executive director of the College Football Association.

People, after all, are the makers of history. The thousands of volunteers, and the staff members (those named here and many others) who cherished the work, set the example. Above all, they served the membership and have made a profound difference in the NCAA story as it is set forth on the following pages.

A century, obviously, is full of history, and anyone setting out to write about one will face the imperative of making choices. The choices in this volume, made with the help of many people, arise from the themes that have dominated the Association's development on a continuing basis. For the NCAA, the principal themes — fundamental at the beginning and fundamental today — are the commitment to amateurism and the connection between education and athletics in which education is the principal partner. Other important themes take their places in relation to these overriding emphases: the century of tension between the changing demands of home rule and the abiding desire for a level playing field; regulatory and enforcement responsibilities; governance and organization; external influences; diversity and inclusion; and the question of where within this complicated framework to put the student-athlete. The interplay among these elements and their evolving relationships with the fundamental themes help tell the story of a hundred years. The story plays out against a background of constant growth and change and periodic, often urgent, calls for reform.

This book emphasizes the Association's last 25 years. However, despite Falla's informative volume, it seemed wise to provide a historical context for the developments of those years. The book, that is to say, needed to begin at the beginning — indeed, before the beginning. Accordingly, the first chapter highlights the origins of collegiate sports, particularly football and including the game's ancestry traced to prior millennia and foreign soil. The late 19th century explosion of interest in campus athletics in the U.S., a corresponding concentration at that time on higher education in general, and the tie between the two, are explored in this chapter. The chapter concludes with the founding of the NCAA (under a different name) in 1906.

The second chapter summarizes the growth and problems of intercollegiate athletics, and the difficulties the Association faced in dealing with these matters, during the period 1906-51. This was a time, as noted, when the organization operated without staff and depended on institutional members and their conferences to protect the primacy of education and the principle of amateurism. College sports became very popular in these years. The institutional stake in them grew ever greater, and violations of basic NCAA policies increased in both frequency and prominence. Eventually, the strategy of dependence on home rule for enforcement proved a failure. By the end of the period, it was abundantly clear that a new approach was required.

That approach is at the heart of Chapter Three, which covers the years between 1951, when Walter Byers became the Association's first executive director, and 1981. At that time — with Byers still in charge — the Association embarked upon the eventful voyage that brought it to the start of its second century. Byers was the dominant figure in this era. He built an organization founded on enforcement of the rules and, as mentioned, a philosophy of service to the members. That entity developed a capacity for a growth and a capability to take on multiple challenges. Battles were fought. Some were lost. Many were won. After its first 75 years, the NCAA had evolved through the vision of Walter Byers. It was bigger, better, stronger — and it needed to be.

The fourth chapter addresses major changes in enforcement and governance since 1981 as well as the birth and growth of a reform agenda. That agenda was constructed around a strategy of enhancing both presidential involvement and educational primacy, the latter through a series of academic-eligibility requirements. Governance changes were a byproduct of increasing differences in the size, scope and cost of athletics programs among the membership. The old idea of like institutions being grouped together for competition purposes still had life and helped produce a divisional (and later, in Division I, a subdivisional) arrangement. "Federation" is the word employed for this arrangement. The word grew in importance as the years passed. The expansion of television's role and reach, as this chapter explains, moved the process along and gave rise to a critical question: Who controls the role and reach?

Continued growth, serious problems and the college game's prominent place in the public consciousness meant that entities outside the Association would take a strong interest in the NCAA's business. Such interest, again, was nothing new. The organization owed its establishment to President Theodore Roosevelt's insistence in October 1905 that campus leaders either stem the tide of violence in college football or eliminate the game. The federal government involved itself occasionally in other ways during the NCAA's first 75 years. But in the last quarter-century, external influences have become both more demanding of the Association's time and resources and more influential in its policy-making. The passage of Title IX produced programmatic, personnel and structural changes on a large scale, and antitrust legislation from the first part of the 20th century came to have a substantial impact in the 1980s and '90s. Other laws, notably in the area of equal protection, also have called the NCAA to account. Congressional hearings occasionally have carried the threat of further federal participation in the work of the Association. In recent years, a number of states have passed, or sought to pass, statutes challenging the NCAA's regulatory authority. And, as the American fascination with torts and courtrooms grew to weighty proportions in the 20th century's concluding decades, the Association often found itself caught up in complex litigation. Multiple eligibility issues, enforcement controversies, limits on coaching numbers and compensation, and equipment concerns are examples of this growing involvement. Interventions by Congress, several state legislatures, and state and federal judicial jurisdictions are covered in Chapter Five.

The NCAA's first 75 years ended, and the next quarter-century began, with a historic decision to bring women's sports into the Association fold. That action both symbolically and substantively introduced the modern era for intercollegiate athletics and the organization that governs them. The committee that recommended the action was chaired by a member institution chief executive, James Frank, who in the same year (1981) was chosen as the NCAA's first African-American president. Chapter Six considers the history of sports participation by college women dated from the mid-19th century. The chapter also examines notable milestones in the gradual growth of ethnic minority inclusion — as participants, coaches and administrators — in intercollegiate athletics. Title IX and the Association's responses to its requirements are discussed here, as are the substantial challenges that remain in achieving the Association's diversity goals.

The final chapter focuses on the arena as metaphor as a way of explaining the NCAA's growth from relatively modest beginnings to the point at which, in 2006, its field of view is worldwide. Roosevelt's observation about the man in the arena, reprinted in this book's prelude, must now at last include, by logical extension, the woman as well. The arena itself, once a place where football and a few other sports were played, has had to expand to allow for the presence of hundreds of thousands of student-athletes engaged in numerous sports in three divisions, many of them participating in the 88 championships the NCAA sponsors. Television has contributed to this growth, of course. Greater exposure has had ramifications for academics and amateurism, finance and governance, diversity and external interventions. Problems are more visible and critics more active. The Association, notwithstanding, has an important story to tell and a bigger picture of its makeup and activities to present. The reform agenda persists, pursued by new leadership within a new organizational structure. Chapter Seven reviews these major matters and the challenges they offer to maintaining the priority of education and the ethos of amateurism in the Association's second century.

Major developments during the first 100 years have had an impact on NCAA nomenclature. One significant adjustment, for instance, is in the title of the NCAA's chief executive officer. Byers was appointed in 1951 to the newly created position of executive director. In the wake of the mid-1990s restructuring, the chief executive designation was changed to president. That title, until then, had been held since 1906 by individuals from the membership whose terms were defined (usually two years), whose service was voluntary and whose office was roughly equivalent to that of a corporation's chairman of the board. Byers (1951-87) and Richard Schultz (1987-93) were executive directors. Cedric Dempsey was appointed to that position in 1994, but his title changed to president in 1998. Myles Brand, the current president, began his service in 2003. Before 1998, 31 men and one woman, volunteers all, filled the position of NCAA president. That position is now often referred to as "membership president," though that terminology is not used here. Relatedly, use of the vice president designation, previously associated with volunteers from the membership, also changed with restructuring and is now a title held by senior staff administrators.

Readers will observe that the print edition of the book does not include notes, citations or bibliography. The online edition, which will be made available in spring 2006, will feature the same text, along with notes, citations, a bibliography and a number of links and appendixes. The print edition does feature a timeline that highlights key developments in NCAA history, including many occurrences not mentioned in the main text.

ACKNOWLEDGEMENTS

IT HAS TAKEN at least a village to bring this book to publication. I owe a very large debt to David Pickle, whose assistance, understanding and wisdom have been exceptional and whose patience I have sorely tried and never once found wanting. I am similarly indebted to Ursula Walsh. Dr. Walsh was the NCAA's first director of research, a position she held for 12 years before her retirement in December 1997. She has served as my principal research assistant on this project, a title that does not begin to describe the extent, quality and variety of her contributions. She and David read every word I wrote (most of them more than once), offered many thoughtful suggestions and provided the kind of encouragement a writer needs when the challenge of the pen (the instrument I still use to commit words to paper) seems to fray the brain almost beyond repair. Ellen Summers, the Association's head librarian and archivist, answered my abundant queries promptly, accurately and cheerfully. She pursued data to remote locations, collected material for me in advance of every trip I took to Indianapolis and got needed documents to me in Reno on a moment's notice. Marty Benson, a master of economical expression and Association style, performed expert service in editing the drafts of an often profligate dispenser of written discourse whose hyphenation is suspect and who has never quite understood the function of a semicolon. Karen Cooper efficiently handled the requisite arrangements for my many visits to NCAA headquarters for research and related purposes.

I set out to interview all four of the Association's chief executive officers. Three responded favorably. I learned a great deal from my conversations with Messrs. Schultz, Dempsey and Brand, and I thank them for their time, candor and discernment. Walter Byers, unfortunately, was not available for an interview, but many people who worked with him and knew him well provided both insight and information on Byers' character and contributions. Others interviewed for the book — usually on a variety of subjects, sometimes including the Byers' era — were typically long-term NCAA staff members or volunteers who have held key positions in the organization. Most interviews were accomplished in person; a few were done via telephone or e-mail. My thanks for their invaluable assistance go to David Berst, Tricia Bork, Mike Cleary, Wayne Duke, Dan Dutcher, James Frank, Tom Hansen, Robert Hemenway, Judie Holland, Tom Jernstedt, Nancy Mitchell, Steve Morgan, David Price, Mike Racy, Wally Renfro, Louis Spry, Ted Tow and Ken Weller. Many of these individuals (Berst, Bork, Duke, Frank, Hansen, Jernstedt, Price, Spry, Tow and Weller) also read one or more draft chapters. I am grateful beyond words for their conscientious efforts to make those chapters better. Other readers, equally helpful, included Myles Brand, Elsa Cole and Judy Sweet from the NCAA, and William Delauder, Carolyn Femovich, Jeff Orleans, Valerie Richardson and Charles Whitcomb, whose Association involvements have been important and extensive. In Reno, I received substantial help on Chapter Five from my daughter Margaret Magera, Professor James Richardson and Randy Myers, librarian of the National Judicial College.

Other people from whose time, conversation or other assistance I benefited were NCAA Senior Vice President Bernard Franklin; Todd Petr, Randy Dick and Clint Newlin of the Association's research staff; NCAA librarians Lisa Greer Douglass and Mary Johnston; Patricia Schaefer of the office of general counsel; Lydia Sanchez, director of executive affairs for Myles Brand; Gary Brown, Jack Copeland and Nancy Ettinger of the publishing division; Greg Shaheen, Division I men's basketball; Chris Farrow, corporate and broadcast alliances; and former staff member Keith Gill. Rich Clarkson, who coordinated production and photography issues, needs to be thanked, along with Kate Glassner Brainerd (design) and Jennifer Finch (photo acquisition). So do Dennis Cryder and John Johnson, key administrators for the Centennial project of which this book is a part. I also need to thank Karl Benson, Western Athletic Conference commissioner; Sheldon Steinbach of the American Council on Education; Richard Lapchick, executive director of the National Consortium for Academics and Sports; attorney Dennis Cross; and, at the University of Nevada, Victor Atkocaitis and Steven Zink of the Getchell Library; sports historian Richard Davies; Faculty Athletics Representative Christopher Exline; Director of Athletics Cary Groth and former directors Chris Ault and Richard Trachok. Also at the university, typing and proofreading help was provided by Kristen Kabrin of the political science department and, from the Reynolds School of Journalism, by Drew Johnson, Chris McQuattie and Robert Stewart. Emily Frega, Tina Lindstrom, Professor Donica Mensing and Mark Smith offered important technical assistance. Barbara Trainor, assistant to the dean of journalism, was always ready to make help and supplies available, and Dean Cole Campbell generously blessed the participation of members of his staff.

There is always a home front in the book-writing business. The writing of this book has demanded copious amounts of patience, understanding and encouragement from my wife Joy. She and I share the good fortune of having our entire family — children and their spouses and children — living in Reno. This is a very close family, and all 15 of its members have been supportive beyond the call. That includes our seven grandchildren, who I hope understand why for a time I had to surrender my grandfather's merit badge.

All of the people listed above, and others as well, are citizens of the village that has raised this book. It is important to point out, as ever in these matters, that they bear no responsibility for any errors or shortcomings. That responsibility belongs exclusively to the author, a village elder of sorts, who steps forward here to accept it in its entirety.

—JOE CROWLEY, September 2005

"It is not the critic who counts; nor the man who points out how the strong man stumbles, or where the doer of deeds could have done them better. The credit belongs to the man who is actually in the arena, whose face is marred by dust and sweat and blood; who strives valiantly; who errs, who comes short again and again, because there is no effort without error and shortcomings; but who does actually strive to do the deeds; who knows great enthusiasms, the great devotions; who spends himself in a worthy cause; who at the best knows in the end the triumph of high achievement, and who at the worst if he fails, at least fails while daring greatly, so that his place shall never be with those cold and timid souls who neither know victory nor defeat."

—THEODORE ROOSEVELT

April 23, 1910

THEODORE ROOSEVELT IN HIS HARVARD SCULLING UNIFORM, CIRCA 1877

doer of deeds...

"It is not the critic who counts; nor the man who points out how the strong man stumbles, or where the doer of deeds could have done them better...

FOUR-TIME DIVISION II WRESTLING CHAMPION
TIM WRIGHT OF SOUTHERN ILLINOIS UNIVERSITY, EDWARDSVILLE.

ALICE BARNES OF STANFORD AT THE 2005 DIVISION I WOMEN'S TENNIS CHAMPIONSHIPS.

THE 2005 MEN'S FINAL FOUR NATIONAL ANTHEM CEREMONY PHOTO BY STEPHEN NOWLAND/NCAA PHOTOS

PHOTO BY TREVOR BROWN JR./ NCAA PHOTOS

SYRACUSE'S CHRIS CERCY AND PRINCETON'S KYLE BAUGHER FACE OFF AT THE 2000 MEN'S DIVISION I LACROSSE CHAMPIONSHIP.

THE 2005 WOMEN'S FINAL FOUR OPENING TIP-OFF PHOTO BY JAMIE SCHWABEROW/NCAA PHOTOS

who strives

...The credit belongs to the man who is actually in the arena, whose face is marred by dust and sweat and blood; who strives valiantly...

JUDY GEER, A PIONEER IN WOMEN'S SPORTS, CAPTAINED THE ROWING AND SWIMMING TEAMS AT DARTMOUTH.

who errs

...who errs, who comes short again and again,
because there is no effort without
error and shortcomings...

who knows

...but who does actually strive to do the deeds; who knows great enthusiasms, the great devotions; who spends himself in a worthy cause...

the triumph

*...who at the best knows in the end
the triumph of high achievement,
and who at the worst if he fails...*

NAKITA LEWIS OF SLIPPERY ROCK COMPETES IN THE TRIPLE JUMP
AT THE 2000 DIVISION II WOMEN'S TRACK AND FIELD CHAMPIONSHIPS.

THE 200-YARD BACKSTROKE (LEFT) GETS OFF TO A FAST START
DURING THE 1997 DIVISION III SWIMMING AND DIVING CHAMPIONSHIPS.

while daring greatly

...at least fails while daring greatly,
so that his place shall never be with those cold
and timid souls who neither know victory nor defeat.

1983 POMMEL-HORSE CHAMPION DOUG KIESO OF NORTHERN ILLINOIS PHOTO COURTESY OF THE NCAA

ANCESTRY

FOOTBALL SPAWNED the NCAA, but how that sport started is another question. To some extent, the answer is shrouded in the mists of history. Evidence springs from the distant past of sporting contests around the world involving the convergence of foot and ball, though the latter object may have been an animal bladder, an animal or human skull, or even an entire human head. The Greeks of old had such a game (*harpaston*), as did the Romans (*harpastrum*). The Ts'in and Han Dynasties had their own form of football-type competition in the third century B.C., and such games may have been played in China even earlier. The ancient Egyptians, Japanese, Berbers, South American Indians, South Seas islanders and Arctic Eskimos are all part of the historical picture, as are the British, whose football tradition extends to the Middle Ages. The British game employed pig bladders, was played in the countryside as well as in the cities, was exceptionally violent and was banned by a string of monarchs beginning with Edward II in 1314. Team numbers varied, with dozens or even hundreds of members playing on fields sometimes several miles long. The contests endangered life, limb, property and the public order, and they kept the yeoman players from perfecting the archery and other skills the kingdom needed for warfare. A 16th century observer wrote that, for the players, "footeball" meant:

> *Sometymes their necks are broken, sometymes their backes, sometymes their*
> *legges, sometymes their armes, sometymes one parte thrust out of joynt,*
> *sometymes another … And hereof groweth envie, malice, rancour, cholour,*
> *hatred, displeasure, enmitie, and what not els. And sometymes fightying,*
> *braulying, contention, quarrel picking, murther, homicide, and great effusion*
> *of bloud, as experience daily teacheth.*

Still, neither adverse publicity, nor routine violence, nor royal bans kept British men from sustaining the game for several centuries.

Football of the pig bladder variety arrived on American shores (Virginia and New England) with the first colonists. In Massachusetts, the new arrivals were surprised perhaps to discover the natives playing a sport they called *Pasuckqualkohwog* (meaning, "they gather to play football"). The British Colonial variety was wild and perilous, just as it had been across the Atlantic. The Puritans, as one author suggested, were "a dour lot for whom frolic was akin to sacrilege." That view may have explained football's banishment from Boston in 1657 and why the game eventually disappeared as a common American pastime for nearly two centuries. Students at Princeton in the 1820s played ballown, a game that began with the fist as a feature and later incorporated the foot. Intramural competitions of various sorts were staged on campuses in the 1840s and '50s, including Harvard's freshman-sophomore free-for-alls forbidden by the faculty in 1860. Still, it was not until after the Civil War that football (in assorted forms) became a major college sport.

Walter Camp — the famous Yale player and coach, principal arbiter of the rules for three decades, the man who founded and for years selected the annual All-America team, and reputedly the model for the fictional Frank Merriwell — said that football in this country could be dated to the early 1860s, when a 17-year-old boy named Gerritt Smith Miller got some of his fellow students at Boston's Dixwell Latin School to join him in forming the Oneida Football Club. The Oneidas played, among other opponents, a team composed of boys from the Boston Latin and Boston English schools. This game, played in 1863, is still commemorated by a monument on the Boston Common. Miller's team was undefeated, untied and unscored upon for four years. The sport seems to have been more soccer than anything else. Indeed, the National Soccer Hall of Fame claims the Oneidas as that sport's first organized club in America and houses the ball

PHOTO COURTESY THE NCAA

WALTER CAMP, YALE PLAYER AND COACH

WALTER CAMP AT THE 1921 CONVENTION: At "Princeton College in 1787 there was a law which said, 'Whereas the game played on the rear campus by the boys with the bat and ball is rude and unbecoming to gentlemen and tends to injure the health of our young men, it is forbidden.' I cannot find that the law was ever erased,…but the young men came up and pushed it off the boards."

MONTANA'S JOSH BRANNEN (21) GETS TIED UP IN THE
MARSHALL DEFENSE DURING THE 1995 DIVISION I-AA FOOTBALL CHAMPIONSHIP.

THE BALL USED IN 1863 BY BOSTON
HIGH SCHOOL BOYS WHO HAD RECENTLY
FOUNDED THE ONEIDA FOOTBALL CLUB,
THE FIRST FOOTBALL CLUB IN THE U.S.
COURTESY CAPITAL HISTORIC NEW ENGLAND / SPNEA

PAINTING OF CHARLES GOODYEAR
PHOTO COURTESY GOODYEAR TIRE & RUBBER CO.

used in that famous 1863 game.

That relic was made from vulcanized rubber, Charles Goodyear having designed and produced the first such balls in 1855. His invention clearly separated football — whether soccer, rugby or the American game — from its pig bladder past and paved the way for the explosion of contests that shortly began to capture the attention of sporting enthusiasts. On November 6, 1869, Rutgers and Princeton met in New Brunswick, New Jersey, for what came to be regarded as the first intercollegiate football competition in American history. Princeton football, it was reported, had been "born under [the] benevolent gaze" of the institution's new president (a Scotsman named James McCosh). The teams played 25 men to a side. The ball again was of the soccer type. Scoring was done by goals. The National Soccer Hall of Fame asserts that what happened that afternoon was the first American intercollegiate soccer game (though there were also some rugby features in the rules of play that day). Whichever sport truly owns this game, the players called it football. There was much more to come.

Columbia fielded a team in 1870, Yale in 1872, Harvard in 1874 and Pennsylvania in 1876. As in 1869, Princeton and Rutgers played two games that latter year and again the rules differed from one game to the other. Rules generally were in a chaotic state at the time, although these two teams, along with Yale and Columbia, made an effort at standardization beginning in 1873. In 1876 two important rules changes debuted — a leather oval ball and 11 players to a side. Amos Alonzo Stagg was, with Camp, the most famous football figure of the era of growth that stretched from the last third of the 19th century through the first decades of the 20th. Stagg believed American-style football started in 1876. Others, perhaps including Camp, pointed to 1874. That was the year McGill University came from Canada to play Harvard and persuaded the Crimson to adopt their Northern neighbor's rugby-like approach. That sport bore a much closer kinship to the game into which American football would evolve.

CHAOS AND CONTROL

FOOTBALL WAS NOT, of course, the only sport offering intercollegiate competition during these years. Harvard and Yale raced boats as early as 1852, and the first multi-college regatta was held in 1859. Baseball made its college debut that same year when Amherst, playing under "Boston" rules, beat Williams, 73-32. The sport that was to be known as the national pastime emerged from the Civil War as a very popular game on U.S. campuses. Because the game was typically played by college teams using non-students and professionals, baseball produced serious challenges to rules reformers later on. Other college sports, football included, employed similar practices, but baseball's hired-gun customs proved especially resilient. Intercollegiate track and field appeared in 1876. That same year, the Turf Exchange in New York City provided a kind of parimutuel wagering on the college regatta at Lake Saratoga. This was not the first example of gambling on college sports, and rowing was not to be the only sport affected.

The pig bladder variety of football may have been only an artifact of history by this time, but brutal play was still very much in vogue. The so-called mass (or mass-momentum) plays appeared in the 1880s. The "v-trick" became the celebrated wedge formation, which evolved into the flying wedge, with options that included the turtleback, the Minnesota shift and the notorious hurdle play. As for the latter, Benjamin Ide Wheeler, president of the University of California, gave us a colorful description:

> Two rigid rampart-like lines of human flesh have been created, one of
> defense, the other of offense, and behind the latter is established a catapult
> to fire through a porthole opened in the offense ramparts a missile composed
> of four or five human bodies globulated about a carried football with a
> maximum initial velocity against the presumably weakest point in the
> opposing rampart.

These globulated bodies could actually be the launching pad for the hurdle play. The carried football required a carrier, and that individual was the missile that was to conclude its flight on the other side of the defense. The job of the defense, then as now, was to find a way to stop whatever new wrinkles had been installed by the offense. The answer was to launch a defensive missile. The result, as NCAA historian Jack

Falla described it, was a "midair collision" likely to put both player-missiles in pain and out of the game.

Mass plays, in almost universal use by the early 1890s, were nearly the death of football. Serious injuries abounded because of the absence of adequate protective padding, along with what seems to have been the individually optional use of insubstantial helmets. The Intercollegiate Football Association (IFA), formed in 1873, changed some rules in 1876, moving away from soccer and toward rugby, but was largely ineffectual in stemming the violence that was so characteristic of the game in the 1880s and '90s. It was difficult even to keep the four members of the IFA on the same page regarding rules and practices.

This was true nationwide since the long-standing principle of home rule made it difficult for associations such as the IFA first to agree on something and then to follow through. One or another IFA member occasionally left the group over a disagreement, or dropped football for a season or two. When Harvard and Columbia withdrew in the early 1890s, leaving only Yale and Princeton as members, the Intercollegiate Football Association collapsed.

A successor organization, the American Football Rules Committee, was soon established. It made further alterations in standards and procedures, but — apart from rather modest efforts to eliminate or moderate abusive behaviors — it was able to do little to curb the brutality. Meanwhile, two other problems — recruiting and subsidization — needed attention. The student groups who typically took charge of intercollegiate sports in the post-Civil War period (raising and allocating funds, hiring coaches, scheduling games, filling rosters and, in general, managing the enterprise) hired players and allowed them to compete as non-students. The students were often aided by alumni, who sometimes were part of the organization (and sometimes were themselves the principals). These organizations frequently resisted attempts to alter the questionable practices. In many cases, they also fought attempts to curb the game's violence.

A set of circumstances involving three Midwestern universities is instructive. In 1894, Indiana believed Purdue to be recruiting the Hoosiers' football captain from the year before and to have made a financial offer to enhance its chances of success. Indiana tried to retain the player, but he ended up at Michigan. In 1893, according to coach Stagg, the Wolverines had seven football players who were not enrolled in classes. This use of "ringers," wrote Stagg, "was duplicated in most colleges at that or earlier periods."

Fielding Yost's brief career as a ringer provides another enlightening example. Yost was the "point-a-minute" football coach at Michigan (1901-26), whose teams had a record of 55-1-1 and a scoring margin of 2,821-42 during his first five seasons. He became a strong supporter of strict academic and eligibility standards in his later coaching years. But as a star player at West Virginia in 1896, he transferred to Lafayette in mid-season, expressing an interest in the engineering program there. He played one game, against that institution's traditional rival (undefeated Pennsylvania), then — the attraction of engineering apparently having diminished — transferred back to West Virginia the next week. Lafayette, with much help from Yost, won the game.

It's not clear whether James Hogan was a ringer, but at age 27, at the turn of the 20th century, he was doing well for himself as a football player at Yale. That institution paid his tuition and gave him a luxurious suite of rooms, free meals at the University Club, a $100 scholarship and (shared with two others) all profits from game-day program sales. He also was made the New Haven agent for the American Tobacco Company, receiving a commission for every package of cigarettes sold in that city. And, during the fall semester, but after the football season, he was awarded a 10-day vacation in Cuba.

Practices such as these sounded increasingly louder alarms elsewhere on college campuses. Faculty members, who had had little say on athletics matters at most institutions, started to assert themselves in the 1890s. At Harvard, a faculty committee sought to discontinue the football team in 1893. That effort failed, although Harvard did drop the "demoralizing ... and extremely dangerous" sport after the 1894 season. Similar endeavors were underway in the Midwest. At Wisconsin, faculty members, considering football to be a menace, attempted to have it abolished shortly after the turn of the century. Student management of athletics had left the program in difficult financial straits and general disarray. For three years, football's fate in Madison was uncertain. A similar situation occurred at Michigan and other institutions in the region. In 1906, faculty representatives from Wisconsin, Michigan and other institutions in the then-Western Conference met in Chicago to discuss possible changes, and recommended several. These ideas included one year of residency before eligibility to play (and thus only three years of allowable competition); satisfactory academic performance by players; coaching appointments restricted to institutional staff members (no "professional" coaches)

PALMER PIERCE AT THE 1907 CONVENTION, CITING PRESS CRITICISM OF ABUSES DURING 1905: "For instance, one prominent player was said to have derived hundreds of dollars from the privilege of furnishing programs for games; another received the profit from a special brand of cigarettes named after him; a third was the ostensible head of an eating club, while others were in the employ of rich college graduates."

FIELDING YOST WAS A STAR PLAYER FOR WEST VIRGINIA IN 1896.

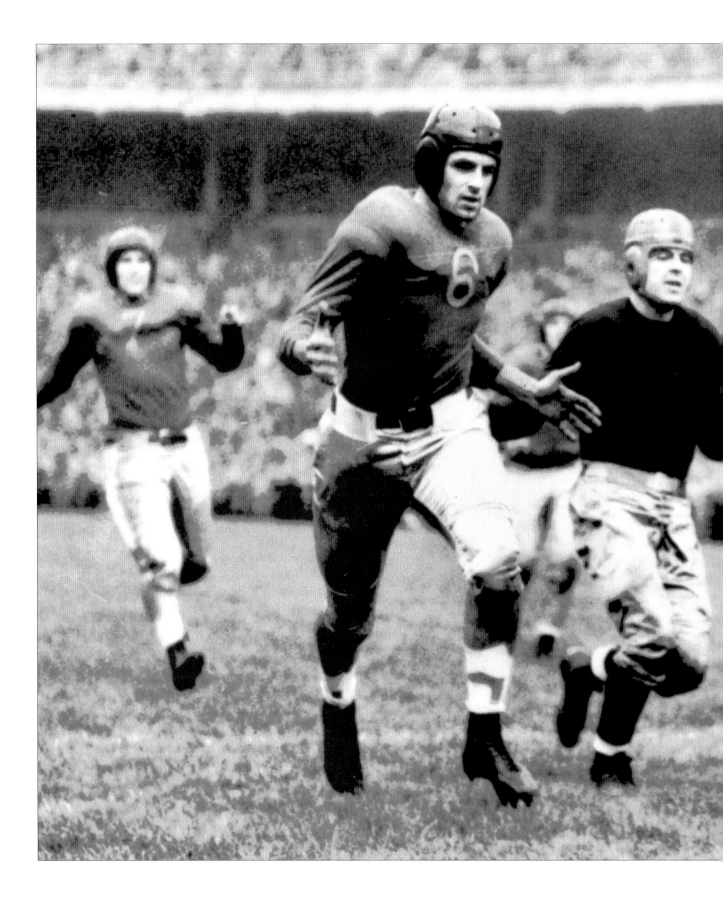

WILLIAM HOWARD TAFT AT THE 1915 CONVENTION: "It is not possible for a man to grow old in college athletics by studying first for one degree and then another until he becomes a man of thirty or thirty-five. That was a great abuse in my day. A man could go through the academic department, then through the scientific department, and then through the law school, and then through the divinity school, and then through the medical school and continue to win victories on the diamond or the football field until he had nearly passed the military age."

NOTRE DAME'S ANDY PILNEY (IN DARK SHIRT) FUMBLES AGAINST OHIO STATE, 1935.

PHOTO COURTESY THE NCAA

AMOS ALONZO STAGG

at regular faculty salaries; cost reductions; and cheap fees for student admission to athletics contests. The meeting was also directed toward developing stronger faculty control over athletics programs.

When these ambitious changes were brought back to the Michigan campus, a "storm of indignation" from students, alumni and university regents ensued. The latter group in 1907 abolished the faculty Board in Control of Athletics, which had pushed for the changes, and created a new entity friendlier to the cause of less stringent reform. As a result, the conference removed the university from membership in 1908.

Earlier, faculty boards of control were encroaching on the students' long-held territory at a number of institutions. Charles Eliot, Harvard's nationally prominent, veteran president, had established the first one in the 1880s. Others followed. Multiple member organizations were forming in this period (notably the Western Conference — formally established as the Intercollegiate Conference of Faculty Representatives in January 1895 — and the Southern Intercollegiate Athletic Association, which began life three weeks earlier). Brown University led an effort to bring faculty representatives from the Ivy Group together to produce a reform agenda. These initiatives were not only aimed at increasing faculty influence over athletics programs but also were intended to restore the principle of amateurism and move toward a greater standardization of rules.

PRESIDENTIAL PERSPECTIVES

SINCE THE QUESTION of when football or other college sports reached a point of crisis has arisen on virtually every occasion down through the decades, one might ask where the campus presidents were in this era of change and challenge. The answer is unclear, at least in terms of there being at the time a single, overarching theme describing presidential feelings about football. Some examples from around the country illustrate that point.

Harvard's Eliot was probably typical of many of his presidential colleagues. He was an advocate of physical culture, which played out in his time as a commitment to strengthening both mind and body. He had been a rower as an undergraduate, and he remained interested in that sport, and others such as track and field, during his 40 years in the presidency. But he had disdain for the popular sports, born at least in part of his devotion to the amateur ideal and his opposition to the paying of players and commercialization of the game. He thus was anxious about the direction football was headed. Eliot regarded the sport as "more brutalizing than prize-fighting, cock-fighting or bull-fighting." It was, he wrote, "an undesirable game for gentlemen to play, or for multitudes of spectators to watch." His creation of a faculty board of control for athletics has been noted, although he ultimately preserved an ample role for students and alumni on that body. Despite Eliot's misgivings and his periodic efforts to ban the game from his campus, Harvard took football seriously. For example, William Reid was recruited from the state of California to serve as coach in 1905 at a salary and expense allowance of $7,000. That sum exceeded the compensation of every faculty member. For the game with Yale that fall, 43,000 fans filled the two-year-old Harvard stadium. Some claim a place for Eliot as a leading reformer in athletics matters, probably because he was assuredly a spokesman for major higher education reform and perhaps simply because he was a Harvard man. Other college presidents of the time were more involved.

For instance, Michigan's James Burrill Angell strongly supported reform, amending and standardizing rules, and enhancing faculty control. He was not ready to abolish football, as some faculty leaders wanted, but he was committed to significant change. He was a central figure in gathering Western Conference faculty representatives for the aforementioned 1906 reform meeting. His peer at Wisconsin, Charles Van Hise, adopted a similar position. At Chicago, President William Rainey Harper took a more complex, bolder tack.

Harper brought an amazing record of accomplishment with him when he became Chicago's founding president in 1891 at age 35. This brilliant, charismatic, creative visionary was a risk-taker and a man in constant purposeful motion. His view of the role of athletics in the academy set him apart from most other presidents. Stagg was one of his first hires, becoming the director of the nation's first department of physical culture and athletics. Harper anchored both the department and Stagg firmly in the academic structure of the institution. The new director was appointed as a faculty member and was paid like one. He taught classes. He coached three sports. He also played two of them, a common practice in the early 1890s. He was, in effect if not in title, the director of athletics. He was to be eventually something of a national figure in the cause of reform, even if he was not ready at the outset of his tenure to embrace the elimination of mass plays (and, indeed, asserted ownership of the turtleback idea).

Harper famously stated that "the athletic field, like the gymnasium, is one of the university's laboratories and by no means the least important one." He wanted a well-rounded athletics program for both men and women but understood that football was the marquee game. He placed great value on the sport as a way to build ties with the community. He occasionally visited the Chicago dressing room at halftime to cheer his boys on. And yet he was clear and emphatic that Chicago's players were expected to compete in the classroom as well as on the field, that there would be no hired athletes and that he was not disposed to join the march toward ever-bigger stadiums. ("It is not," he said, "the function of the university to provide at great cost spectacular entertainment for enormous crowds of people.") The Maroons played their games at what Stagg called a "home-made field."

Back East, the undergraduate Woodrow Wilson was one of the directors of Princeton's football team as an undergraduate in the late 1870s. As a young professor at Wesleyan (Connecticut), he served as a coach, helping the team captain develop plays. He was also an enthusiastic fan. On at least one occasion, when Wesleyan was losing to Lehigh, he played the role of cheerleader. Later, as president of his alma mater (1902-10), his cheerleading experiences behind him, he became a determined athletics reformer.

Yale's president during Wilson's tenure as Princeton's leader was Arthur Twining Hadley. He was cut from a cloth somewhat similar to Wilson's, except that Hadley's strong attachment to football in his presidential years was more comparable to the future U.S. president's youthful and exuberant embrace of the sport during his Wesleyan appointment. Hadley attended football and other contests regularly. He also went to practices. His letters to his children contained references to the abilities of various players and his thoughts about the prospects for the team. He was absolutely a football devotee. Camp was Yale's coach, which probably contributed to Hadley's strong support for athletics. Camp's standing as a leader in developing new rules — even while protecting against major changes — also may have contributed to the president's espousal of certain reforms.

Out West, David Starr Jordan, Stanford's founding president, was not aboard the reform bandwagon. He had displayed distaste for football during his seven years as president of Indiana, and his attitude had not changed when he moved to Palo Alto. Jordan was a member of the sound-mind/sound-body school. He played on the faculty baseball team until he was 58 years old. Football reform did not interest him. He found the game's violence intolerable and described the sport as "fundamentally a battle between hired gladiators." His goal was abolition. When he had the opportunity early in the 20th century, he was the key person in getting football dropped at a number of California universities. Rugby became the Golden State's game of choice for several years, which pleased Jordan's colleague at Berkeley. President Wheeler thought rugby, and soccer, to be "the heartiest and manliest of the Anglo-Saxon sports."

However much campus presidents influenced the course of events for American-style football, whatever the degree of faculty involvement, and no matter what efforts conferences and other bodies made to clean up and standardize the rules, football remained in serious trouble as the 1890s wound down. Yes, the sport was still wildly popular. Game-day crowds grew, and more universities were fielding teams. However, football was staring hard at the prospect of demise. The choice offered by President Roosevelt in 1905 was at hand: reform or abolish. How had American higher education gotten itself into this predicament? Why in this country, unlike elsewhere in the world, had universities developed such a

MICHIGAN'S ADOLF SCHULTZ, 1907

PHOTO COURTESY THE NCAA

PALMER PIERCE AT THE 1910 CONVENTION: "If we succeed in eradicating the 'win-at-any-cost' spirit on college athletic fields, the civic life of this country undoubtedly will be wonderfully benefited."

close association with an intercollegiate sport that provided entertainment and spectacle on a grand scale while seemingly having little relationship to the noble purposes of the academy?

It's a fair question, one that generations of critics have asked; a question that, in various guises, would arise in assorted assemblies of the NCAA for a century to come.

THE GAME AND THE ACADEMY

FORMER NCAA EMPLOYEE Kay Hawes has written that the Association's "father was football and its mother was higher education." This was, she noted, an "almost unintentional union," brought about in part by the proclivity of students to play games. They demonstrated that bias through their increasing numbers of on-campus matches and melees in the pre-Civil War years. Young Mr. Miller offered further evidence with his Oneida club and its interscholastic contests in the 1860s. Intercollegiate competition seemed a natural outgrowth of these activities. The role of alumni in supporting, financing and even administering college teams helped cement the tie between institutions and their athletics programs. Alumni associations were often born in the late 19th century precisely out of a shared commitment to the control and promotion of these programs. Competition with each other was known among the great British universities, which served for so long and in so many ways as the model for American higher education. In turn, those universities, anchored in the traditions of classical education, owed much to the Greeks.

The mind and body were entwined in Greek philosophy and practice. Education had among its missions the proper development of both. The British universities, committed to the education of gentlemen, held similar views and passed them on to their institutional progeny in America. Small wonder, then, that an American professor at West Point would observe to an appreciative audience at the third annual Convention of the Intercollegiate Athletic Association of the United States (IAAUS) that:

> The Athenian Greek was the most perfect natural man that history records; certainly the most consummate physical being the world has known, and in his education the care and development of his body came first. In the Palestra, the Gymnasium, … the Greek youth was taught to make his body a perfect habitation for his mind …

The professor went on to state his claim for American colleges and universities "that the body deserves the same compulsory systematic training at the hands of educators as does the mind." The "spectacle of skilled athletes matching their powers in a fair, generous, courageous struggle for mastery is inspiring," he remarked and, further, "athletics on a high ethical basis are a splendid training in self-restraint, in chivalric bearing, [and] in decision of character …" Even so, he concluded, here in America the ethics of athletics were flawed. Imbedded in the mind-body relationship, in these values — fairness, generosity, courage, character, self-restraint, chivalric bearing, high ethical standards — is that noble amateur ideal. The professor spoke for a legion of college educators, presidents included, in proclaiming these values and that ideal, and the shortcomings of American higher education in achieving it. Here, as in the old country, Americans were in the business of educating gentlemen. That remained a goal in Britain. On this side of the Atlantic, by the time the professor addressed the 1908 Convention of the IAAUS, other goals had begun to get in the way.

The decades after the Civil War came to be regarded as the first Golden Age of American higher education. The classical curriculum imported from Britain in the 17th century was under siege in those years. The curriculum was rigid, made up of required courses, and the route to an undergraduate degree at most colleges was largely the same for all students. Apart from medicine and law, education in the professions — business, engineering, agriculture, journalism and the rest — had been relatively rare. These curricula were being added. Eliot introduced a radical change at Harvard by permitting students to take elective courses. Institutions of higher education were no longer the almost exclusive preserve of small numbers of young white males. Black colleges were established during the Golden Age, as were colleges for women. The American college, now with many more programs to offer, was turning into a university. Following the objectives set forth by Sen. Justin Morrill in his ambitious 1862 legislation, land grant universities, designed to reach the masses in a variety of ways, were being organized in every state.

Wealthy men deployed large resources toward the founding of major institutions, such as Chicago, Stanford, Cornell and Johns Hopkins. Graduate programs based on the Continental concept were instituted. Scholarly research consequently took on new meaning on American campuses.

In retrospect, this era was almost revolutionary. Hallowed traditions and philosophies were altered, bent and broken at what was for universities an astonishing speed. The old British model endured, of course, but it gave up a lot of ground. Borrowing ingredients from other countries and inventing some of its own, the fundamentally democratic American model of higher education took root during this time. The country was not geared toward just educating gentlemen anymore. We were building a system that ultimately would be open, in one venue or another, to anyone who wanted to come through the door.

With all that happened in higher education's Golden Age, it is understandable that the ancient ideal of amateurism gave way in some measure. Football was involved in that journey. Along with other popular sports, the game that was championed by some and despised by others emerged in a boisterous era, when the meaning of American higher education changed dramatically. Campuses expanded their landscapes and aspired, as the poet said, to contain multitudes. Sports were part of the change of meaning, part of the expansion and among the multitudes. Carnegie Foundation President Henry Pritchett took rather unhappy note of this development in his preface to the foundation's 1929 study of American college athletics. What happened to football, he wrote, could "only be understood by a review of the transformation of the… college of 50 years ago into the present-day American university." Pritchett's perspective was elitist. He frowned upon what had happened to both football and higher education.

For the Greeks as for the British, amateurism was a central component of elite education. In America, the amateur ideal provided an anchor, a tie to the past, perhaps a symbol of continuity. That ideal would need to change and stretch as higher education became a major vehicle of democratization, with college sports playing a key role. The continuing challenge for American colleges and universities, emerging as part of Pritchett's historic transformation, was to preserve the fundamental principle and ethical essence of amateurism while applying it in a thriving democratic environment. That too would be the NCAA's constant challenge.

REFORM OR ABOLISH

HAWES WAS CORRECT in observing that the union of football and higher education was "almost unintentional." No one set out to be matchmaker. The NCAA's parents were not starry-eyed lovers. They had a troubled relationship from the beginning. They were trying to make a go of it, after all, in circumstances beset with cross-purposes and conflicting principles. Many reforms were offered, and some implemented, to try to make the union work. Reformers made some progress in curbing recruiting and subsidization abuses. Modest but important advances were made in standardizing the rules of football. The chaos and financial irregularities so often a part of student control of athletics abated considerably as faculty committees assumed stronger oversight. Institutional presidents were more involved in seeking solutions to the dilemmas of college sport. But, despite improvements made to protect players through rules changes and the prohibition of certain behaviors, the specter of violence still haunted the game as the 20th century arrived. Mass play was still popular. Injuries were still common. Death was becoming a factor. The 18 fatalities and 149 serious injuries of the 1905 season brought critics out in force. Condemnations from the press were plentiful. Outrage grew among the American people. Something had to give.

In October 1905, Theodore Roosevelt invited representatives from Harvard, Yale and Princeton (known then as "the Big Three") to the White House. A month earlier, he had been the key person in ending the Russo-Japanese War, winning the Nobel Peace Prize for this

1906 (March 31) —The first constitution and bylaws of the IAAUS are issued.

1906 (December 29) —First Convention of IAAUS is held at Murray Hill Hotel in New York City (first report of Football Rules Committee).

1907 —**James Naismith**, credited with the invention of basketball, steps down as men's basketball coach at the University of Kansas, where his teams compiled a 55-60 record beginning in 1898.

PHOTO FROM NCAA FILES

1909 —IAAUS football rules change in response to 33 football-related deaths; movement to abolish the sport is stopped.

1910 (December 29) —IAAUS changes name to National Collegiate Athletic Association.

1914 (November 21) —Yale Bowl opens with Yale vs. Harvard football game.

1916 —Brown University's Frederick "Fritz" Pollard becomes the first African-American back named to an all-America team in football.

PHOTO COURTESY BROWN UNIVERSITY ARCHIVES

1918 —Future actor, singer and activist **Paul Robeson** concludes athletics career at Rutgers University, in which he earned 12 varsity letters in four sports and is selected as a football all-American.

1921 (June 17-18) —The first NCAA-sponsored championship, the National Collegiate Track and Field Championships, is conducted at University of Chicago. Sixty-two teams participate.

1922 (December 28) —Ten-point code adopted (conferences, amateurism, freshman rule, ban on playing pro football, three-year participation, no graduate students, faculty control, anti-betting, ban on playing for noncollegiate teams).

1924 (April 11-12) —First National Collegiate Swimming Championships are conducted at the U.S. Naval Academy).

PHOTO COURTESY OKLAHOMA STATE UNIVERSITY SPORTS INFO OFFICE

1928 (March 30-31) —First National Collegiate Wrestling Championships are conducted at Iowa State University. **Oklahoma A&M University** (now Oklahoma State) wins first of 11 team titles between 1928 and 1940 under coach E.C. "Ed" Gallagher.

1931 (December 31) —First "round table conferences" conducted at Convention.

1935 (June 21-22) —Ohio State University's **Jesse Owens** becomes the first (and remains the only) athlete to win four individual titles in one year at  the NCAA Outdoor Track and Field Championships (held at the University of California, Berkeley);a year later, he repeats the feat (in Chicago) to become the first and only athlete to win eight career outdoor individual titles.

THEODORE ROOSEVELT AT THE WHITE HOUSE, 1903.

PHOTO COURTESY THEODORE ROOSEVELT COLLECTION, HARVARD COLLEGE LIBRARY

accomplishment. Now, he faced the challenge of bringing some peace to football. He was a fan, but he knew the need for change. Roosevelt gave his visitors a hard charge: Reform the game (or, he implied, abolish it!). The Big Three accepted the challenge, but the American Football Rules Committee, with Camp in command, was not so sure. On November 25, a New York University football player was killed in an effort to stop a mass play. NYU's chancellor, Henry MacCracken, sent a telegram that evening to Harvard's Eliot, urging him to call a meeting of college presidents to address the football problem. On November 26, Eliot declined.

Undaunted, MacCracken moved ahead, gathering the next day with NYU faculty and students to call for either the abolition of football or major rules changes because of the game's "homicidal" nature. Having failed with Eliot, he invited representatives of institutions NYU had played recently to attend a conference and, in effect, make the choice Roosevelt had presented. Thirteen colleges and universities sent delegates. They voted to get back together with a larger group later that month.

This meeting was held December 28, with 62 institutions represented by faculty members. Others expressed interest but did not attend. Some simply declined, including the Big Three. President Wilson of Princeton declared his support for major reforms (and listed several) but also noted a reluctance to work with a large number of institutions to achieve them. Yale indicated that since alumni rather than faculty controlled athletics in New Haven, it would be inappropriate to send a representative. Eliot, then in the 36th year of his Harvard presidency, wrote to say he favored "separate action by individual colleges" and abandonment of football for one year to develop these actions. His institution, he said, would work on its own solutions.

Nevertheless, the National Football Conference of Universities and Colleges met, elected its own rules committee (with individuals from Dartmouth, Haverford, Minnesota, Nebraska, Oberlin, Vanderbilt and Army) and instructed it to seek amalgamation with Camp's committee. The latter group (Yale, Harvard, Princeton, Cornell, Pennsylvania, Navy and Chicago), as noted, was concerned about making major rules changes. But Roosevelt once more entered the picture, promoting the formation of a joint committee, which his influence helped bring about. The conference also appointed an executive committee to draft a constitution and bylaws for a new entity and later changed its name, in part to assure that this body would deal with more than one sport. The drafts were approved in March 1906, and the first Convention of the organization was held at the Murray Hill Hotel in New York City in December of that year. The Intercollegiate Athletic Association of the United States was the new name, one that would be changed again four years later. The National Collegiate Athletic Association was born. ●

JOSH SUMNER CELEBRATES TEXAS' 1992 COME-FROM-BEHIND WIN OVER HOUSTON.

PHOTO ©AP

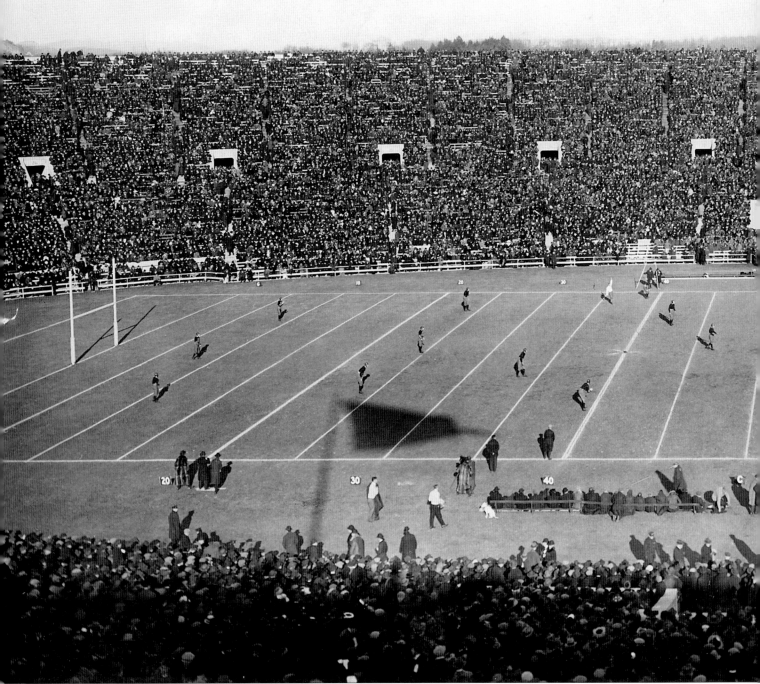

YALE VS. HARVARD AT THE YALE BOWL

Power and Pageantry

Football was present at the NCAA's birth, and it remains among the Association's most prominent sports. More than 43 million fans attended games in 2004.

COACH KNUTE ROCKNE (LEFT AND ABOVE) LEADING THE FIRST DRILL OF THE SEASON, SEPTEMBER 1930

AMOS ALONZO STAGG, CHICAGO FOOTBALL COACH

THE 2003 FIESTA BOWL (ABOVE) NATIONAL ANTHEM. ST. JOHN'S (MINNESOTA) PLAYERS CELEBRATE THEIR VICTORY (BELOW) IN THE 2003 DIVISION III FOOTBALL CHAMPIONSHIP.

JAMES MADISON COACH MICKEY MATTHEWS GETS DRENCHED DURING
THE 2004 DIVISION I-AA FOOTBALL CHAMPIONSHIP.

JIM LANNIGAN OF BLOOMSBURG CELEBRATES A FUMBLE RECOVERY AGAINST
DELTA STATE DURING THE 2000 DIVISION II FOOTBALL CHAMPIONSHIP.

WIDE RECEIVER SHANNON HAYES (ABOVE) OF WESTERN KENTUCKY MAKES A RECEPTION AGAINST MCNEESE STATE DURING THE 2002 DIVISION I-AA FOOTBALL CHAMPIONSHIP.

CHRIS GAMBLE OF OHIO STATE (ABOVE) STIFF ARMS JEREMY LESUEUR OF MICHIGAN DURING THE 2002 MICHIGAN VS. OHIO STATE GAME AT OHIO STADIUM. OHIO STATE DEFEATED MICHIGAN, 14-9, TO ADVANCE TO THE NATIONAL TITLE GAME.

THE TEXAS A&M FOOTBALL TEAM LISTENS INTENTLY TO THE FINAL WORDS FROM THE COACH MOMENTS BEFORE TAKING THE FIELD FOR THE OPENING KICKOFF AGAINST TEXAS, 1989.

GRAND VALLEY STATE COACH BRIAN KELLY HUGS RUNNING BACK REGGIE SPEARMON
AFTER DEFEATING VALDOSTA STATE DURING THE 2002 DIVISION II FOOTBALL CHAMPIONSHIP.

DEFENSIVE BACK MARCEL DILLARD OF GRAND VALLEY STATE AND HIS MOTHER MARCETTA DILLARD
CELEBRATE THE LAKERS' 2003 DIVISION II CHAMPIONSHIP VICTORY OVER NORTH DAKOTA.

MONTANA RUNNING BACK BEN DRINKWALTER IS WRAPPED UP BY GEORGIA SOUTHERN'S
JAMAR JONES (97) AND DAVID YOUNG (18) DURING THE 2000 DIVISION I-AA FOOTBALL CHAMPIONSHIP.

JAMIE SCHWABEROW / NCAA PHOTOS (BOTH)

CHAPTER TWO

HOME RULE 1906-51

THE ORGANIZATION THAT became the nation's principal regulatory and enforcement body for intercollegiate athletics did not start out that way. Nearly 50 years passed before the NCAA claimed a significant enforcement role. Although regulation was set forth as an objective (and regulatory language appeared) in the Association's founding documents, the real authority was vested in the member institutions. The athletics activities of American colleges and universities, according to the first constitution, were to be "maintained on an ethical plane in keeping with the dignity and high purpose of education." The founders expected that "a high standard of personal honor, eligibility and fair play" would be preserved and any abuses remedied. The foundation was amateurism, with its principles and rules enumerated in the bylaws. For instance, recruiting players, offering inducements and playing those who were not really students or who had not matriculated for one year (or were not, in fact, amateurs) was prohibited. Unsportsmanlike conduct would not be condoned.

DELEGATES (ABOVE) AT THE MURRAY HILL HOTEL, 1905, AS PICTURED IN THE NEW YORK DAILY TRIBUNE.

The Association, however, did not bear responsibility for enforcing these principles and rules. As noted earlier, this was the province of the member institutions, and later of the conferences as well. Those entities were to be the guardians of amateurism because the NCAA was intended to be a predominantly educational body. As a result, home rule would be the standard governing the division of labor. The possibility of establishing a stronger central authority was proposed during discussions of the original Executive Committee, but the idea was abandoned. Local control became the organizing principle. This decision was both sensible and attuned to the political and philosophical realities of the time, but, as Falla noted, the choice carried with it a built-in tension between the organization's commitment to amateurism and its reliance on the member institutions to honor that goal. The diversity of the membership complicated the achievement of this ideal even then. The schools were spread over a wide geography, had differing traditions and served varying audiences. Given those still-present factors, establishing trust in each other among the members would be a challenge from the start, continuing to the present day.

BEGINNINGS

THAT INITIAL EXECUTIVE Committee, which served during the year (1905-06) of design and planning that preceded the first Convention, had six members. Three were institutional chief executives — a chancellor, a president and an acting president. The latter individual, once back on the faculty, continued to be active in the Association, but it would be a long time before a college president or chancellor again found a place at the top of the governance structure. Those attending that first Convention (representing 28 institutions) were almost all faculty members, as were visiting delegates and others who came to watch. Faculty would predominate at the annual Conventions and on the committees for many years, an appropriate mode of operation for an organization that regarded faculty control at the campus level as essential.

The message of faculty paramountcy was conveyed early and often. At the 1908 Convention, Professor Clarence Waldo of Washington University (Missouri) spoke forcefully on the subject:

THE MEADOWLANDS ARENA (LEFT) IN EAST RUTHERFORD, NEW JERSEY, DURING THE 1996 MEN'S FINAL FOUR.

DEAN LEBARON BRIGGS, AN NCAA PRESIDENT (1914-16), discussing the trickery employed in football at an earlier time of "barbarity and rancor and low cunning:" "I shall never forget the appreciative satisfaction with which one excellent fellow told of another whose peculiar talent for the game...was in holding his adversary so cleverly that his adversary appeared to be holding him."

*What in its essence is the proper control? Is that the right kind which helps
an educational institution to occupy the most space in the sporting columns
of a metropolitan daily? Which gratifies sporting alumni …? which builds
immense and costly stadia and collossea that our young gladiators may
disport themselves before great masses of non-academic people? …which
tends to recruit the ranks of professional athletes from the class of our young
men who are the unfolding bud and promise of our nation …?*

No, Waldo said, we want to "secure an athletic spirit throughout the whole student body, a spirit that thrives on generous, wholesome, honest, glorious rivalry." He maintained that this can happen only if the direction of campus athletics is vested in the faculty.

The next year, a committee chaired by Waldo reported its conclusions to the annual Convention in even more emphatic terms. While there is room in the control picture for a measure of student involvement, he said, a committee selected "from among the strongest men in the faculty," and thus possessed of "the greatest available wisdom and experience," must have the prevailing authority. This committee's task was to "promote among its students honesty, chivalry, genial good fellowship and the fine manners of the ideal gentleman." If the campus committee succeeds, it will thereby:

*eliminate many bad things and practices, such as coaches afflicted with
professional notions, recruiting, inducing, falsifying, overtraining,
overindulgence in athletics, excessive specialization, hippodroming, …
immorality, indecency, profanity among students and athletics as a
business.*

Waldo's words reflect a conviction that intercollegiate athletics in these initial years faced truly dire straits, a perspective shared by Dr. R. Tait McKenzie of the University of Pennsylvania. McKenzie, speaking at the 1910 Convention, was an unabashed champion of the view that the modern inheritors of Greek amateurism were "the two great Anglo-Saxon races." These people, he said, were responsible for "spreading civilization, law and order to … Egypt, India, Africa, Cuba and the Philippines," and it was their commitment to

ROUGH PLAY AT THE GOAL LINE

PHOTO COURTESY THE NCAA

honorable physical endeavor that made the concept possible. In the realm of athletics, he observed, this commitment expressed itself through the doctrines of amateurism. McKenzie gave the delegates an overview of 1,200 years of Greek athletics history, down to the concluding era of professional sports based largely on their entertainment value. In this country, he suggested, we were dangerously close to that final stage. That end could be averted if the Association continued to work "to avoid the mistakes that in the past have done so much to drag down the ethics of athletic competition among gentlemen." Four reforms in particular were in order: The standard by which excellence is measured should be kept "within the reach of more men," and "the class distinction between athlete and student" should be diminished. Third, "we should consider the player first and not the spectator." Finally, through educational means, it would be important to cultivate in both players and spectators "that wholesomeness of mind … found in clean, honest and manly sport, that makes the sting of defeat nothing when weighed with the consciousness of having won dishonorably or by subterfuge." McKenzie did not say it, but one can assume he would have shared the strong belief of Waldo and other delegates that, in the Association and on the campuses, faculty leadership would be central to accomplishing such reforms. In any case, for Waldo, his colleagues and the Association as a whole, the Greek athletics heritage was imperiled, and vigilance had to be the watchword.

CHALLENGES

McKenzie offered his view of contemporary troubles and their Greek antecedents at the Convention that brought the Intercollegiate Athletic Association of the United States its new name. The NCAA was now in formal operation, but it came close to being stillborn. The concentration on amateurism and faculty control gave way to football problems, which were back in the headlines. The previous year, college football fatalities had set a record. The Football Rules Committee reported at the 1909 Convention that 32 deaths attributed to football injuries had occurred during the fall season, a number well above the total from four years before that had led to the formation of the IAAUS. The committee claimed that the new number considerably misrepresented what had actually happened, blaming inaccurate and sensationalized newspaper accounts.

Whether or not the reported number was credible, the news stirred up the passions. It was clear that the rules would need to be altered. President Edwin Alderman of Virginia, whose institution had experienced the death of a football player, told the Convention he believed that the game was doomed "unless radical changes were made." Professor C.A. Short of Delaware College suggested that legislative intervention was coming and, indeed, that it was possible "the playing of football might, in some states be treated as a crime." Numerous resolutions and related communications from institutions around the country urged major action to confront the crisis. The committee acknowledged that, in the face of a "public stampede," a "wise modification" of the rules was necessary.

The changes were made, and the rules committee reported in 1910 that the game was "comparatively safe and reasonably free from danger." As Falla concluded, despite initial doubts "the committee definitely saved college football, and it may well have saved the NCAA in the process." The preservation of one sport did not mean that the newly named organization's challenges had ended. The old nemeses of amateurism still threatened. Despite the clear language of the NCAA constitution and bylaws, and frequently articulated pledges of allegiance to the amateur ideal, the so-called twin evils of recruiting and subsidizing players continued to plague intercollegiate sports. Football was not the only game affected.

Baseball was an almost annual topic at the early Conventions, one that would continue to surface for years to come. The major issue was the summer game, which was often played for pay by college athletes. Palmer Pierce, the Association's founding president, regularly condemned this practice. Even at the hour of crisis over football fatalities, Pierce said that baseball was the greater problem:

> The moral degeneration that comes from the playing of summer baseball for
> money and then returning to college and deceiving the college authorities
> about this in order to play in intercollegiate contests is deplorable … Such
> practice is all too common.

Four years later, summer baseball was a common subject for Convention speakers. George Ehler of Wisconsin referred to the game as "that ever recurrent specter." E.H. Nichols of Harvard, during an address entirely devoted to the subject, described the problem as "playing baseball in summer for money … and usually lying about it afterwards." Cornell's C.V.P. Young observed that this is an issue that "will not down":

> Articles have been written against it, resolutions passed condemning it, rules
> passed, it was fondly imagined, that would absolutely prevent it, but we still
> hear on all sides that summer ball is being played, and that the net result of
> opposition to date has been a widespread development of lying and
> hypocrisy.

For his part, Pierce's soon-to-be successor, addressing the same Convention, seemed more concerned about what he called "the dark side of sportsmanship." Baseball, LeBaron Briggs said, was among "the most conspicuous and … gratuitous offenders." The practice of seeking

to unnerve an opponent, rattle or ridicule him, to gibe at him "in plain hearing of the umpire without one word of efficient rebuke," bothered Briggs, an academic dean at Harvard.

His concern would never quite be answered. Similarly the greater problem of play-for-pay was itself in 1913 some time away from resolution. That problem, however, had contributed substantially to a gathering consensus that amateurism language needed another look. The 1911 Convention had heard a report from the Committee on Amateur Law that had its origins in discussions of summer baseball in 1907 and 1908. This committee gave considerable attention to the "psycho-social validity of the principle of amateurism," a concept based on scholarship dealing with the human "play impulse." Play, the committee believed, was "nature's method of education," and accordingly, colleges ought to ensure that every student has "a full, normal play life." Further, they "must organize and control athletics as an educational force for the whole student body" and not just "for a few unduly skilled performers." This idea reinforced the traditional claim that sports programs undertaken especially for the most talented athletes, leading to the class distinction McKenzie had criticized and often to a kind of hero worship, were at odds with the amateur creed. As well, it provided a foundation for a concerted effort after World War I to establish a required physical education curriculum in colleges and schools across the nation. For the present, the committee concluded, its idea allowed for formulation of "a positive general law":

> An amateur is one who enters and takes part in athletic contests purely in obedience to the play impulses or for the satisfaction of purely play motives and for the exercise, training and social pleasures derived.

On that basis, the catalogue of sins associated with proselytizing (the old term of art for recruiting) and rewards (the sundry forms of subsidy) led logically to a need for regulations. The Amateur Law Committee proposed a number of them. Baseball was not the only sport covered, despite its prominent role in the committee's establishment. No machinery for enforcement was recommended, however. Home rule stood in the way.

PRESIDENTIAL VOICES

MEMBER INSTITUTION PRESIDENTS and chancellors often were invited to Conventions during these years to share their thoughts on the values and challenges of athletics with the delegates. Their speeches did not necessarily set them apart from their faculty colleagues, and, like those colleagues, they spoke with sometimes conflicting voices. Two instructive examples are Chancellors James Roscoe Day of Syracuse, who addressed the 1909 Convention, and Samuel Black McCormick of Pittsburgh, who spoke two years later.

Day expressed his "confirmed judgment that athletics have an essential place in college work and … are vitally related to scholarship and manhood." They are not, he added, "an excrescence but the fiber and essential integrity of the best educational system and plan." He went on to remark, however, on what he called "this iniquity." The reference was to the use of athletics for advertising and the practices NCAA members engaged in to serve that purpose (recruiting from preparatory schools, soliciting alumni for scholarship assistance and asking talented players to serve as "advertisers"). Institutions "have bribed star athletes away from other colleges. They have played ringers. It is an old story." Beyond that, he said, "gate receipts have been the price at which honor has been sold." Day criticized coaching salaries (often, at least for the time spent on the job, greater than those for presidents) and claimed that many presidents "who are neither fossils nor mollycoddles" were perplexed by the lengths to which colleges were willing to go to "make a spectacle of themselves." The remedy, he said, was to return to an understanding of what made athletics, done the right way, central to the learning experience. Simply put, sports are for all college students, not just for the stars. So the Association had to move back to that core idea. Major reforms were in order lest "parents and guardians and an alarmed citizenship appeal to the legislatures for protection."

Despite his many misgivings and strong strictures, Day showed appreciation for the "magnificent stadium" his trustees had found the money to build at Syracuse.

McCormick did not see intercollegiate athletics in quite the same way. He did not address the issue of sports programs (especially football) being used for institutional advertising purposes, nor did he call the roll of evils, as Day had done, and attempt to justify them. He thought it "the most natural thing in the world that the young man should permit his enthusiasm for sport to carry him too far and that college alumni in their zeal for their college should do things which are neither wise nor good." The answer to evils, he argued, was to "eliminate them if possible; lessen their effect, if they cannot be eliminated, and endure them if their effect cannot be lessened …" Rules can help, but, with patience, instruction and "healthy public sentiment," the problems will eventually take care of themselves.

Meanwhile, he said, we need to stop taking athletics issues too seriously. Presidents have "again and again gotten into a panic" over these issues, and their "fear have been out of proportion to the dangers … It is no better to send forth fulminations against athletics because there are imperfections therein than to inveigh against Nature because sometimes a cyclone sweeps destructively over the prairie." In the tirade against athletics, "a large number of college presidents and professors have joined." They have done so mostly because of the problems, "without considering the immense good" that athletics have accomplished. He took up the banner of the play side of human nature:

> *In play, with all its generous rivalry, with all its splendid forthputting of*
> *energy, with all its eagerness to attain the goal, with the applause of the*
> *thousands of spectators in the athletic contest, is to be wrought out the*
> *great, strong, generous, manly character which is to dominate the world.*

McCormick was hardly unusual in offering a paean to the role of college sports in the development of manly character. Celebration of the responsibility of colleges, through athletics, to bring boys to manhood was a common, self-congratulatory theme in the texts and speeches of the time. Theodore Roosevelt wrote in his "American Boy" essay that "great growth in the love of athletic sports … has beyond question had an excellent effect on increased manliness." McCormick's willingness to tolerate evils in the interest of the greater good, however, was a sentiment seldom publicly offered, by presidents or professors, at NCAA Conventions or elsewhere. Moreover, the speaker who mentioned the importance of campus athletics activity for women was rare. McCormick may have been the first: We are certain, he avowed at the 1911 annual meeting, "that the physical element must hold a high place, not simply for physical perfection, but for the symmetrical development of all the qualities of manhood and *womanhood*."

GROWTH, 1906-20

ALTHOUGH ONLY 28 accredited delegates attended the first Convention in December 1906, the IAAUS had 39 members by that time. Membership numbers expanded steadily, reaching 97 by 1912 and 170 in 1919. In the beginning, member institutions came mainly from the East and Midwest. In 1911, for example, 39 of the 73 members were Eastern colleges and universities, 20 came from Midwestern states (particularly from Ohio), and Southern numbers had grown to 12. The West was represented only by Colorado and the Southwest by Texas. Eastern representation probably would have been greater during these years if not for the continuing baseball controversy. Many New England institutions featured the summer game, so they were reluctant to join an Association that regularly condemned that sport and its custom of paying players.

Notably absent during these early years, for varying periods, were the Big Three universities. They had been represented on the old pre-IAAUS football rules committee, were accustomed to having their own way by and large on athletics matters and were thus reluctant to place themselves under any form of direction from a large national organization with a diverse membership. The Big Three presidents met now and then to discuss athletics matters, though maintaining a united front among themselves proved difficult. Harvard's Abbott Lawrence Lowell and Yale's Hadley held similar views of reform, believing a gradual approach would be best. Wilson, however, was adamant that radical football reforms were needed and, typically

1939 (June 24-29) —Intercollegiate Golf Championships of the United States first conducted under auspices of NCAA (after sponsorship by U.S. Golf Association beginning in 1897). **Vincent D'Antoni** of Tulane University wins the individual title and Stanford University wins the team title.

1939 (December 29) — Longtime NCAA Secretary-Treasurer Frank W. Nicolson of Wesleyan University (Connecticut) resigns after 30 years in position.

1941 (March 29) —First National Collegiate Fencing Championships are conducted at Ohio State University.

1945 (June 25-30) —Francisco **"Pancho" Segura** of the University of Miami (Florida) becomes (and remains) the only three-time singles titlist in NCAA tennis championships (the only other three-time collegiate titlist is Malcolm Chace, who competed in the pre-NCAA Intercollegiate Tennis Championships for Brown and Yale from 1893 to 1895).

1946 (July 22-23) —Conference of Conferences is conducted in Chicago, resulting in "Principles for the Conduct of Intercollegiate Athletics" (five points of the principles — known as "Sanity Code" — formally were adopted in 1948).

1946 (July 23) —$5,000 grant made to National Collegiate Athletic Bureau in New York City for statistics compilation and other record services (directed by Homer F. Cooke Jr.).

1947 (January 6) —Research of head and spinal football injuries is funded.

1947 (June 20-21) —First National Collegiate Baseball Championship played in Kalamazoo, Michigan, where the University of California, Berkeley, defeats a Yale University squad that includes future president **George H.W. Bush** (Bush returned to the final with Yale in 1948, where the team again finished second, behind the University of Southern California).

1948 (March 18-20) —First National Collegiate Ice Hockey Championship is conducted at Colorado Springs/Colorado College.

1949 (April 7-9) —Chuck Davey of Michigan State University becomes the only four-time National Collegiate Boxing Championships individual titlist.

for him, was not prepared to compromise. Harvard was first to depart this fractured alliance, joining the IAAUS in 1909. Princeton followed four years later, Wilson having since left to serve as governor of New Jersey (1910-12) and — in the year of Princeton's admission to the NCAA — as president of the United States. Yale joined in 1915. Stanford arrived the next year, its longtime embrace of rugby as the substitute for its abandoned football program having weakened. President Jordan's distaste for the latter ("in its essence a battle, not a sport, and largely devoid of interest except for the colorful, tumultuous partisanship engendered by it") was not so great an influence after he moved to the institution's newly created chancellor position in 1913.

As the Association's numbers grew, so did its coverage of sports. By 1919, it was directly involved in 11 of them. As this coverage expanded, rules committees were established, and Conventions came to be characterized in part by reports from one or another of these committees. The geographic districts offered annual reports at the meetings, and their number increased from six to nine (then back to eight), each of them entitled to a seat on the Executive Committee. The number of athletics conferences grew, and these bodies (if they had at least seven members) were also represented on that committee. All of these developments meant that the Association's agenda became both more complex and more controversial. The Conventions of 1915 and 1916 are revealing in this regard.

The 1915 gathering was Dean Briggs' second as NCAA president. His address that year struck a negative note, as he told his audience that intercollegiate athletics were now "deservedly" under constant attack. The evils were many and great, he said, and the worst of them was "mutual distrust." At his home institution (Harvard), he said, "rumors are rife of iniquitous practices at Princeton and Yale; at Princeton and Yale rumors are rife of iniquitous practices at Harvard." There were cordial relations among the three schools, but distrust was still a major concern. Briggs observed that when football, the Association's foundation sport, was conducted in the wrong way it "may be all that its enemies declare it, a monstrous growth of brutality and craft over physical and intellectual manhood."

Others attending were not so sure. Professor Robert Corwin of Yale said that the problem was not so much the game as the faculty attitude toward it. The professoriate, he observed, views intercollegiate football and athletics in general as "an insidious malady which threatens the well-being of the body scholastic." Students, in contrast, have a positive view, perhaps because they understand athletics as "a laboratory in the art of living" and "a course in the precepts … of manliness, honesty, self-restraint, persistence, resourcefulness and fair play …" Students were still in charge at Yale, which was a good thing, Corwin thought, in light of the "unsympathetic, not infrequently unintelligent repression" that can accompany faculty control.

William Howard Taft, then on Yale's law faculty after his White House years, appeared at this Convention to voice strong support for college sports. They added much to "the value of college memories and associations." They were:

> *the flesh that clothes and rounds out the frame … The feeling of solidarity and loyalty in the student body that intercollegiate athletics develops … outlasts every contest, and it continues in the heart and soul of every graduate as long as he lives.*

If there were serious problems for the Association to confront in 1915, there was also comfort to be found in its growing presence in areas of the country where it had not previously been strong. The Southwest Intercollegiate Athletic Conference and its eight member schools from the states of Texas, Arkansas and Oklahoma became members that year. So did the Pacific Northwest Intercollegiate Conference, representing institutions in Washington, Oregon and Idaho. Six conferences belonged to the NCAA and, more and more, they were looked upon to shoulder the enforcement responsibility the Association itself was sworn to avoid. Despite Briggs' concern about the game's brutality, 1915 was the year the delegates voted to abandon the football death report given at every Convention since 1906 and to discontinue the Committee on Fatalities Among Football Players that had done the research.

That year, President William T. Foster of Reed College published an article highly critical of the state of athletics on American college campuses. Foster, an innovative educator who had written earlier about the multiplying burdens of the college presidency, took his colleagues to task for allowing their athletics programs to become money-making and advertising vehicles controlled by students and alumni. These programs, he said, served the few at the expense of the many and brought us to an "age so unbalanced nervously that it demands perpetual excitement, … a pathological nervous condition which craves greater excess." What we have, he wrote, was the "maelstrom of college athletics."

Foster's indictment raised hackles at the 1916 Convention. Professor George Johnson of Harvard rose to defend intercollegiate athletics as "an expression of loyalty, an endeavor to maintain and exalt the dignity and honor of the college," and as a program that brings "prestige [to] alma mater." Raymond Gettell of Amherst spoke in a similar vein, but focused his remarks on a single sport. He recited the litany of football's celebrated benefits (self-sacrifice, self-control, etc.) and argued that the game "while retaining the virtues of physical combat, remedies its worst evils by emphasizing organization, cooperation and obedience."

Whether persuaded by Foster's critique, unconvinced by the positive views of Johnson and Gettell or simply of its own volition, the Football Rules Committee responded by adopting a code of ethics in 1916. The committee also asked a large foundation to undertake an overall study of intercollegiate athletics. That work was eventually completed, but only after two major historical developments intervened — World War I and the decade of excess that was the Roaring Twenties.

THE BALLYHOO YEARS

IN HIS CLASSIC history of the 1920s, Frederick Allen wrote of the rise of radio, the popularity of jazz, the boom in movies and automobiles, the great bull market, government scandals, land speculation, flying and flagpole sitting, flappers and bathing beauties, prosperity and prohibition, bootleggers and speakeasies, famous racketeers, gang rule in the cities, the arrival of Freudian psychology on American shores, a "revolution in manners and morals," and, of course, the stock market crash of 1929. He wrote about college sports as well, football in particular, and observed in this regard that:

> Teams which represented supposed institutions of learning went barnstorming for weeks at a time, imbibing what academic instruction they might on the sleeping car between the Yankee Stadium and Chicago or between Texas and the Tournament of Roses at Pasadena.

HOME-RUN KING BABE RUTH PRESENTS A MANUSCRIPT OF HIS AUTOBIOGRAPHY TO YALE BASEBALL TEAM CAPTAIN AND FUTURE PRESIDENT GEORGE H. W. BUSH, 1948.

These were, Allen said, the ballyhoo years for the country, an era of immoderacy in assorted walks of life. Large, expensive stadiums were built and filled with fans on Saturday afternoons on many campuses. Colleges often paid for these structures over time with gate receipts, which could also produce profits, which in turn could finance further growth for athletics departments.

The introduction of radio fueled public interest in college sports. Overall radio sales grew at a staggering rate during the decade, from $60 million in 1922 to more than $842.5 million in 1929, an increase of 1,300 percent. The first football broadcast was of a game between Princeton and Chicago in October 1922. A month later the Harvard-Yale game aired. Although data are lacking, it is probably safe to say that during the next

NOTRE DAME PLAYS CHICAGO AT UNIVERSITY OF CHICAGO GYMNASIUM, 1930.

MICHIGAN PLAYS CHICAGO AT UNIVERSITY OF CHICAGO FOOTBALL FIELD, 1904.

COLORADO COLLEGE FOOTBALL STADIUM (ABOVE), 1927. THE OLDEST COLLEGE FOOTBALL STADIUM WEST OF THE MISSISSIPPI, THE STADIUM IS STILL IN USE TODAY.

THE KANSAS BASKETBALL TEAM (LEFT) PRACTICING IN ROBINSON GYMNASIUM, 1908.

1950 (January 6) —Standard awards for athletes placing in NCAA competition are approved.

1950 (March) —City College of New York becomes the only team to win both the National Invitation Tournament and NCAA basketball championship in the same year.

1950 (April 4) —Basketball tournament is expanded from eight to 16 teams; automatic qualification for 10 conferences is approved.

1951 (January 12) —Sanity Code is revised (financial aid and enforcement provisions).

1951 (October 1) — **Walter Byers** becomes full-time executive director of NCAA (after serving since 1947 as part-time executive assistant).

1952 (January 11) —Limited television plan is adopted.

1952 (July 28) —NCAA office moves from Chicago to Kansas City, Missouri.

1953 (August 12) —Basketball championship is expanded to 24 teams (15 automatic qualifiers) effective in 1954.

1954 (January 4) —Baseball championship is reorganized (32-team field, eight-team double-elimination final).

seven years the growth of game broadcasts was nearly as great as the increase in radio sales. Newspapers also expanded their coverage of college sports during the decade. Some sportswriters rose to fame in these years, often by satisfying the public mania for college football. Although Knute Rockne was already a legend (aided and abetted by the press), the public immortalized reporter Grantland Rice in part because he wrote of Rockne's 1924 backfield as the Four Horsemen of Notre Dame.

At its 1918 Convention, soon after the Armistice in November ended the war, the NCAA set out on a major effort to convince member institutions and public school systems of the need for compulsory physical education programs for their students. Congress was asked to support this effort. Letters were sent to state legislatures seeking statutory assistance and to school boards requesting their cooperation. The focus was on elementary and secondary schools as well as on higher education, and the program was to cover both males and females. The Association emphasized the connection between the ideal of exercise for all and "effective citizenship." A special committee was organized on "Extending the Influence of the Association" and charged with initiating the process of implementation. The initiative required all member institutions to ensure that the program in "Physical Training and Athletics be recognized as a department of collegiate instruction, directly responsible to the college or university administration." Stagg had come to Chicago under just such an organizational plan almost 30 years earlier, and the desirability of that arrangement had been often asserted in the intervening period. Significant progress was made during the 1920s, and the concept, now anchored on many campuses, became something of a restraint on the ever-beckoning temptation to find a way around restrictive rules. Where it worked best, the special committee provided a vehicle for enhanced institutional control of athletics activities. The initiative to require physical education at all educational levels was successful, too, as millions of students across the generations came to understand, if not to appreciate.

Other notable advances took place during this time. The first NCAA championships were held — track and field in 1921 and swimming in 1924. The Association outgrew the "Executive Committee as sole authority" approach, establishing the NCAA Council in 1922. This body remained a key component of the governance structure for three quarters of a century. That same year, the Convention approved a 10-point code, reiterating and reemphasizing long-held principles and objectives: sectional conferences, the freshman rule, a three-year participation limit, a prohibition of graduate student and "migrant" player participation, suppression of "the betting evil," and "absolute faculty control," among others. The fundamental principle, of course, was still amateurism, a definition of which was promulgated in 1916 and amended six years later. The 1922 version provided that an "amateur sportsman is one who engages in sport solely for the physical, mental or social benefits he derives therefrom, and to whom the sport is nothing more than an avocation."

The supporters' intention behind these several measures, as always at these Conventions and as often echoed by the Association's leadership, was good. But strong countercurrents persisted. Baseball's play-for-pay problem remained unresolved. The membership's hoped-for utilization of conferences to serve as rules enforcers had yet to take anything close to full effect. Those new stadiums often drew capacity crowds, commercial motives were increasingly evident, and the old challenges of recruiting and subsidizing athletes were still on prominent display. President C.A. Richmond of Union College (New York) deplored "the high cost of athletic victories" in a 1921 speech. He criticized the competition for bigger, better programs as something "like the contest in dreadnoughts" that characterized the international situation in the years before the war. We have on our hands, he said, a "race of armaments." And it would not be the last one.

Professor C.W. Savage of Oberlin described himself as an appalled friend of intercollegiate athletics at the 1923 Convention. It is clear, he said, that:

In practically all of the great colleges and universities … there are being built up great intercollegiate machines, great athletic systems, commercialized and professionalized in spirit, that are fast assuming the proportions of stupendous Juggernauts … which are threatening to crack every bone in our academic bodies, and to crush out of our scholastic veins every drop of the blood of idealism and inspiration.

Dartmouth President Ernest Hopkins defended the state of intercollegiate athletics in 1925, suggesting that colleges had both a curriculum life and a community life. "No agency of undergraduate life so powerfully binds the college community together nor … so advantageously permeates its ideals," he insisted, " as do the undergraduate sports."

Two developments collided that year to tell at least part of the story of college sport in the 1920s. One occurred when the NCAA appointed another special committee and charged it with studying the overemphasis on football and the problematic impacts of the sport's professional version. The other development, which probably produced the special committee, was the story of a hero (not all that unusual in a decade that deliriously celebrated the feat of a young pilot named Charles Lindbergh). The subject of that story was Harold E. "Red" Grange. Red Grange was a phenomenon. He played for Illinois, where he competed without an athletics scholarship (an award more and more in evidence by this time). He was the "Galloping Ghost." In October 1925, he scored six touchdowns against Michigan in Illinois' spacious new stadium. On November 11, his fans circulated a petition nominating him for Congress. (He was too young.) Ten days later, he played his final college game. The next day, Grange signed a professional contract with the Chicago Bears. On November 26, he played his first game with the Bears, for $12,000. He barnstormed the country with that team in the following weeks, earning additional money and helping cement a place in the public mind for the new and struggling professional game. On December 7, Grange agreed to a $300,000 movie contract. The next day, he was presented to Calvin Coolidge, president of the United States.

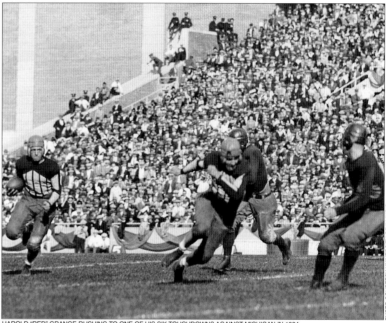

HAROLD "RED" GRANGE RUSHING TO ONE OF HIS SIX TOUCHDOWNS AGAINST MICHIGAN IN 1924.

It was hardly a surprise that four years after Grange's great adventure, the Carnegie Foundation for the Advancement of Teaching delivered to the NCAA, and the country at large, the critical, empirically based report, "American College Athletics." The study had been authorized by foundation trustees in early January 1926 — perhaps not coincidentally just one month after Grange shook hands with President Coolidge — at the request of several major national associations. The NCAA was one of them. The foundation's study team collected abundant factual information during visits to 105 American campuses, 18 secondary schools and some Canadian colleges as well. The findings were well documented, carefully explained and, for the most part, expected. The Carnegie report concluded that campus faculty control had failed too frequently. The concept, the report said, was something that existed "in name but scarcely in fact" and was "often a mere subterfuge."

The NCAA more than likely did not anticipate the finding that students did not have much say over athletics and should be entrusted with an increasing and major share of the responsibility. But other major conclusions could not have been surprising to the Association. The fundamental issues, the report's authors argued, were twofold: "commercialism and a negligent attitude toward the educational opportunity for which a college exists." The defects of contemporary athletics programs, particularly as they imposed heavy burdens on the athletes, included disproportionate time requirements, isolation from the rest of the student body and highly compensated "professional" coaches whose focus often was not on the education of their players. The report prominently revisited the old twin evils of player recruiting and subsidization:

The recruiting of American college athletes … has reached the proportions of nationwide commerce…Its effect upon the character of the schoolboy has been profoundly deleterious. Its influence upon the nature and quality of American higher education has been no less noxious.

As for the subsidy problem, the authors again minced no words. "The subsidized college athlete of today," they stated, "connives at disreputable and shameful practices for the sake of material returns and for honors falsely achieved." Regarding the campus rules intended to eliminate the twin evils, they were both subtle and clear: Whatever regulations on recruiting and subsidizing "may be in vogue, they must be regarded as ideals … which a very large number of institutions have not yet attained."

The 383-page report also commented on sportsmanship, eligibility, amateurism (the definition of which institutions honor in the breach) and worsening professionalism, health questions, the "sorry role" of institutional alumni and excessive publicity. The press was taken to task for the notoriety it gave to "schoolboy athletes" and the undue and growing coverage given to the games: "Much of the distortion of the popular attitude toward the college has flowed from the fact that intercollegiate contests appear to be the only phase of college life that is regarded as news."

The authors said that effectively combating the emphasis on commercialism required nothing short of a change in campus values. The report maintained that commercialism must be reduced and college sport enhanced so that it is:

PHOTO COURTESY UNITED STATES MILITARY ACADEMY

CADET PALMER PIERCE OF THE UNITED STATES MILITARY ACADEMY, CLASS OF 1891.

esteemed primarily and sincerely for the opportunities it affords … to exercise at once the body and the mind, and to foster habits both of bodily health and of those high qualities of character which, until they are revealed in action, we accept on faith.

Educational opportunity also was in part a matter of values. And of will: "The American college must renew within itself the force that will challenge the best intellectual capabilities of the undergraduates," athletes included.

At the next year's Convention, a special committee assigned by the NCAA to study the Carnegie publication made its report. In general, it looked upon that earlier work as a constructive review, "friendly and useful," and one that institutions "can wisely use … as a check on their own situations." The committee was careful to point out that the NCAA remained "primarily a consultative and advisory body [that was] not expected to lay down detailed rules of action" for the member colleges and universities. The Carnegie report commented not only on problems but also progress. The NCAA committee concurred — there were reasons to be encouraged as the Association moved into a new decade. James R. Angell, president of Yale and the Convention's featured speaker that year, devoted his speech to the problems of athletics. He was the son of James Burrill Angell, the reform-minded president of Michigan in an earlier era. The son had similar goals. He was a gradualist, heartened by the spirit of change in the air and confident that the problems would be resolved. He offered his own "creed" on athletics issues. Like the Carnegie report, his speech stressed the old values: the mind-body relationship, physical exercise for all, wholesome games, dedication to amateurism principles and the rest. Angell's creed had no room for high-priced coaches, for winning as the highest priority, or for recruiting, subsidizing or advertising. The Carnegie report authors preferred athletics to be intramural and free of commercial influences. Games were to be played and watched both honorably and for the fun of it. The young Angell agreed. His father would have as well. By 1930, however, college sports were headed in the opposite direction.

PALMER PIERCE

THE NCAA HAD no staff members during its first quarter century and would have none on a full-time basis until 1951. But there was a leader in this founding period, a man who held the office of NCAA president for 21 of those years. The leadership of that man, Palmer Pierce, was consequential even before the Association was established. Pierce, then an army captain and teaching at West Point, made his presence felt at the December 1905 meeting of football-playing institutions called by President MacCracken. He offered a number of resolutions that were adopted at the meeting, and he was instrumental in the decision to form a national organization. Pierce was appointed to that body's executive committee, chaired the first Convention of the IAAUS, continued in his role as president for eight years and returned for 13 more in 1917. The 1891 West Point graduate commanded a brigade of the Third Army Corps in World War I and was a brigadier general by the time the war ended.

Pierce was a strong believer in the values of sport that gave substance to the first constitution and bylaws, that were embraced consistently by Convention speakers and that formed the basis for the Carnegie Foundation's 1929 report. In his presidential addresses, he spoke often and forcefully of the need for what he called a rational approach to intercollegiate athletics. The word "sane" was among his favorites in commending this approach to Convention delegates and the Association membership. He was a passionate champion of home rule and the attendant role of the NCAA as an educational (and not an enforcement) organization. Indeed, in 1907 he said that the NCAA was, above all else, a "League of Educated Gentlemen," implicitly incorporating into that label his view of both the fundamental values and the basic responsibilities of the Association.

Among other causes for which he was a leading spokesman were faculty control; the integration of athletics into the academic structure of member institutions; the need for compulsory physical education in schools and colleges; the initiation of national championships; and, in 1921, the possibility of establishing a central office (and presumably a staff to man it) for the growing entity he led. That growth was in ample measure attributable to Pierce's energetic efforts. He was visibly and vigorously involved in a long and bruising battle — a jurisdictional dispute encompassing all the years of his presidency — to break the Amateur Athletic Union's self-proclaimed ownership of amateur sports and sportsmen.

Pierce was candid in his assessment of serious problems, yet always optimistic and encouraging. For example, he was able to put a positive spin on the dramatic increases in stadium gate receipts in the 1920s by suggesting that they were needed to help pay the high costs of compulsory physical education programs for all undergraduates. Withal, he was a man for his long season, and while in a sense events had passed him by at the end of that season, Pierce left a major mark on the NCAA.

THE JOURNEY TO ENFORCEMENT

PIERCE'S SERVICE AS president came to a close in 1929, the same year the stock market crash ended the ballyhoo era and its extravagance. The Carnegie Foundation report published that year documented both the record of excesses of intercollegiate athletics and offered reasons for hope that the future would bring a restoration of traditional amateur values and practices. The Association developed something of a dual personality in the next two decades. These amateur values and practices remained in place on paper and in rhetoric, and to some extent member institutions applied them. On the other hand, the serious challenges that prompted the Carnegie study were not going away, so a change of course was necessary. The NCAA's commitment to the classic amateur ideal was so deep that such a change could be neither sudden nor comprehensive. It would take time. It would be a journey requiring relatively small steps at first, bigger ones later and a few setbacks along the way. In the end, the grip of home rule would be weakened and the NCAA finally would take on enforcement authority.

A different understanding of the problems of recruiting and subsidizing, and of how to deal with them, emerged as the NCAA moved into this role. Howard Savage, the Carnegie report's principal author, spoke at length at the 1930 Convention on ways to eliminate these long-lived twin enemies of amateurism. The result, he thought, would be "a stage in the evolution of a better American sportsmanship." Evolution was soon to be on the march, but it would ultimately reach a stage different from what Savage envisioned.

Pierce's successor, Charles Kennedy of Princeton, told the Convention the next year that the Association was experiencing a "period of readjustment … a vital reconstruction of college sport …" In a way, this echoed Savage's 1930 comments, but Kennedy added a new idea. He proposed a study of whether the NCAA's interests "would be promoted, and its influence increased, by the establishment of a permanent headquarters and the appointment of a salaried executive officer." Pierce had mentioned the possibility in passing, and there had been some discussion of it in the past. For nearly a half-century the Association could come no closer to permanent staff positions than Pierce's long tenure as president and Frank Nicolson's three decades (1909-39) as secretary-treasurer. Pierce, however, was a volunteer. So was Wesleyan's Nicolson. Kennedy believed something more was needed. He may not have appreciated his proposal's potential meaning for home rule or its implications, from the staffing perspective, for enforcement. Still, his idea was prophetic. Twenty years would pass before the prophecy — replete with office, staff and a vehicle for enforcing compliance — would be realized.

The first step came a few years later, in the wake of a report by the Special Committee on Recruiting and Subsidizing. The committee had recommended what became a seven-part code of "unjustifiable" practices, based largely on conventional amateur doctrine. This group also recommended a survey of member institutions to determine the extent to which they practiced what this code preached. The replies, sent in by two-thirds of the membership and reported at the 1935 Convention, were instructive. About 36 percent of the respondents said they approved and were enforcing the code. A slightly higher percentage expressed approval but also some doubt regarding the ability of institutions to enforce all of the code's elements. A quarter of the members indicated disapproval of one or more of the seven points. The responses included pessimistic statements about the practicability of requiring compliance, "impossible" being perhaps the most-used descriptor of one or another of the points. One president expressed his judgment that colleges and universities "cannot be prevented from using persuasion in bringing athletes to their institutions." Several conferences reported they were considering whether the offering of scholarships was acceptable. Some had already decided it was — and they were doing it. Obviously, home rule was not getting the job done.

Noted writer Paul Gallico bade a famous farewell to his sports beat in 1937 with a scathing indictment of college athletics. Football especially incurred his wrath "as the leader in the field of double-dealing, deception, sham, cant and organized hypocrisy." It had degenerated into "the biggest and dirtiest sports racket the country has ever known …" As for amateurism, he wrote: "If we have any conception of the real meaning of the word 'amateur,' we never let it disturb us. We ask only one thing of an amateur and that is that he doesn't let us catch him taking the dough."

The year before, an Association committee issued its report on the threat posed by recruiting and subsidizing practices among the members. Such abuses, the report indicated, were the NCAA's "most pressing problem." The committee described the by-now familiar reasons, criticizing other activities and behaviors (bowl games, gambling, drinking) and noting that the organization "has no police powers." But the committee recommended no changes to deal with the old twin evils. The committee's critique was late because change, perhaps influenced by Gallico's harsh commentary, was coming already. Though it was not necessarily their intention to do so, college presidents were helping to make it happen.

Carnegie's Savage had produced a study in 1925 blaming presidents for the confusing state of affairs in college athletics. This judgment received further emphasis in the foundation's report four years later. In 1931, Pennsylvania President Thomas S. Gates said:

> An institution has today the kind of athletic system … its president wants it
> to have or permits it to have. It is all very well to blame the abuses upon
> the public or the alumni or the emphasis given in the newspapers. But in
> the last analysis, the president is responsible.

The survey responses reported by the Special Committee on Recruiting and Subsidizing, pointing to a considerable variety among institutions in dealing with amateurism standards, at least implicitly supported Gates' observation. If explicit testimony was needed, it came in Executive Committee member comments during a discussion of the amateur code at the 1940 Convention. Although a large number of presidents had responded affirmatively to a letter from the Association asking for assurances that the code was being enforced on the campuses, the facts indicated otherwise. Clearly, violations were both widespread and "matters of college policy approved by the presidents." Accordingly, an Executive Committee member said, "We are now confronted with the problem as to whether the college presidents have been fooled by the conditions of their own institutions or whether [they] intend that the code should be interpreted differently than most of us understand it …"

The situation seemed to demand an expansion of the Association's authority to handle the growth of violations. That year (1940) the Convention gave the Executive Committee investigative and interpretive powers in relation to the code. As Falla pointed out, there was now "acceptance of the concepts of investigation and adjudication," but a decision to add enforcement to these concepts was "not yet on the horizon." World War II clouded that horizon for the next half-decade. In 1946, however, the NCAA moved one step closer to assuming a responsibility to compel compliance. The Association called for a Conference of Conferences to be held in Chicago that year.

During the war, the military used many college campuses for training purposes. Athletes played under the banners of these training programs, for army camps and naval base teams, and — with great success — the two service academies. War had diverted the sporting public's attention from amateur-code issues to matters of much greater moment at home and around the world. With the peace came a GI Bill that sent hundreds of thousands of veterans to school, and with them came a considerably expanded sense of the importance of financial aid for college students. Sports pages once again trumpeted (and criticized) the college game. Gambling scandals were back as well, or at least looming, when the conferences gathered. They assembled a first draft of a document, "Principles for the Conduct of Intercollegiate Athletics" and, in keeping with long practice, sent it to NCAA member institutions as a questionnaire. The principles — five of them — were largely reformulations of the old amateur ethos, covering financial aid, recruitment, academic standards for athletes, institutional control and the principle of amateurism itself. Campus response was positive. With some editing and revising, the five principles were adopted by the delegates at the NCAA's 42nd Convention in 1948. They became known as the "Sanity Code," that title suggesting an intention to return sanity to college sport and also recalling Pierce's frequent references to the need for sane governance of intercollegiate athletics.

The Sanity Code was not just another in a long line of codes put in place through the decades by Association reformers. This one had teeth. The Executive Committee created by regulation a three-person Constitutional Compliance Committee with authority to interpret the constitution and to determine whether "stated practices, actual or contemplated, are forbidden by, or are consistent with," its provisions. A Fact-Finding Committee was also established to investigate possible violations. The only penalty for institutional violators was expulsion from membership, an action requiring a two-thirds vote of Convention delegates. That standard proved to be a problem.

Two years later, a constitutional crisis occurred. Seven universities were determined to be guilty of code violations, but only a 111-93 majority favored expelling them. A fair amount of criticism had been leveled at the new code since its enactment, much of it coming from campuses anxious about the limits it placed on recruiting and financial aid. The combination of anxiety over these provisions, concern about the severity of the expulsion punishment and the failure to gain the required two-thirds vote in 1950 led the 1951 Convention to repeal the Sanity Code. Still, enforcement had made a public appearance, and it was not going away. The

1957 (March) —Dartmouth College's **Chiharu Igaya** becomes the only student-athlete to win six career individual titles in the National Collegiate Skiing Championships.

1957 (March 13-15) —First College Division Basketball Championship is conducted at the University of Evansville.

1957 (March 23) —The University of North Carolina, Chapel Hill, defeats the University of Kansas in a triple-overtime final at the NCAA University Division Basketball Championship.

1958 (November 15) —First College Division Cross Country Championships are conducted at Wheaton College (Illinois).

1959 (August 27) —Ownership of National Collegiate Athletic Bureau is authorized.

1959 (November 28) —First National Collegiate Soccer Championship played at the University of Connecticut; **Saint Louis University** wins the first of 10 championships between 1959 and 1973 (five under coach Bob Guelker, five under coach Harry Keough).

officers of the Association, as if to underline that point, decided that while the seven offenders could not be expelled, a majority of delegates had found them guilty. The leadership thus decreed that the seven would be classified as members "not in good standing." There would be more to come in 1952. In October 1951, a young man who had been serving as a part-time assistant since 1947 was appointed as the Association's first full-time executive director. His name was Walter Byers. He would have offices to house him and his staff. He came to the position with an optimistic belief in the potential of college sports and a determination to prove Gallico wrong. He remained in charge for 36 years.

There were, of course, other consequential developments in the 1930s and '40s. Membership grew steadily. By the 1951 Convention, nearly 400 institutions and conferences belonged to the NCAA. Radio broadcasting had grown substantially, producing concern about possible effects on game attendance, a concern of greater magnitude once television became common. The evolution of broadcasting — its problems, promises and impacts — is covered in detail in later chapters. Suffice to say here that no one could have envisioned the huge role electronic media would play in intercollegiate athletics when the NCAA sponsored the first men's national basketball championship in 1939. It was held in March that year, minus the madness. It was not televised. It produced a loss of $2,531.

EXECUTIVE DIRECTOR WALTER BYERS (LEFT), NCAA MEMBERSHIP PRESIDENT HUGH WILLETT (CENTER) AND NCAA SECRETARY-TREASURER KENNETH L. WILSON (RIGHT) CONFER DURING THE 46TH NCAA CONVENTION.

PHOTO COURTESY THE NCAA

Neither would most have anticipated then that college basketball would become the focus of gambling scandals that shocked the nation a decade later. Point-shaving claims were investigated in New York City, involving institutions in that area and others in the Midwest and South, seven in all. Trials followed, and a number of players were found guilty. Institutional control was clearly lacking on the affected campuses. This was major news, and further evidence of the need for stronger rules compliance and enforcement. The Court of General Sessions in New York mounted a probe led by Judge Saul Streit, who issued a statement describing his findings in unsparing language. Streit recounted the pattern of abuses on the campuses involved in the scandals, concluding that commercialism in football and basketball was "rampant." These are, he wrote, "no longer amateur sports." Athletes "are bought and paid for." Scouting and recruiting violations are "almost universal." Academic standards are evaded through "trickery, devices, frauds and forgery." Responsibility for the scandals "must be shared not only by the crooked fixers and the corrupt players, but also by the college administrators, coaches and alumni groups who participate in this evil system …" Finally, he said, presidents and faculty members must take charge of their athletics programs, and the NCAA must "reorganize and revitalize …"

Walter Byers had been in office for one month when Streit issued his damning assessment. Plenty of work awaited him. ●

DUKE CENTER CARLOS BOOZER PUTS UP A SHOT OVER ARIZONA FORWARD MICHAEL WRIGHT DURING THE 2001 DIVISION I FINAL FOUR CHAMPIONSHIP GAME.

WRIGHT
2

DUKE

Above the Rim

Each spring, the national frenzy of March Madness builds to a celebration of basketball at the Men's Final Four. The Division I Men's Basketball Championship is the Association's most-attended event—and the most-watched on television.

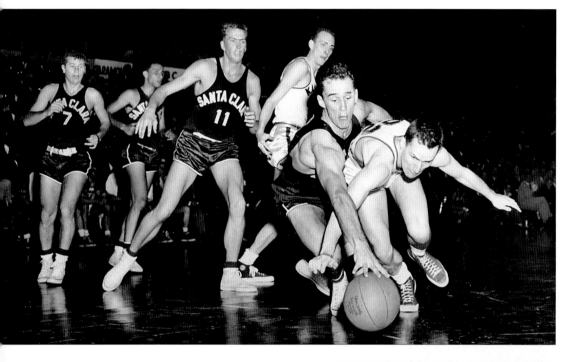

DEAN SMITH (ABOVE) AS A KANSAS PLAYER (DIVING FOR BALL IN WHITE JERSEY) AT THE 1952 FINAL FOUR AND AS A CHAMPIONSHIP COACH (RIGHT) OF NORTH CAROLINA AT THE 1993 FINAL FOUR.

COACH TUBBY SMITH (TOP MIDDLE) AND THE 1998 KENTUCKY WILDCATS CELEBRATE THEIR NATIONAL TITLE.

COACH ADOLPH RUPP'S KENTUCKY TEAM (TOP RIGHT) WATCHES IN DISMAY AS THE TEXAS WESTERN TEAM ACCEPTS THE 1966 BASKETBALL CHAMPIONSHIP TROPHY.

KENTUCKY'S STEVE MASIELLO (FAR RIGHT) LEAPS THROUGH THE AIR AS UTAH'S DREW HANSON LOOKS FOR AN OPEN TEAMMATE DURING THE 1998 MEN'S FINAL FOUR CHAMPIONSHIP GAME.

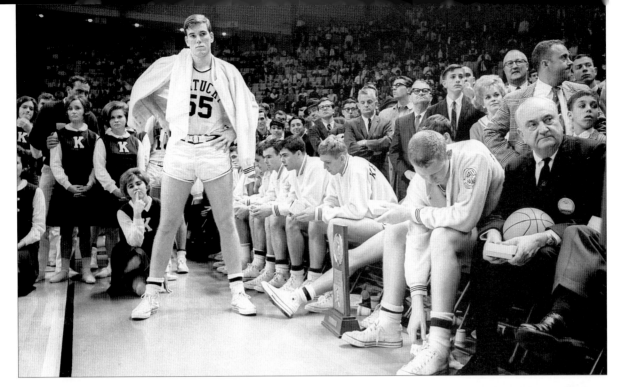

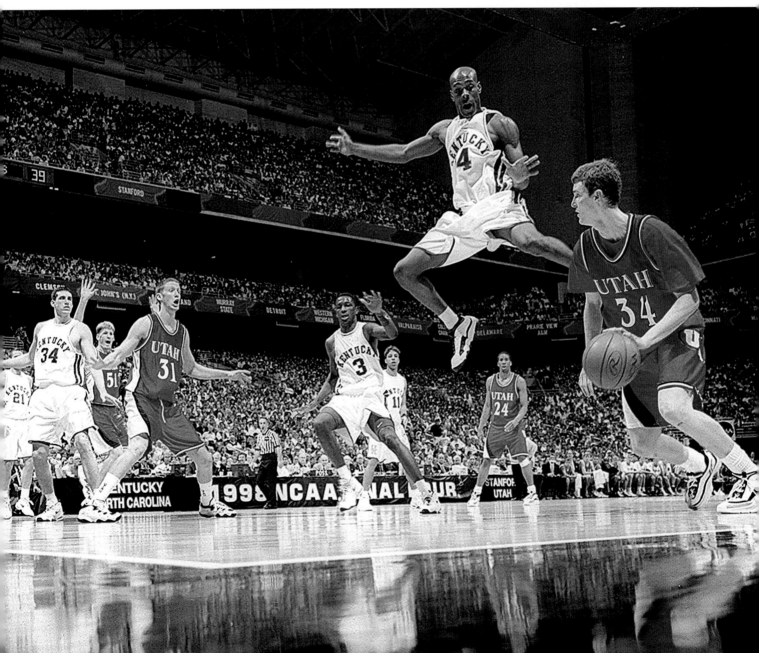

UCLA COACH JOHN WOODEN WITH SIDNEY WICKS, 1971.

DUKE'S GRANT HILL IN THE 1994 FINAL FOUR.

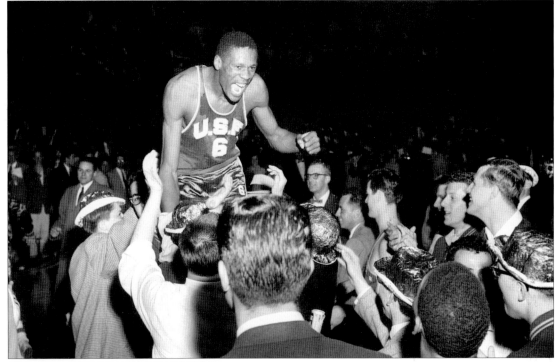

SAN FRANCISCO'S BILL RUSSELL (ABOVE) GETS A RIDE OFF THE
COURT BY FANS AFTER DEFEATING LA SALLE, 77-63, TO WIN
THE 1955 FINAL FOUR CHAMPIONSHIP GAME.

UCLA'S LEW ALCINDOR (LEFT) AND HOUSTON'S ELVIN HAYES BATTLE
FOR THE BALL DURING THE 1967 FINAL FOUR SEMIFINAL GAME.

Teamwork and Passion

The Division I Women's Basketball Championship celebrates its 25th anniversary in 2006, building a strong national following attracted by ever-greater athleticism and a commitment to team play.

TENNESSEE COACH PAT SUMMITT (ABOVE) DURING A 1997 WOMEN'S FINAL FOUR SEMIFINAL GAME.

CONNECTICUT GUARD DIANA TAURASI (RIGHT) DRIVES TO THE HOOP AGAINST TENNESSEE DURING A 2002 DIVISION I WOMEN'S FINAL FOUR SEMIFINAL GAME.

JIM GUND / NCAA PHOTOS

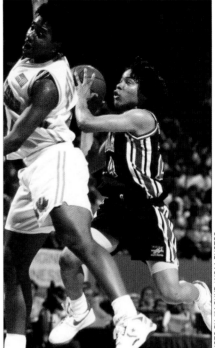

CHERYL MILLER OF SOUTHERN CALIFORNIA (ABOVE) DRIVES TO THE BASKET AGAINST GEORGIA DURING A 1983 WOMEN'S FINAL FOUR SEMIFINAL GAME. UNIVERSITY OF VIRGINIA'S DAWN STALEY (ABOVE RIGHT) WAS NAMED MOST OUTSTANDING PLAYER OF THE 1991 DIVISION I WOMEN'S FINAL FOUR CHAMPIONSHIP GAME.

STANFORD AND GEORGIA BATTLE (ABOVE) FOR THE REBOUND DURING THE 1996 WOMEN'S DIVISION I FINAL FOUR SEMIFINAL GAME. RUTH RILEY OF NOTRE DAME AND KELLY SCHUMACHER OF CONNECTICUT (RIGHT) JUMP FOR THE OPENING TIP-OFF DURING A 2001 WOMEN'S FINAL FOUR SEMIFINAL GAME

CONNECTICUT COACH GENO AURIEMMA SHOUTS INSTRUCTIONS TO HIS TEAM
DURING THE 2004 DIVISION I WOMEN'S FINAL FOUR BASKETBALL CHAMPIONSHIP GAME.

NOTRE DAME (ABOVE) CELEBRATES ITS VICTORY OVER PURDUE DURING
THE 2001 DIVISION I WOMEN'S FINAL FOUR BASKETBALL CHAMPIONSHIP.

BAYLOR'S JORDAN DAVIS AND LATOYA WYATT (LEFT) CELEBRATE THEIR VICTORY
OVER MICHIGAN STATE DURING THE 2005 WOMEN'S FINAL FOUR CHAMPIONSHIP GAME.

CHAPTER THREE

THE BYERS YEARS

THE NEW EXECUTIVE director got a sense of what the position would be like during the years he served as a part-time assistant, with a full-time secretary, working out of a remodeled hotel room in Chicago. He attended the New York Convention at which the Association had been unable to muster the two-thirds majority needed to expel the seven institutions that had violated the Sanity Code. He recalled the eight-column *Chicago Tribune* headline declaring, as a consequence of that failure, that the NCAA was dead.

Byers was at the 1951 Convention when the Code was formally repealed, and he was aware of the work of an interim committee that year in developing a new approach to enforcement. Given the organization's history of regulatory reliance on the members, and the powerful testimony that the Code's demise offered to the continuing influence of home rule, he certainly recognized the difficult road ahead. If he harbored any doubts about that, they would disappear when — in his first month on the job — it became clear that a sizable scandal was about to envelop the nation's premier college basketball program.

DEATH IN LEXINGTON

KENTUCKY WAS ONE of the seven institutions targeted by Judge Streit in his condemnatory public statement. The university's basketball teams had won national championships in 1948 and 1949. Players from those teams had been instrumental in earning the gold medal for the United States in the 1948 Olympics. Some were household names. Five went to jail, convicted of point-shaving in highly publicized federal trials. Their coach, the storied Adolph Rupp, was criticized by Streit for his relationship with a bookmaker. Kentucky's basketball teams, the judge observed, had become "commercialized enterprises."

The convictions and rebukes of the early 1950s followed a period during which the university — with strong support from the state, the institution's governing board and president, and the legion of Kentucky fans — had devoted considerable attention, energy and money toward strengthening its athletics program. The football stadium's seating capacity had almost doubled and the team's winning reputation was greatly enhanced under new coach Paul "Bear" Bryant, who would eventually become legendary himself. The state had committed funds to build a large new basketball facility. Control over the sports program had been vested in an entity — the University of Kentucky Athletic Association, Inc. — that was separate from the university, though with several of the institution's employees on its board. These developments had led a consulting firm, hired by the state to examine the university's possible role in economic growth, to question the direction intercollegiate athletics was taking. The firm noted in its 1947 report that the program at Kentucky, "as in other universities, has become professionalized" and recommended a return to "an amateur sports basis" as soon as such a change could be effected. The recommendation was not endorsed by the state and not pursued by the university.

UNIVERSITY OF KENTUCKY COACH ADOLPH RUPP

In August 1951 the NCAA Council approved a new code, covering long-standing concerns — limits on practice seasons and numbers of games; postseason competition; curriculum matters and academic progress; financial assistance; eligibility; and adherence to the rules, among others. Included was a call to member institutions, echoing down the corridors of decades past, to "enlist the support of true lovers of wholesome college athletics … to reduce undesirable recruiting." This code provided a basis on which to build a more practicable approach to enforcement, which the membership approved at the 1952 Convention. The new code estab-

CONNECTICUT'S KELLY SCHUMACHER SWATS AWAY ONE OF HER NINE BLOCKS DURING
THE 2000 DIVISION I WOMEN'S FINAL FOUR CHAMPIONSHIP GAME.

lished a Membership Committee and a Subcommittee on Infractions as well as roles for the NCAA Council and the annual Convention. The Membership Committee (the NCAA president and eight district vice presidents) was to examine complaints about violations, which then were to be investigated by the subcommittee. The findings of the latter body would be presented to the Council, which could suspend a member institution or place it on probation. Reinstatement was provided for. The Council could request that the Convention terminate membership in certain cases.

This was the structure within which Byers, as subcommittee chair, filed Case Report No. 1, the first formal action of the Subcommittee on Infractions, in September 1952. The party charged was the University of Kentucky. Byers' challenge was stern. The case would test his ability, and agility, as the NCAA's first CEO. It would determine whether nationally imposed regulations could work.

Report No. 1 charged that 10 players had received illegal financial aid. Rupp, it was said, knew about some of the offers. One prominent member of the 1951-52 team was thought to have been ineligible, though there was no such finding in his case. The Southeastern Conference commissioner suspended Kentucky from conference basketball for one year. The Council, through its Membership Committee, banned the program from all intercollegiate competition for that year. The central question was how to enforce this punishment. The answer — a "shaky death penalty," Byers called it — was to take advantage of constitutional language requiring that members compete only against institutions compliant with the Association's rules. Letters were sent to the membership asking for the cancellation of games with Kentucky. Considering the stature of the university's basketball program,

NCAA EXECUTIVE DIRECTOR WALTER BYERS (RIGHT) PRESENTS THE KANSAS BASKETBALL TEAM WITH THE CHAMPIONSHIP TROPHY AFTER THE 1952 MEN'S FINAL FOUR CHAMPIONSHIP GAME.

PHOTO BY RICH CLARKSON / NCAA PHOTOS

"A university fires its losing coach frequently without conscience and only occasionally with due process. But when a college cannot control a winning coach, the NCAA must step in to do the university's job."
—WALTER BYERS, IN HIS BOOK "UNSPORTSMANLIKE CONDUCT"

the refusal by its supporters and the state's governmental leadership to accept Judge Streit's conclusions, and the vigorous resistance to NCAA sanctions emanating from Kentucky media such as the Lexington Herald, the Association anticipated significant difficulty in carrying out the Council's decision. However, in the end, the university accepted the punishment. The NCAA's new standing as a vehicle for enforcement gained credibility. And Byers earned hard-won recognition for his leadership.

BUILDING AND BALANCING

DEVELOPING THE POWER to enforce the rules clearly and consequentially distinguished the new organization from the one that preceded Byers' appointment. Enforcement, the executive director said, "is the bedrock upon which the NCAA edifice is based." The resulting structure would have to be enlarged over the years as both the athletics enterprise and the Association grew; as the rules expanded and, commensurately, the temptation to break them; and as the college game increasingly captured the nation's fancy. Of course, other forces were at work as well.

Membership growth inevitably led to differences in the size, complexity and ambition of athletics programs among the institutions. Recognition of these differences eventually came in the form of periodic restructuring that introduced the word "federation" to the NCAA vocabulary. Cost issues, in terms of both expansion and containment, became an almost constant preoccupation. Growth also strained the most essential of Association relationships — the one that incorporates athletics into an educational framework. Eventually that problem would be addressed through academic-eligibility standards, although this development did not necessarily alleviate the strain. Conflict was a natural by-product of these considerations, as was the need to balance competing interests. Accommodations had to be worked out between national mandates and home rule; between the components of a federated structure; between the student and the athlete; and, constant equalizing efforts to the contrary notwithstanding, between the several levels of the playing field. Television was at the heart of the building and balancing, fueling the process of growth, extending the Association's reach, filling its treasury and exacerbating its tensions. Some saw a road to ruin, or at least to big trouble, in these developments and issued calls for reform. In particular, the American Council on Education (ACE) became involved, issuing critiques and recommendations on two occasions.

This chapter covers the NCAA's evolution during the three decades after Walter Byers' assumption of authority in 1951, and the executive director's stewardship as well. Enforcement will perforce be a focus. Federation, cost considerations, academic concerns and the interrelationship among these factors will be examined. The inevitable conflicts and compromises arising from the diverse nature of the membership will be reviewed. The role of television also will be evaluated. That topic, given its ever-expanding role, is a proper place to begin.

PHOTO COURTESY OHIO STATE UNIVERSITY ATHLETIC DEPT

THE GATE DEBATE

THE RAPID INCREASE in sports-event broadcasts in the period between the two world wars created uneasiness in college athletics departments. Attendance had dropped by the mid-1930s. The Depression was likely a significant contributing factor to this decline, which stood at 15 percent for football in 1934. But there was a strong enough feeling that radio was the culprit for the NCAA to establish a special committee to review the issue and report its conclusions in 1936. A committee survey of athletics directors yielded no clear answer regarding radio's impact on gate receipts. The exception was a belief by smaller programs that the widespread airing of major-college games demonstrably reduced their attendance. In any case, the individual institutions sold their own broadcast rights. Home rule was still a basic principle and practice. The NCAA, accordingly, did not have the franchise for radio. Television would be different.

The first telecast of an intercollegiate contest was NBC's airing of a Columbia-Princeton baseball game in May 1939. Football came next, with the 1940 Maryland-Pennsylvania game from Franklin Field in Philadelphia. However, not until the late 1940s did televised sports receive serious interest from the Association. There was again a concern about the impact on attendance, should television expand its scope as radio had done earlier. The NCAA Television Committee was created by the 1950 Convention to examine the gate question and other issues. The committee asked the National Opinion Research Center (NORC) to assist. The NORC reports confirmed that there was an adverse impact from TV and that the loss of attendance was especially prevalent in areas where television had a large presence. Elsewhere, attendance grew. The Association decided to pursue a partial television moratorium for the 1951 season to determine the effect of blackouts in each geographic area. Gate numbers again declined. A policy developed to provide limited telecasts under NCAA control was passed by the 1952 Convention, 163-8. As a result, a specific plan for the 1952 season was presented to the membership in a mail referendum. Again, the margin of passage (185-115) was impressive. Despite the overwhelmingly favorable votes, stern and vocal opposition remained.

The principal dissenters were Pennsylvania, whose team had played in that first televised game, and Notre Dame, whose renowned football program suggested to its leaders the benefits of pursuing an independent course. Their stated underlying principle was home rule, but the bottom line was money. These two institutions displayed their strong feelings from the outset. Each had televised its home games for several seasons. Pennsylvania signed a television contract for its 1951 games and seemed poised to ignore the partial moratorium that year.

1960 (March 19) —An Ohio State University team featuring four future Basketball Hall of Fame selections – Jerry Lucas, Bobby Knight, John Havlicek and coach Fred Taylor – wins the NCAA Basketball Championship.

1960 (April 7-9) —San Jose State wins its third straight National Collegiate Boxing Championships team title under coach Julie Menendez in the final competition before the championships are discontinued.

1960 (April 27) —NCAA cancels alliance with Amateur Athletic Union.

1961 (January 11) —National Collegiate Boxing Championships abolished.

1963 (March 15-16) —First College Division Wrestling Championships are conducted at the University of Northern Iowa.

1963 (June 6-8) —First College Division Tennis Championships are conducted at Washington University of St. Louis.

1963 (June 7-8) —First College Division Track and Field Championships are conducted at the University of Chicago.

Confronted with threats of reprisal from the NCAA, and boycott from fellow Ivy League institutions, the university backed away. Notre Dame pursued a course of energetic criticism rather than confrontation. Its president, Father John Cavanaugh, took note of what he believed to be the policy's "very dubious principles and procedures" and the NCAA's "dictatorial powers." The policy and plan for the 1952 season was revisited and an updated proposal was advanced at the 1953 Convention. Cavanaugh had since moved to another position, but his successor, Father Theodore Hesburgh, held the same outspoken views regarding NCAA control.

Francis Murray, Pennsylvania's athletics director, had been appointed by university President Harold Stassen in 1950. Stassen was interested in big-time football for the university. Murray thought television could be an important contributor. During a round table discussion at the Convention, describing himself as a "vehement member of the opposition," Murray criticized the NORC research, observing that polling data pointed to strong public support for unrestricted football television. He said the data suggested that limiting telecasts and thereby forcing people to buy tickets to see the games was "a bad example of commercialization in collegiate sports." Centralized control, he said, was inconsistent with the NCAA constitution and "contrary to the basic principles of free institutions." Notre Dame's athletics director, Edward

PHOTO COURTESY THE NCAA

ROONE ARLEDGE AND ABC CAMERA CREW.

Krause, followed Murray. He emphasized that nothing less than the public interest was at stake in the television decision. That position was echoed by the university's vice president, Father Edmund Joyce, who argued that the NCAA's approach "depicts a socialistic tendency." In the Cold War setting of the 1950s, this kind of claim was inflammatory. At other times, the charge of socialism was repeated by Hesburgh and by Krause, who took the allegation a step further. "Our stand," he said of NCAA control, "is that it is Communistic." And, more colorfully if less politically incendiary, he remarked that it was as if "someone tried to come into your home and steal your furniture." It would not be the last time in the long struggle over TV controls that the property rights banner would be run up the flagpole.

The 1952 plan provided for one national telecast each week for 12 weeks with wide geographic distribution, allowance for games of regional interest to be added or substituted and a stipulation that member institutions could appear on television no more than once during the upcoming season. A total of 51 teams had their games aired that fall. NBC paid a rights fee of $1.14 million, the great majority of which went to the members whose games were televised. Nationwide, attendance fell. The Association leadership, blaming the decline again on television, was determined to retain the restrictive policy for 1953. This set of circumstances gave focus to the lively debate that followed at the Convention that year. Speakers from the Television Committee held that growing a relationship with the new medium should be a process of "learning to crawl before we walk." They said that ideally the walk should be along "the middle road between those institutions who would ban television completely and those … at the other extreme who would … permit [its] monopolization … by the very few." This, the Television Committee representatives observed, was the "course of moderation and reasonableness."

The committee's proposal was approved by the delegates, 172-13. The detailed plan, once more submitted to the membership by way of referendum, was approved by a 95.3 percent majority. Restrictions on the number of games and institutional TV appearances continued. The rights fee from NBC for the 1953 season was $1.72 million. The NCAA felt comfortable that it was on sound ground legally, although several speakers suggested that, in fact, the restrictive policy violated the Sherman Antitrust Act. Serious discussions of that question were to come.

EXPANSION AND DISSENT

FOOTBALL ATTENDANCE DECLINED again in 1953, lending further support to the already widely held view that the restrictions imposed by the Association were necessary to preserve both the game itself and the gate receipts. Nevertheless, from that point forward, national football attendance grew every year from 1954 through 1981, excluding only a slight hiccup in 1974. The rights fee charged in 1954 was $2 million, and attendance increased that fall by nearly two percent. By 1981, the fee was $31 million, and 35.8 million fans went through the turnstiles that year. Although NBC was the dominant partner during the first 14 years, the other two major networks won occasional contracts. ABC started its 16-year run as the TV king of college football with the 1966 season. Rights fees, which were at $7.8 million that first year, stood at $31 million for the 16th season. Television sets in millions of homes were tuned in to the games. The expansion of ABC's football reach was the work of Roone Arledge. The increase in rights fees was the work of Walter Byers.

Arledge, the head of ABC Sports, almost literally changed the face of televised football. He brought instant replay, the split screen, the zoom lens, and lots of cameras and camera angles to the games. He involved the announcers more in telling the story. Byers said he admired him for his "sheer technical mastery," his "hyped-up genius" and his "indefatigable energy." Indiana professor and college athletics critic Murray Sperber wrote that the ABC head saw "college football as pageant and fable." Others said he saw it as "showbiz." For his part, Byers came to be regarded as a negotiator without peer. He downplayed negotiating skill as a significant factor in the periodic contract discussions, but, in this regard at least, he did not see himself as others saw him. The quadrupling of rights fees in the ABC era, the huge increases that followed in the subsequent two years (1982-83) and the even more impressive revenue brought in by the airing of NCAA postseason championship basketball are tributes to the talents he brought to the table.

Television revenue was the principal contributor to the Association's financial growth under Byers. In 1956, before these dollars began to make a big difference, the organization's treasurer reported that, for the first time in its 50-year history, the NCAA was financially stable. Stability was one thing; growth was quite another, particularly for a body now charged with rules-making, interpretation and enforcement; with administering more championships; and with managing diverse other responsibilities. The latter included the army of volunteers from the membership who served on the committees, councils, commissions and liaison groups whose critical recommendations — and, in some cases, decisions — became policy and procedure for the NCAA. More staff, greater expertise in certain areas, and bigger and better facilities were needed. Revenue from member dues helped meet the need, but television dollars provided the bulk of the funding. Football rights fees contributed to the establishment of postgraduate scholarships for student-athletes, subsidized championships travel, supported a statistical service and paid for the construction of a new headquarters building. By 1970, fees from the ABC contract supported a dozen different NCAA functions. Although the Association kept 12 percent of the rights fee the first year (1951), when Westinghouse had the football contract, the amount it routinely took thereafter ranged from three to five percent.

The Association's share of the net receipts from the Division I Men's Basketball Championship was a more significant source of support for NCAA operations than the football television assessments. Until 1980, net receipts of the basketball tournaments were split 50-50 between the NCAA and the competing teams. Thereafter, most of these net receipts went to conferences and institutions, with shares based on allocation formulas determined by the Executive Committee. Beginning with the 1981-82 academic year, the teams took 60 percent of the net and the Association 40 percent, giving the teams (and their conferences) approximately $10.7 million and the NCAA $7.1 million. Football TV assessments for 1981-82 were $2.3 million. The Association did not control regular-season telecasting in basketball. Distribution of the basketball championship funds was not a source of major continuing conflict; however, as the football rights fees grew, so did the arguments.

The major programs, seeing the opportunity to enhance their visibility and increase their treasuries, wanted additional appearances and the resulting money. The smaller schools, watching others' wealth swell, wanted a larger share. The Association, retaining control and

RICH CLARKSON / NCAA PHOTOS

1963 (June 12-14) —First College Division Golf Championships are conducted at Southwest Missouri State University.

1964 (March 20-21) —First College Division Swimming Championships are conducted at Grove City College.

1964 (March 21) —The **University of California, Los Angeles**, finishes an unbeaten season and wins the first of 10 basketball championships between 1964 and 1975 under coach **John Wooden**.

1964 (April 18) —32 $1,000 postgraduate scholarships for varsity letter winners authorized.

1964 (April 19) —Special Committee on Women's Competition is appointed.

1964 (December 12) —First College Division Regional Football Championships are conducted at Sacramento; Abilene, Texas; Murfreesboro, Tennessee; and Orlando.

1965 (January 12) —1.600 rule for initial academic eligibility is adopted.

1965 (March 12-13) —First National Collegiate Indoor Track Championships is conducted in Detroit.

staying with the principle of broad participation, continued to receive mostly strong backing from the membership. It opted for two-year network contracts in football in 1960, experienced closer voting in the 1961 and 1963 referendums, but received 96.1 percent majority approval for the ABC 1966-67 agreement. The number of permissible institutional appearances had grown to two in 1955 and, much later, to three. The mail referendum for the 1974-75 television contract was approved by 330 institutions, with 10 opposing. Even so, by the mid-1970s, there was much unhappiness about how the football television revenue was being allocated. The 1960s were relatively peaceful, in NCAA television sports terms. The conflict had not altogether subsided, but public interest in and excitement about college football, and its attendant financial advances, kept the discord manageable. It helped that by 1974-75, the NCAA was certifying 11 postseason bowl games, which provided an aggregate $8.2 million to the participating teams. By then, though, a number of institutional athletics departments were facing substantial deficit problems.

The cost of fielding competitive football teams had grown. Title IX, which became federal law in 1972, brought about a need for greater funding without attendant new revenues. The Association, while sustaining a pattern of membership growth, sought to recognize the growing differences in size, funding, attendance and mission among its members. The process was exacerbated by contention about how the Association distributed television dollars. Stephen Horn, president of Long Beach State, launched what came to be known as his "Robin Hood" initiative in 1975. He proposed cutting grants-in-aid for football from 105 in 1976 to 65 in 1978. He suggested that 50 percent of the net proceeds from football television be provided to Division I (which generated virtually all of the revenue) and 25 percent to each of the other divisions. His idea went nowhere, except onto a lengthening list of concerns shared by the leading institutional critics of the Association's television controls.

As the first three decades of NCAA TV involvement wound down, no one could reasonably deny the remarkable changes in the sports-watching habits of the American public. Nor, from a purely financial perspective, could anyone doubt that the Association's policies had made its members richer. But there were many more members now, and as their number grew, so did the distinctions between them. Old ideas regarding commonality of program and purpose were under strain, as was the basic operational standard of broadly spreading the TV opportunities. That new word — *federation* — entered the discussions of NCAA governance in the early 1970s. It was pushed into prominence by membership growth, the evolving divergence of institutional program and purpose, and, assuredly, by an increasingly impassioned debate about TV dollars. Television played midwife in the birth of a competing organization that soon dramatically altered the broadcast landscape. This group, the College Football Association (CFA), listed greater federation as one of its most important goals.

DIVIDING THE HOUSE

IT COULD BE argued that federation began its long and episodic journey in 1957, when the NCAA initiated championships in basketball and cross country for its then-College Division. The Association took this action because of the increasing difficulty of maintaining a level playing field between smaller-budget schools and those with major athletics programs. Growth, and the widening differences in resources, had reduced equitable access to championships. As these conditions evolved, further changes would be needed. Thus, in 1968, the NCAA asked all institutions to identify their programs as belonging to either the College Division or its University big brother, with the expectation that the members of each classification would compete mainly against one another. Then, during the 1972-73 academic year, the Association expanded the number of College Division championships to 10 and set up six regional postseason football bowl games for the members. None of these developments included rules differences between divisions. All NCAA institutions continued to meet and legislate together. The need to provide separate meeting opportunities had been acknowledged, but there was not yet a federated approach to rule-making. By 1973, the time for that was about to arrive.

In 1971, the Council created a Special Committee on Reorganization. The committee brought to the 67th Convention, in January 1973, a recommendation that would in effect make the two divisions distinctive entities for certain legislative purposes. The basis for such separation was the greater number of sponsored sports in Division I and a major emphasis in at least two of these sports, one of which had to be football or basketball. The committee's proposal was turned down by the delegates by a six-vote margin. Various reasons

STEPHEN HORN, PRESIDENT OF LONG BEACH STATE AND FATHER OF THE "ROBIN HOOD" INITIATIVE.

PHOTO COURTESY OF NCAA

were offered in opposition, one being the perceived inadequacy of a bipartite reorganization. There was now more diversity than two divisions could reasonably handle.

Despite the rejection in January, the demand for change continued. The Council immediately determined that the issue required a Special Convention — the Association's first — to revisit the possibilities. Such a meeting was called for August 1973. That assemblage put in place the three-division alignment that, with consequential adjustments along the way, still serves as the NCAA's basic organizational framework. The Association now had a federated structure, with each division empowered to establish its own membership criteria. Guarantees were provided for championships at all levels, and changes were made in the key governance entities — the Council and Executive Committee — to reflect the new framework. Certain areas, such as recruitment and financial aid, could be covered by different rules for each division. Much of the Association's business would still be accomplished together. The numerical result of this first successful effort at federation was that 233 institutions aligned themselves in Division III, 194 chose Division II and 237 elected Division I as their home. Of the latter number, 111 did not sponsor football. Of the 126 that did, most operated major programs in the sport. Many, though, did not. This difference proved to be significant.

With the 1973 legislation, federation became a principal battleground in the football television debate. From the perspective of a large number of major football powers, establishing the new Division I did not solve the problem. It was seen as being too big and, with so many members not sponsoring the key sport, it lacked a clear focus on football. It did not alleviate concerns about comparability and did not promise for the major powers what they considered to be their rightful share of the television wealth. So they sought a tighter drawing of the lines. In December 1976, 56 of them met in Dallas to discuss ways of separating legislatively from the rest of the pack. They viewed stadium size, a tougher scheduling requirement and an attendance minimum as possible standards. The objective was to arrive at a figure — around 80, it was thought — that would assure these institutions the financial and program comparability results they desired. After the meeting, 78 universities were invited to join the organization that would seek to achieve these results. Sixty-one of them attended the July 1977 gathering that put the CFA in business. At the 1978 Convention, a proposal was made, with CFA support, to subdivide Division I for football-playing institutions. Criteria similar to those discussed in Dallas, including a sports-sponsorship requirement, were to provide the dividing line between what would be called Division I-A and I-AA programs. The attendance rule (a 17,000 average, with alternative paths allowed for achieving it) proved to be the most contentious question.

Subdividing a division that had been only recently and controversially created was difficult for the delegates and tested the mettle of the Convention's parliamentarian. On one part of the proposed legislation, for example, a motion was made to vote by secret ballot. That was followed by a motion to vote by secret ballot on whether to have a secret ballot, which in turn produced a substitute motion for a roll-call vote. Next came a roll-call vote on whether to have a roll-call vote. The delegates favored the latter alternative and then, by roll-call vote, approved the passage in question.

This was town-meeting democracy in action, though it also illustrated the kind of Convention maneuvering that drove some delegates to distraction and, nearly two decades later, helped fuel a new federation movement and a different process for decision-making in Division I. Among the results in 1978 was the approval of an amendment, put forward by the Ivy League, to exempt from the attendance requirement institutions that sponsored a minimum of 12 sports. The amendment passed, 73-70. With this exemption, the I-A/I-AA legislation was approved, but, in the immediate aftermath, it produced only a small reduction in the number of members competing at the highest level of football. That new number was 137, a long way from the CFA's hoped-for 80. The battle, with federation and TV dollars pointed-

1966 (January 11) —First Honors Luncheon conducted at 60th Convention (honors 50 government officials, including three cabinet members, 17 senators, 30 congressmen).

1966 (March 11) —Kentucky Wesleyan University wins the College Division Basketball Championship, the first of eight Division II titles between 1966 and 2001.

PHOTO BY RICH CLARKSON / NCAA PHOTOS

1966 (March 19) —**Texas Western College** (now the University of Texas at El Paso) defeats the University of Kentucky in the basketball final with a starting team consisting entirely of black players.

1966 (April 23) —The National Collegiate Athletic Bureau is separated into publishing and public relations functions. The new College Athletics Publishing Service is moved to Phoenix.

1966 (April 23) —The Theodore Roosevelt Award, the Association's highest honor, is established. Dwight Eisenhower receives first award at 1967 Convention, where 12 astronauts who won varsity letters also are honored.

1967 (March 17) —Winston-Salem State University, led by most outstanding player Earl Monroe and coached by Clarence "Big House" Gaines, becomes the first historically black institution to win an NCAA basketball title (College Division champion).

PHOTO COURTESY OF INDIANA STATE UNIVERSITY

1967 (September) —Indiana State University becomes the first member institution to install an artificial playing surface (AstroTurf).

1967 (October 24) — Committee appointed to study feasibility of establishing development/supervision of women's intercollegiate athletics.

1968 —James "Doc" Counsilman publishes "The Science of Swimming" during period of success for his Indiana University, Bloomington, swim teams.

PHOTO COURTESY OF NCAA

1968 (January 20) —The University of Houston defeats the University of California, Los Angeles, in Houston's Astrodome before largest basketball crowd ever.

ly in play, was now joined in earnest.

Even with the quarrelsome conclusion to the 1978 subdivision discussion, and with CFA spokesmen expressing great disappointment at the outcome, some quarters said the Association had taken a regrettable step toward the creation of a super-powers classification for college football. An observer from Sports Illustrated disagreed. The decision, he wrote, "was neither a massive elixir nor a massive knockout drop. It will neither solve all the problems of the strong nor start a funeral march for the weak." What it did start, for the CFA, was an attempt to undo the perceived damage by finding a way to substantially decrease the number of I-A institutions. This effort began while the organization sought to negotiate its own television football contract. The CFA was back at the 1979 Convention, trying without success to repeal the Ivy League amendment. It was also working on its television initiative, hoping to bring into the fold the two powerful conferences it lacked —the Big Ten and Pacific-10 — that had refused the initial invitation to join.

The Association was understandably concerned at the prospect of a competing TV contract. It seemed to some that the likely consequence of losing NCAA control would put the networks in charge at the bargaining table and the institutions in financial peril. CFA leadership, on the other hand, believed that breaking the NCAA's grip would mean bountiful rewards for its members. As the dispute moved closer to the courtroom for resolution, Byers and his colleagues considered what might be done to further balance the equities, with regard to both federation and the television dollars.

On the matter of dollars, the executive director was involved in complicated discussions with more than one network. ABC's 16 consecutive years of sole ownership were about to end. Instead, a four-year contract was assembled, involving both ABC and CBS, with a two-year agreement for the Turner Broadcasting System. The total broadcast rights return exceeded $281 million. For the first year (1982), the rights fee was $64.8 million, more than doubling the $31 million ABC paid for 1981. The 1983 total was $74.2 million. The NCAA saw this as a bonanza for all members, including the major football institutions. In addition to the greater subsidy available for televised games, the number of appearances allowed was increased to three. The other bit of balancing the Association was prepared to undertake was support for further federation that could substantially reduce the number of I-A members. To accomplish that purpose, with litigation looming and the CFA at a serious stage of negotiations with NBC, the NCAA called a Special Convention for December 1981.

Put simply, the federation proposal at this conclave was to repeal the Ivy League exemption amendment, which had given refuge to many other universities, and to resurrect the attendance and stadium-size requirements that the exemption had effectively nullified in 1978. This action was expected to reduce the number of I-A members from 137 to about 95 and grow the I-AA classification from 50 to approximately 90. The proposal passed. However, it was not enough for the CFA, which had attempted to place on the agenda an item that would create a Division IV, to be composed of the paramount football powers. This effort failed, as did a related one from the University of Texas raising the question of institutional property rights in relation to television football controls. On this subject, the Council submitted a resolution, passed by a wide margin, that led to renegotiation of the 1982-85 television contracts and a sweetening of the kitty for Association members.

The various changes adopted at the December Special Convention dealt with the concerns of the football elite. Byers wrote later about his hopes for these changes: "If we satisfied [their] complaints and gave the football powerhouses more control, perhaps they would reject the lure and illusions of the CFA." That didn't happen. Earlier, the Association had made clear that any members violating the football TV regulations by developing their own contracts would get the speedy attention of the Committee on Infractions, and those found guilty could expect serious penalties. That pronouncement was reinforced by a motion passed at the January 1982 Convention that the NCAA would continue to "control all forms of … telecasting [and] cablecasting." These actions severely hampered the CFA's ability to rally its members in support of a proposed agreement with NBC. The federation initiative having been deemed insufficient and CFA television options looking bleak, no other avenues remained for resolving the differences within the NCAA family. The next venue for debate would be a federal courtroom in Oklahoma City.

SEA CHANGE

THE DRAMA THAT unfolded in Oklahoma City, and its historic final act, will be covered in Chapter Four. At this juncture, it is important to understand the changing environment in which that drama was rooted and within which the discussions of federation and television controls took place. New rules, amendments and continuing efforts to stretch rules of whatever vintage virtually transformed the landscape of intercollegiate athletics during the two decades that followed a weighty 1956 decision on financial aid. Much of what transpired during that period revolved around that recurring issue. Other developments — freshman eligibility, platoon football and rapidly rising costs — also played key roles in this transformation. By the end of the period, with financial bottom lines in trouble on campus, the NCAA approved a set of contentious recommendations on cost containment. The landscape was also meaningfully modified by this action.

In its effort to hold fast to the principle of amateurism, the defunct Sanity Code had proscribed the awarding of financial aid based on athletics ability. Economic need and academic talent were the only acceptable reasons for assistance covering tuition and fees. When the Code disappeared in the early 1950s, there was no specific standard governing aid awards. However, the subsidization of college athletes having been an old and varied (if often condemned) practice, institutions still found ways to help their players financially. There was a wide disparity in both method and amount. As before, ample criticism and concern arose, as did calls for reform. Some said that having all institutions on the same page would protect amateurism by ending the sundry assaults on the principle.

Others took this argument to be naïve. But both sides agreed that protection would be essential if the alien and potentially expensive notion of athletes as employees were to gain currency around the country. A 1953 Colorado court decision presented just that kind of threat. The result — an "experiment" in Byers' estimation — was a constitutional change enacted at the 1956 Convention. Henceforth, members could make awards for all "commonly accepted educational expenses," subsequently defined as tuition, fees, room, board, books, and a small monthly stipend for laundry and like expenses. The "full ride" grant-in-aid became the law of the land for intercollegiate athletics. The question of whether this was, in effect, an abandonment of amateurism and an endorsement of "play for pay" would be a subject of endless future debate. The reformers, by and large, were pleased.

The NCAA's founders could perhaps have been permitted a synchronized rolling over in their graves at this turn of events. But the sacred text they and their successors clung to during the Association's first half-century could no longer square (if indeed it ever had) with the changing realities of college athletics. The grant-in-aid was now in place. Critics would attack it from differing directions. Amendments would be passed to strengthen or weaken it. Reformers would learn that it was not all it had been expected to be. It did not stop cheating any more than the eloquent indictments of subsidization had in an earlier era. Institutions would discover ways to bend its provisions without eliminating them. But it became and remained the standard. The grant-in-aid provided common guidance, and a means of constraining excesses and defending the level playing field. It has stood for 50 years.

Another long-standing doctrine in the book of college sports began its journey into obsolescence in 1968. Even before the NCAA arrived on the scene in 1906, the idea of playing freshmen had been regarded as perverse by some institutions. That sentiment found a receptive home within the Association. Except in time of war, freshmen simply were not eligible for intercollegiate competition. Freshman teams were common, and first-year athletes might find a spot on the junior varsity. But beyond these opportunities, it was generally an article of faith that freshman participation was wrong. The first year was for adjusting to college life and continuing the process of mental, emotional and physical maturation. By the mid-1960s, increasing numbers of people concluded that times had changed; freshmen were ready to play, and institutions were prepared to play them. A 1965 survey determined that 64 percent of the responding colleges and universities believed that freshmen should be eligible for intercollegiate competition. Such a proposal failed in a close vote at the 1967 Convention. Western Athletic Conference Commissioner Paul Brechler argued at the time that, because of

PHOTO COURTESY OF UCLA

higher academic standards, students (athletes included) were now "better able to do university work." Travel took less time than it used to, he said. On the subject of time, he said "athletics today don't take any more [of it] than other campus activities." Further, freshman teams, with more grants-in-aid available and high attrition rates occurring, were expensive. Brechler's position was that first-year students ought to be eligible for winter and spring sports, but not football.

At the next year's Convention, a freshman-eligibility proposal was again put before the delegates for all sports except football and basketball. This time, after strenuous debate, the proposal passed, 163-160. Four years later, the membership added the two excluded sports. It was not fair, according to the proponents, for freshmen to be kept from competing in the two major sports when they were able to do so in all the others. Also, since first-year students had been receiving grants-in-aid, and playing on freshman teams, it made economic sense for institutions to play freshmen on their varsity teams. A tradition that dated back to an initiative taken by former Harvard President Eliot in 1903 was now abandoned. Coaches, Byers maintained, led the way in getting the change passed.

The membership made another important adjustment of the rules at the 1973 Convention. This one abolished an important component of the 1956 grant-in-aid legislation. That constitutional change included language allowing for the award of grants for up to four years. The language was permissive, however, and institutions and conferences applied it differently. Some adopted a four-year approach; others offered assistance on a one-year, year-to-year basis. The classic consequence was a tilted playing field, or so it was perceived. The programs using the four-year option had the advantage, it was claimed, though that alternative was open to all. A one-year rule would be more cost-effective and would give the student-athletes who did not perform well under multiyear awards an incentive to do better. So went the argument. The proposed change had been considered before, in 1967, and voted down. By 1973, though, institutions were feeling the financial pinch. Savings were available from passing a one-year grant-in-aid limit. The two-thirds vote required to change the constitution, where the grant-in-aid was anchored, was achieved, making the one-year rule a reality. Byers, who strongly opposed this amendment, observed that, with its passage, the "freshman tryout had been legalized."

The point about saving money had merit, given the circumstances. Athletics had become a costly proposition for members. Television and its promise to substantially enhance both visibility and monetary resources had engendered a zeal for spending. Institutions had spent. The authorization of athletics grants had complemented this zeal. Increases in student-athlete numbers, in numbers of coaches, in recruitment expenditures, ancillary benefits to the players (separate and sometime luxurious athletics dormitories, for example) and other areas had precipitated a near financial crisis on some campuses. Among the drivers of the expanded expenditure trend were increased squad sizes and the level of grant-in-aid support necessary to sustain them. Among the causes of greater squad size was the move to two-platoon football in 1965.

The platoon idea, like freshman participation, took root during World War II when, ironically, a shortage of talented players (many of whom were on military service) led coaches to spread responsibilities among the less capable athletes on hand. The talent shortage led to specialization, with offense and defense becoming separate pursuits. After the war, coaches having become enamored with platooning, the practice continued. This development was unpopular among veteran fans and those observers of the game who measured the worth of football against the model of the athlete who could do it all. One eleven, playing both ways, with few substitutes — this was the way it had almost always been. Specialization did an injustice to the treasured norm. It was also a milestone on the road to swollen budgets.

Still, coaches fought to keep the platoon system and its cousin, unlimited substitution. Byers and his associates in the NCAA leadership found a way around this formidable opposition. In 1953, the Council recommended a return to the one-platoon game. The proposal did not go to the Convention floor, however, but to the Football Rules Committee, where, at the time, athletics directors rather than coaches predominated. This was, as one critic described it, an end run. It worked. The committee endorsed the recommendation. Amid loud cries of protest, the game returned to its roots.

But not for long. Free substitution became a rallying cry. Gradually, modifications of the rule were devised and implemented. In 1965, after a 12-year absence, two-platoon football came back to stay.

THE BOTTOM LINE

PLATOONING'S PROPONENTS SAID the practice provides more opportunities for student-athletes and adds quality to the game and excitement for the fans. Its restoration, they argued, was a relevant development for an age in which specialized performance had become a necessity in many fields. But in the 1970s, a time when more institutions were dropping football for financial reasons, platooning also became a symbol of prodigal spending. Another such symbol was the growth of the grant-in-aid, the "scholarship" that had no relationship to scholarly endeavor nor to the financial need of the recipient. The possibility of changing to need-based grants attracted plenty of interest in the 1970s and led to several dedicated efforts to establish that idea as the governing principle for financial assistance. Cost control was a fundamental reason for pursuing this alternative. Such had been discussed and rejected in the 1950s, but with the bottom line now much on the minds of the members, the idea received a more thorough airing. It saw the light of day without a vote at the 1972 Convention, made the agenda and lost in 1973, and came to the floor once more in 1976. This was another occasion of major controversy for the Association. After a three-and-a-half-hour debate, and the first roll-call vote in NCAA history, the need proposal lost in both Divisions I and II. The margin was close in Division I, though, where 112 delegates voted in favor and 120 against. Perhaps the proposal failed this time because of a lessened membership appetite for cost containment after the substantial cutbacks the Special Convention produced the summer before. The football powers, equating need-based aid with de-emphasis, voted against it by a four-to-one margin. The closeness of the Division I vote led one writer to suggest that major college football was at risk:

> It wouldn't take you long to realize the sport is in danger of wilting on the vine because some of its self-professed expert gardeners keep crimping the water hose .… That danger will remain as long as your Yales, Fairfields, Pepperdines and New Hampshires continue to vote on policies for the likes of Texas, Oklahoma, Alabama and Nebraska.

Concern about spiraling costs prompted the NCAA to schedule the second Special Convention in Association history for summer 1975. Cost-containment alternatives dominated the agenda. The Council sponsored legislation in several areas, seeking and gaining reductions in various expenditure categories: numbers of coaches, grants-in-aid (total and annual), expense-paid visits by recruits and recruitment visits by coaches. The legislation limited squad sizes as well. Many coaches were unhappy with these actions. Some sued, hoping to undo the damage they saw done by the legislation. Staff reductions were a particular sore point, which was hardly surprising given the growth in, say, assistant coach numbers in football. At Alabama, for example, there were 17 coaches by this time. Now there could be only eight, plus two graduate assistants. Grant-in-aid allowances were also controversial: There would be a limit of 95 in Division I, where previously there was none. At Pittsburgh in 1973, a first-year coach had 83 grants to offer to his recruiting class. The Special Convention set 30 as the annual limit. Division I basketball would henceforth be held to 15 total grants, and, after football and basketball, a total of 80 would be permitted for all other sports. The Division II limits — 60 in football, for instance — were less contentious.

As the years passed, the membership eased squad-size limits and institutions found ways to expand coaching staffs. Recruitment reform became a hardy perennial. Probably the most consequential components of the 1975 legislation were the 95/30 football grant-in-aid specifications. The 95 number was further reduced (to 85) later; 30 was cut to 25 as the annual scholarship limit. Aside from whatever cost savings were realized through these reductions, one clear result as the years went by was increased parity among Division I programs. Most of the football powers of the mid-1970s remained powerful, but they could no longer stockpile large numbers of scholarship players. Some of those athletes would become available to the institutions for which stockpiling, for financial reasons, had not been an option.

All the litigation — four suits, in Alabama, Oklahoma and Indiana — failed at either the original or the appeals court level. Still, NCAA officer J. Neils Thompson expressed concern about "the continued tendency of some member institutions [and] some staff members of member institutions to frustrate the application of the NCAA rules by testing their validity through … court proceedings." Using the courts, he wrote, "it would be possible for a college with an ineligible player to win a conference championship and compete in the NCAA tournament before the matter could be finally adjudicated …" He may not have known it at the time, but Thompson was not just describing a current problem. He was anticipating a wave of the future.

1.600

PERHAPS LOOKING TOWARD a balancing of interests, the delegates approved an important academic reform measure at the same Convention (1965) at which they gave their blessing to the return of two-platoon football. Certainly, these delegates were aware that the admission of athletes with questionable academic credentials was an increasingly problematic practice. They could reasonably expect that problem to grow with the availability of unlimited substitution. In any case, they strongly supported an amendment establishing the "1.600 rule." This was an expedition into territory the borders of which had long been guarded by home rule. The amendment attempted to give an academic dimension to determining athletics eligibility.

ROBERT RAY AT THE 1975 NCAA CONVENTION.

PHOTO COURTESY OF NCAA

The 1.600 designation arose from the provision that incoming and continuing student-athletes must have "a predicted minimum grade-point average (GPA)" of 1.600 (on a 4.000 scale). The methodology for making such predictions was both complex and, to a degree, flexible. Then-NCAA President Robert Ray called the amendment "a national minimum academic expectancy." This approach was formula-driven, combining high school rank or GPA and standardized-test performance derived from ACT or SAT scores. Although various "tables" — institutional, conference or national — could be used to determine the best route to predictability, the objective was to have a student-athlete population with an academic standing comparable to the general student population at each college or university. The national-minimum piece of the legislation was critical. Conferences and institutions could exceed the minimum based on their own standards. Finally, the new eligibility rule was, in a sense, permissive; however, any institution that did not use it would forfeit eligibility to participate in national championships competition. Within the first 15 months after passage, 86 percent of the Association's 571 active members were in compliance.

But some institutions not only had not complied, they had no intention of doing so. The Ivy League announced that its members would not compete in NCAA championships. Three of those members — Harvard, Yale and Pennsylvania — informed the Association that they would not apply the new rule. Their teams that otherwise had qualified for postseason events were barred from competing. Headlines followed. And despite the ample margin of initial approval of the rule, opposition was not confined to the Ivy schools.

Criticism of the new standard began almost immediately, and it came from several quarters. The NCAA leadership continued to express strong support. President Ray regarded the rule as a principal reason why the 1965 Convention was "without question one of the most important in … history." His successor, Everett Barnes, told the delegates in 1967 that "nothing this Association has done in my memory ranks with its efforts to establish a common minimum academic standard." Byers was a constant and emphatic supporter. Atlantic Coast Conference Commissioner James Weaver agreed with NCAA officers that the 1.600 rule was "one of the most constructive pieces of legislation" ever passed by the NCAA. Alan Chapman of Rice, who would also soon serve as Association president, argued that eliminating the rule "would be a severe blow to intercollegiate athletics" because the determination of eligibility was now made by proper institutional authorities and not by the athletics department. "It is very valuable," Chapman said, "that a man approaches the registration office first, rather than the gymnasium."

But others felt otherwise, voicing varied arguments against the rule. Some believed it was simply wrong for the NCAA to involve itself in a decision that historically and appropriately resided with an institution. This was the standard home rule position, given added authority by its proponents' insistence that the national body was interfering with admissions. That position was not well founded in this instance since the question here was eligibility, not admissions. However, that counter-argument failed to convince the dissenters. Some 1.600 opponents expressed concern about the message being sent by the standard, which, they said, implied that a C- average was sufficient for college athletes. Others cited competitive concerns. They said a conference that used eligibility criteria exceeding the 1.600 minimum faced a comparative disadvantage when playing teams from conferences using the minimum standard. As the debate moved into the late 1960s, an assertion took hold that the rule (and standardized tests in general) showed a bias against economically disadvantaged students. These students were being increasingly courted by colleges and universities whose leaders believed that, given the temper of the times, they had an obligation to admit and assist them. This contention may have been the one that, in the end, tipped the balance.

The 1.600 discussion and discord continued for eight years after the 1965 vote. The NCAA leadership successfully resisted several attempts to terminate the standard during that period. The Association eventually passed an amendment to meet the concern about economically disadvantaged students, but divisiveness over the issue just got worse. Finally, at the 1973 Convention, opponents of the 1.600 rule prevailed. The rule was discarded, 204-187, and replaced by a requirement for only a minimum 2.000 GPA for athletics eligibility. The absence of a standardized-test connection, or some additional provision that could balance the wide variety of factors involved in comparing high school GPAs, rendered the new standard undemanding. Byers was depressed about the outcome:

> *Losing the 1.600 rule was one of the most painful experiences in the 22 years I had then served as executive director. It was a terrible day for college athletics. Supposedly responsible educators had voted for sports expediency .... For a decade afterward, the weak requirement ... would provide recruiters an open door to solicit whomever they wanted ...*

Lessons would be learned from the 1.600 experience. Reformers did not give up on the idea of creating a fair, reliable instrument for measuring athletics eligibility. Indeed, it would one day come to preoccupy the Association's leadership. For the moment, while opponents wore down support for a minimum national academic standard, the American Council on Education (ACE) geared up to launch a serious effort to rehabilitate college athletics. A similar effort by the organization in the early 1950s had fallen well short of that goal. The new decade's undertaking ultimately produced important changes, one of which was a set of academic-eligibility requirements known to history as Proposition 48.

PRODDING THE PRESIDENTS

JUDGE STREIT'S 1951 denunciation of the state of college athletics, and the gambling and other scandals that brought it on, led to ACE's conclusion that this subject needed urgent

1970 (June 18) —The **University of Southern California** wins the first of five straight Division I Baseball Championship titles under coach Rod Dedeaux (who coached the Trojans to a total of 10 titles between 1958 and 1978).

1971 (January 13) —Freshman eligibility in all championships except University Division basketball and postseason football is approved.

1971 (March 25-27) —The Association stages its first basketball championship in a domed stadium — the Astrodome in Houston — where the University of California, Los Angeles, defeats Villanova University for its fifth straight title.

1971 (June 5) —First National Collegiate Lacrosse Championship is conducted (Hofstra University).

1972 (January 8) —Freshman eligibility in basketball and football is approved.

1971 (May) —Florida Southern College wins the College Division Baseball Championship to claim the first of eight Division II baseball titles between 1971 and 1995 (three times under coach Hal Smeltzly, two times under coach Joe Arnold and three times under coach Chuck Anderson).

1973 (January 12) —First Silver Anniversary and Today's Top Athletes awards presented at Honors Luncheon.

1973 (January 13) —1.600 legislation is abolished.

PHOTO COURTESY OF WAYNE STATE UNIVERSITY

1973 (March 15) —Diver **Dacia Schileru** of Wayne State University (Michigan) becomes first female to compete in any NCAA championship during the College Division Swimming and Diving Championships.

1973 (April 6) —NCAA occupies new national office building in Mission, Kansas.

1973 (June 5-9) —The University of Oregon's Steve Prefontaine becomes the first student-athlete to win an NCAA University Division Outdoor Track and Field Championships event four straight years with his victory in the three-mile run; later in the year, he also becomes a three-time cross country champion.

attention. Since ACE is guided by institutional presidents, the committee the organization assembled to examine the issues was composed of campus chief executive officers. Notre Dame's Cavanaugh was a member, as was A. Whitney Griswold of Yale. Nine other presidents and chancellors sat on the committee, including John Hannah of Michigan State, who was chosen as chair. Hannah had taken a college of previously limited eminence and, in relatively short order, turned it into a big university with significant national recognition. He had help, of course, and some came from the institution's football team. By 1949, propelled in part by that team's success, Michigan State became a member of the Big Ten. A decade into his 28-year tenure in East Lansing, Hannah was the leader of the Special Committee on Athletic Policy, helping develop an agenda for athletics reform.

The committee's report was promptly issued. Its language was strong. The ACE document said that, despite adherence to "the highest standards" by many institutions, "serious violations not only of sound educational policies but also of good moral conduct are not … uncommon." The benefits of athletics competition, the report observed, were threatened by "proselytizing, subterfuge and distorted purpose." The committee's broad goals were to relieve external pressures on athletics programs, protect institutional control, develop strong enforcement measures and "suggest general standards of acceptable practice." Much of the remainder of the report was cloaked in the language of prior generations: Athletics departments should be part of the university's regular education structure, a la Stagg's situation at Chicago in the 1890s. The same admissions standards should apply to athletes and non-athletes alike. Freshmen should not be permitted to participate on the varsity. All financial aid must be administered by the institution and none should be awarded for athletics ability. These principles, and others noted by the committee, had been around since the NCAA's founding. They were still worthy in 1952, even though for years many colleges and universities had observed them only in the breach. Specific ACE proposals included eliminating football bowl games, postseason tournaments, out-of-season practices and expense-paid recruit visits to campus. The group also recommended the involvement of regional accrediting bodies to help assure adherence to sound standards.

The NCAA's reaction was lukewarm. The Association had no ground to stand on in opposing the principles and no reason to seek any since they were in essence already valued pieces of NCAA philosophy. The specific recommendations were another story. The Association would be willing to study proposals like the banning of postseason competition, but it held little hope its members would support that particular idea. Some limitations on out-of-season practices — spring football was the target — could be considered. Recruiting was always fair game for discussion. Nothing would be gained, the NCAA said, by involving accreditors. That was an enforcement matter, and the Association at this juncture in its history was becoming an enforcement organization. One was enough. Under these assumptions, NCAA leaders indicated they would be pleased to discuss mutual interests with the special committee and the ACE leadership.

Hannah, who attended the 1952 Convention (when football television was the topic of choice), apparently considered the NCAA's stance to be something of a compromise. Later that year, the ACE sponsored a symposium at which both Hannah and Association President Hugh Willett were speakers. Hannah criticized the press for focusing on bowl games and spring football, which were "minor phases," he noted, of the "total recommended program." He said he thought the NCAA would need time to follow up on the committee's principal proposals, notably the "standards of acceptable practice." Willett said that the NCAA would be "pleased to endorse the committee's objectives" and most of its recommendations since they were "the accepted policy" of the Association "and the established practice of a large majority of … members." What we need, he added, is "*more observance of the standards and legislation we already have …*"

The Hannah Committee disappeared from the scene forthwith, its efforts having availed little. Hannah himself became the target of criticism for his performance as chair. Professor Sperber wrote of him as an "ACE traitor" who "would carry the corpse of reform [and] bury it in an unmarked grave." In Sperber's view, the NCAA's role in the proceedings was to "subvert," not assist in, the cause of reform.

A representative of the Football Writers Association also spoke at the ACE symposium and offered a candid commentary on the troubled nature of contemporary athletics. He agreed that there were serious problems and that sportswriters did not have the answers. But he placed a large share of the blame on college administrators. An institution's president, he said, "can minimize whatever evils there are." That individual "can let his athletic director and coaches know that violations of rules or ethics … will not be tolerated." College presidents "have been in charge of athletics for many years," he added, and we cannot "overlook the result of their administration." As for the press and the proposed agenda for reform, he concluded, "we must remain as cynics and skeptics until we see whether college presidents mean business this time."

The reporter's observations, some might suggest, could just as well have been offered two decades later when the ACE came knocking again at the door of reform. Most of the major changes in intercollegiate athletics discussed previously were products of the intervening decades. The problems — and now, in the 1970s, especially those of a financial nature — were getting worse. There were those times when protest was in the air, as in the opposition to freshman eligibility, one-year grants or platoon football. There were occasional voices sounding the alarm, calling out the litany of sins and seeking a rebirth of the amateur credo. The annual Convention roundtables offered a platform for such declamations. At the 1961 Convention, for example, distinguished historian Henry Steele Commager demonstrated how the reform message was kept alive during these years. He spoke of the "terrifying consequences of present malpractices," particularly in relation to the old tradition of English and American games. Sports, in those gallant days of yore belonged "to the boys in the school or to the gentlemen in college." In that era, there were no finances involved, no admission charged, no expensive facilities and no handsomely paid coaches. Now the games have been taken away from the students, and college sports have become "heartily professional." In half a century, he declared, "or even less, we have repudiated and indeed reversed the tradition and the purposes of athletic games." But the situation could be remedied, he said: Remove "the dollar sign;" discontinue payment for athletics scholarships; stop the "junkets to faraway schools;" call a halt to bowl games. Coaches, he argued, should be full-time faculty members. Give the games back to the students. These changes can return sports to the niche in college life where they belong, he said.

Given those suggestions, Commager could have served happily with Palmer Pierce, written the 1929 Carnegie report, or contributed to the Hannah committee recommendations from 10 years earlier. He did not indicate that he intended his remarks to be heard by college presidents. Even if he had, it is not clear that in 1961 many of them would have been listening. Commager's speech had much the same result as many others of his day; the same result, by and large, as the ACE report had in 1951-52. Not much happened on the reform side in the 1950s and '60s. Such efforts did little more than remind NCAA members of the roots of college athletics in America. Meaningful positive change would remain out of reach until somebody could ground reform within the challenging realities of the last half of the 20th century. And bring the presidents to the table for a longer stay, for more than just a quick study of the problems and passing reproofs of a noble venture gone awry. That was ACE's aim in its next quest for athletics renewal.

With funding support from the Ford Foundation and Carnegie Corporation, the organization initiated a pilot study of athletics and higher education. George Hanford, a vice president of the College Entrance Examination Board, led the effort. His 1974 report — "An Inquiry into the Need for and Feasibility of a National Study of Intercollegiate Athletics" — was not a lamentation of the abandonment of hallowed principle. Rather, it was an insightful review of present issues and future possibilities. Hanford took pains to point out that looking to the past would not solve the problems. Amateurism "in its purest form," he argued, "disappeared years ago." That ideal form had become popular when athletics were "very much the privilege of the upper class." Today, he said, the definition is both elusive and controversial, lending weight to the question of whether pure amateurism "is consistent with the principle of equality of opportunity." The report noted that presidents had been criticized "with astonishing regularity" for "ignoring intercollegiate athletics." In Hanford's view, an earlier generation of campus CEOs had abdicated its "responsibility for the ethical conduct of college sports" and recent generations had continued the practice. The committee's inquiry yielded the impression that "the majority of presidents of big-time sports institutions tend to avoid paying direct attention to athletics ..." At this juncture, the report concluded, "there are problems of sufficient magnitude" to warrant involvement of these previously inattentive leaders.

The Hanford report gave particular coverage to "the economic plight" of college sports; the relationship among commercialism, entertainment and ethical shortcomings; and the need for a re-examination and strengthening of the fundamental tie between athletics and higher education. Future challenges were laid out with considerable foresight — the rise of litigation and the role of state governments, for example.

PHOTO COURTESY OF NCAA

CENTRAL (IOWA) PRESIDENT KENNETH WELLER AT 1992 COMMITTEE ON REVIEW AND PLANNING MEETING.

The need to bring women and minorities into the athletics mainstream would have to be faced. So would student-athlete medical concerns. The perplexing question of public attitudes about sports, especially the paradoxical tendency for athletics prominence to be "equated in the public mind with academic reputation and prestige," would need to be explored. The report repeated the Hannah committee preference for the inclusion of college sports programs in accreditation self-studies. A national assessment was needed, and there were plenty of difficult topics to consider. The vehicle for undertaking this task, the committee suggested, could be a Commission on College Athletics under the sponsorship of ACE. Soon after the Hanford team presented its report, the Ford Foundation gave the organization $200,000 to fund the work of this commission.

Those expecting the Hanford inquiry to produce a mandate for change that the NCAA would quickly embrace would be disappointed. Neither this inquiry nor the policy proposals from the commission that came next created a sense of urgency in the Association. The findings of the commission were reported in 1979, two years after its formation. Their familiar point was that higher education had to come to grips with the central question of where athletics fit in the collegiate scheme. Simply put, "do they constitute integral, adjunct or auxiliary parts" of the higher education mosaic? The commission, and the ACE, wanted an answer. "Until the college and university community decides this question," the commission concluded, "the problems of intercollegiate athletics will remain essentially unsolved."

The commission's report was printed in the fall 1979 issue of Educational Record, an ACE journal. Robert Atwell, the organization's vice president and soon to be its CEO, wrote in that publication about the need for campus presidents to assume the leadership role in athletics reform. If the relationship between higher education and college sports was to be articulated to suit the closing decades of the 20th century, the presidents, he asserted, would be critical to the task.

The NCAA News published the commission's report in its January 1980 Convention issue. Thompson wrote a commentary in this issue expressing disappointment with the report. He had been the Association's liaison representative to the commission, and he was especially concerned that some of the members of that body lacked understanding "of the impact, contributions and importance of collegiate athletics ..." He and Central College (Iowa) President Kenneth Weller prepared their own paper on the strengthening of NCAA programs and objectives, which made a point, often overlooked through the years, that the Association "is in essence a reflection of the thinking of its constituent members." That simple, truthful statement, though its authors may not have intended as much, identified a meeting ground where the ACE and NCAA could do business together.

Some observers expressed criticism that the two ACE reports, like their 1951-52 predecessor and the Carnegie effort of 1929, did not measure up to the mandate of bringing about large-scale change in a time of serious trouble. However, the ACE did not end its reform labors in 1979. As the next chapter recounts, follow-up endeavors led to two salient initiatives in the 1980s. One spoke to the question of the athletics/higher education relationship by making academic performance a test of student-athlete eligibility to compete. The other, proceeding from Hanford's findings and Atwell's urging, would help put campus presidents — after three-quarters of a century and not to the extent the ACE desired — in a leadership position in the NCAA.

MIDFIELDERS JEN BUCZKOWSKI (9) OF NOTRE DAME AND JILL OAKES (19) OF UCLA
BATTLE FOR THE BALL DURING THE 2004 DIVISION I WOMEN'S SOCCER CHAMPIONSHIP.

NCAA EXECUTIVE DIRECTOR WALTER BYERS (1951-87) IN HIS OFFICE IN MISSION, KANSAS

Walter Byers

THE ASSOCIATION REACHED its three-quarter century birthday in 1981, when Byers completed three decades as executive director. He still had six more eventful years to serve, as the next chapter reveals. That period challenged the strength, flexibility, character and even the existence of the organization Byers had built. He had assumed office at a time when the NCAA was under severe challenge. The immediate post-World War II years had seen an upsurge in the popularity of college sports, particularly football and basketball. But there was a similar increase in the kinds of problems the Association was then ill-suited to handle: proliferating bowl games, recruitment transgressions partially traceable to the return to college campuses of tens of thousands of World War II veterans and the gambling scandals that told a story of rampant disregard for the governing tenets of intercollegiate athletics. The future of the college game had been turned over at that point to a 29-year-old former undersized high school athlete who had been a journalism and English major at two universities and a sports reporter for United Press International. Daunting was hardly the word for the task confronting him.

By the time Byers retired in 1987, NCAA membership had grown from 381 to 1,003, employee numbers from two to 143, and championships from 11 for men only to 74 for men and women. He could take credit for football television contracts that began with a $1.1 million payout in 1952 and grew to a rights fee of $74.2 million for the last one he negotiated. TV revenue for the Division I men's postseason basketball tournament increased from $550,000 to $36 million between 1970 and 1987. He had resolved a decades-long conflict with the AAU decidedly in the Association's favor. Beyond those impressive accomplishments, Byers had developed a substantial NCAA enforcement capability — a principal charge when he took the job — that had punished many cheaters and doubtless held in check others who otherwise may have been sorely tempted to cut illicit corners. He had put together a staff committed to excellence in performance and service to the membership.

Most of that work was behind him by 1981. His successes had given his name great visibility, though his person was almost never out front. The fact that the modern NCAA was an outgrowth of his vision and priorities, coupled with the circumstance that the organization had a strong regulatory emphasis, meant its leader would come to be regularly reviled. The NCAA investigated possible violators. It meted out controversial punishments. It published rules interpretations that sometimes tied the hands of people seeking a competitive edge. It was in charge of maintaining (or trying to maintain) the elusive level playing field. It had to contend with the well-anchored tradition of home rule. The Association, Byers wrote, "was the only cop on the block — target of all the blame." He carried the sentinel image. He was the chief enforcer.

Many critics perceived him as a dictator, or something worse. A 1985 article in The Sporting News noted that he had been "compared to J. Edgar Hoover and the Ayatollah Khomeini, to Howard Hughes and Adolf Hitler…" A more recent publication portrayed him as a person of "cold, calculating aloofness" who "built the NCAA into a "coldly efficient organization." His was a "shadowy presence," and the "arrogance and mind-boggling inflexibility" of his enforcement staff was a reflection of Byers' "personality and his rigid sense of duty." He was "a symbol" of the Association's "unchecked power and apparent unaccountability."

The hyperbolic character of such descriptions exposes, perhaps unwittingly, a simple, important truth about the organization, one that assuredly bears Byers' signature. The NCAA is a regulatory body. The membership asked him to build it that way, and he did. And that body has the charge of regulating a field of endeavor more visible than most and one whose practitioners can too often be attracted by the notion that chicanery pays. The executive director understood

BYERS (ABOVE) TALKS WITH CBS SPORTS PRESIDENT NEAL PILSON (LEFT) AT HALFTIME OF THE 1987 FINAL FOUR.

BYERS WITH THE EMMY FOR TV COVERAGE OF THE FINAL FOUR.

that. He took for granted that disparaging commentary would disproportionately come his way. This acceptance came from his deeply held belief that the NCAA was at heart a service organiza-

INCOMING EXECUTIVE DIRECTOR RICHARD D. SCHULTZ AND WALTER BYERS

PHOTO FROM NCAA FILES

"The experiences of my good friends among conference commissioners convinced me that only a national organization, insulated from local and regional power politics — the NCAA, to be precise — had even a faint hope of doing the enforcement job. I suppose that is why I earned a reputation as a puritanical dictator."
—WALTER BYERS, IN HIS BOOK, "UNSPORTSMANLIKE CONDUCT"

tion, and one of its services was to function as a lightning rod for the membership.

There is great irony in language depicting the Association as a "cold" and "unaccountable" entity, imbued with arrogance and distant from its members. Byers staffed it with people who knew, and acted on the knowledge, that service was job one. This wasn't rhetoric. It was an operational imperative. From the vantage point of the early 21st century, the office rules may seem antiquated. Daily attendance was taken. At one time employees could not take coffee breaks, eat in their offices, or have drinks or foodstuffs atop their desks. A dress code for both genders was enforced. Women could not wear jeans, but tailored slacks were acceptable. Men wore coats and ties, though they could shed the coats and loosen the ties while working in the building. Everyone was expected to work a full day. These rules were set, Byers said, to promote a businesslike atmosphere and because "we had to earn the respect of our member colleges." Office policies included working on Saturday mornings, initially required of all staff members and later based on a system of taking turns in accord with a monthly calendar. When returning from Conventions or other important meetings (where spouses were not

allowed to accompany their working mates), Byers expected staff to go to the office before going home in order to tend to whatever urgent business the meetings generated. Byers viewed his rules and policies as the necessary attributes of a professional organization, put in place, again, to send that message to the members.

Employees may have grumbled a bit, but they accepted the office protocols the executive director laid down. That's just the way it was — a condition of employment. There were no real morale problems. As one former Association administrator put it, "the fact that [we were] so eager to please and do right by him was not a measure of our fear, but rather our respect for him." And the advantages of working at the NCAA, and for Byers, were considerable. Long-serving staff members, some still with the Association, are virtually of one accord on that matter. Byers was "the most insightful person I have ever worked with," one of them observed. "He was the single brightest person I ever encountered," said another. "The smartest man I ever met," said a third. He was "brilliant," a former employee reported, "so far ahead of everyone. Sitting in his staff meetings for a year was like getting a Ph.D." He was demanding, thorough, fair, witty, shy rather than arrogant, tolerant of disagreements and intolerant of incompetence. If one wished to disagree with the executive director's position on an issue, wisdom suggested that one should have all the facts at hand and the aptitude to offer a persuasive recitation of them. What people especially recall, and appreciate, about working for Byers is that — as one of them put it — "he stretched you to the limit of your capabilities. He drew out your best." He insisted that correspondence and other information that left the office en route to member institutions be full of meaning and free of error. Clear communications were essential, which was another feature of the service mentality and testimony to the importance of professional performance.

Byers did not crave the spotlight. He was a behind-the-scenes leader, and an effective one. People from the membership — the officers and committee chairs — spoke for the Association. They were the leaders, the out-front individuals. Byers emphasized that. The staff did not make policy. They implemented it. He included himself in the implementing category. Neither he nor they were decision-makers. The members made the decisions, and that was that. He was, however, a major contributor. The important decisions usually carried his imprint. He worked with the leadership on the issues, providing his ideas, assessments and counsel. In that way, he influenced outcomes. The membership furnished the leaders, and they were certainly not puppets. But there was seldom doubt that Byers was the man in charge. In a few areas, television contracting being one and AAU relations another, he was the visible leader. Otherwise, he led from inside the councils of governance.

Byers also had a hard edge, probably in some measure a product of enduring so much external criticism. He handled the personal attacks, as one writer said, with "infuriating silence." The business he was in, which offered ample opportunity to witness the nether side of a popular pastime, likely made him more skeptical at the end of his tenure than he was at the beginning. Some of the people closest to him believe that he was not a particularly happy man, that he came to expect the worst from people (though not from his employees), that he was both idealist and iconoclast. From the beginning, he "passionately believed NCAA rules could preserve the amateur collegiate spirit [he] so much loved …" He sustained that belief through most of his years with the Association. It informed his sense of the 1950s and '60s "as a romantic era" for college sports. A quarter-century into his appointment, he was still positive about the power of enforcement. It was still that "bedrock of the edifice" for him. He had come to perceive recruiting as the "Achilles heel" of intercollegiate athletics, but he was persuaded that the "competitive spirit of youth," the importance of higher education and the recent changes in the rules would ultimately prevail.

By the mid-1970s, he had experienced that series of defeats — freshman eligibility and the rest — that, despite his lingering confidence, clouded his horizon. A decade later, he was talking publicly about the high percentage of cheaters among the major schools, the chronic violators and his conviction that "intercollegiate athletics are out of control." He was by that time two years away from retirement, with a decade to go before he published a book that seemed to call his whole NCAA career into question. He used the publication to excoriate both the enterprise he loved and the organization he had built to govern it. The language of the book is often acerbic. Byers describes a system "biased against human nature," controlled by "overseers" and "supervisors" at the expense of the "plantation workers." He blames the campus presidents (overseers), the coaches (supervisors), and the pervasive and destructive influence of big money. He expresses strong support for student-athletes (the workers). The Association has become a "centralized bureaucracy" that believes a national body "can do a better job than the local people." He argues on behalf of "deregulation" and, recalling the way athletics did its business well before the NCAA came along, concludes that "it is time to give back to the students who play sports the freedoms they deserve."

Walter Byers had reason to feel bitter as his first 30 years on the job came to a close. The passage of initiatives he so strongly opposed had divorced intercollegiate athletics from some prized traditions. Increasing federation, which had the effect of widening the divide between the haves and have-nots, threatened the underpinning of the NCAA as an association. Television had become a force beyond his control. A rival organization (the College Football Association), led by an individual he had hired, whose career he had helped advance, was camped outside the gates. Byers still had six years to serve. They would be good years for him in some ways. There were signal accomplishments yet to come. But one more disappointment awaited, perhaps the most embittering blow of all. That was the loss of the football television court case.

Whatever happened to drive the Association's first chief executive officer to such deep-felt disillusionment about the line of work to which he devoted the best and biggest years of his life, there should be no dispute that he left to college sports a legacy uniquely his own. The NCAA remains in so many ways the house that Byers built. It is a house of many more mansions than were there when he began, but those mansions still bear his mark. On the occasion of his retirement, his good friend Don Canham, long-time Michigan athletics director, paid Byers homage: "He is a complex character," Canham said. "He is a great leader, … a perfectionist, [and] he has unquestionable integrity and great vision." He is "loyal to the organization and … to his friends and foes … He is tough." He will be "revered and respected and remembered."

One hopes the remembrance is first of his 36 years of leadership and then — with the trappings of obloquy removed — of the wisdom that lies between the covers of his book. ●

RICHARD D. SCHULTZ,
EXECUTIVE DIRECTOR, 1987-93

PHOTO FROM THE NCAA

CEDRIC DEMPSEY,
EXECUTIVE DIRECTOR, 1994-02

PHOTO FROM THE NCAA

MYLES BRAND, PRESIDENT, 2003-PRESENT

PHOTO FROM THE NCAA

Tradition

The Men's College World Series has been played at Omaha's Rosenblatt Stadium each year since 1950 – by far the longest tenure for an NCAA championship at a particular site.

PHOTO BY JAMIE SCHWABEROW / NCAA PHOTOS

TEXAS FIRST BASEMAN JEFF ONTIVEROS BREAKS UP A DOUBLE-PLAY ATTEMPT BY SOUTH CAROLINA SHORTSTOP DREW MEYER DURING THE 2002 MEN'S COLLEGE WORLD SERIES.

PHOTO BY RICH CLARKSON / NCAA FILES

THE COLLEGE WORLD SERIES OF 1956 DREW MOSTLY SCOUTS (ABOVE) WHILE TODAY'S EVENT PACKS EVERY SEAT (RIGHT). THE EVENT HAS BEEN PLAYED AT ROSENBLATT STADIUM IN OMAHA, NEBRASKA, SINCE 1950.

CAL STATE FULLERTON PLAYERS RUSH THE FIELD TO CELEBRATE THEIR 11-5 VICTORY
OVER SOUTHERN CALIFORNIA DURING THE 1995 MEN'S COLLEGE WORLD SERIES.

360

WRIGHT
13

RIGHT FIELDER RAY WRIGHT OF LSU STEALS A HOME RUN FROM EDMUND MUTH
OF STANFORD DURING THE 2000 MEN'S COLLEGE WORLD SERIES.

DANE BUBELA OF RICE IS TAGGED OUT BY CATCHER RYAN GARKO OF STANFORD DURING THE 2003 MEN'S COLLEGE WORLD SERIES CHAMPIONSHIP GAME.

DAVID MAROUL OF TEXAS IS CONGRATULATED BY HIS TEAMMATES AFTER HIS HOME RUN AGAINST FLORIDA DURING THE 2005 DIVISION I COLLEGE WORLD SERIES.

Momentum

The Women's College World Series annually adds to the national following for women's softball. The WCWS ranks among the Association's most popular televised championships.

ARIZONA CELEBRATES ITS VICTORY OVER UCLA DURING THE 2001 WOMEN'S COLLEGE WORLD SERIES CHAMPIONSHIP GAME.

PHOTO BY CHRIS LANDSBERGER / NCAA PHOTOS

LINDSAY JAMES OF CALIFORNIA BEATS THE TAG BY UCLA CATCHER EMILY ZAPLATOSCH DURING THE 2004 DIVISION I WOMEN'S SOFTBALL CHAMPIONSHIP.

PHOTO BY BRYAN TERRY/NCAA PHOTOS

PITCHER NANCY EVANS OF ARIZONA DURING THE 1998 NCAA DIVISION I WOMEN'S SOFTBALL CHAMPIONSHIP.

UCLA CELEBRATES ITS VICTORY OVER CALIFORNIA DURING THE 2003 DIVISION I WOMEN'S SOFTBALL CHAMPIONSHIP.

2002 NCAA DIVISION II
CROSS COUNTRY CHAMPIONSHIPS
510

2002 NCAA DIVISION II
CROSS COUNTRY CHAMPIONSHIPS
511

2002 NCAA DIVISION II
CROSS COUNTRY CHAMPIONSHIPS
506

Adams State

CHAPTER FOUR

ORGANIZATION, ENFORCEMENT, REFORM

WALTER BYERS, WISE as he was, probably could not have foreseen all the developments that, in the six years preceding his 1987 retirement, would significantly change the organization he had built during the previous three decades. From a longer-term perspective, it is unlikely he could have anticipated the array of forces and factors and resultant modifications that gave the Association a dramatically altered architecture and challenging new priorities by the time it made ready to enter its second century. One can make a reasonable case that much, maybe even most, of what has transpired in the last 25 years had a precedential presence in the activities and emphases of the NCAA in the period of Byers' tenure leading to 1981. He had helped facilitate the absorption of women's programs into the Association's structure and processes, which would lead to major roles for women within the organization and on the member campuses. The enhancement of the enforcement responsibility over the last quarter-century proceeded from Byers' long-standing championship of that responsibility as a fundamental one. The arrival of ambitious academic-eligibility legislation in the 1980s, initially through Proposition 48 and related amendments, was at least in part an outgrowth of the problematic efforts to set basic standards in this area in prior years.

There had been stirrings of greater presidential participation earlier, and Byers had been supportive, but one wonders whether he thought of them as a starting point for initiatives that would ultimately give the presidents control of the Association. In light of the decades-long controversy over management of football television he probably would not have been surprised by the escalation of that issue in the early '80s. It seems doubtful, however, that Byers (or anyone else for that matter) could have fully understood the profound difference that the subsequent loss of this management authority would make for the NCAA and intercollegiate athletics in general.

This chapter focuses on rules-making, enforcement and governance since 1981, particularly Proposition 48 and successor legislation on academic eligibility. Other rules-change initiatives dealt with in this chapter include financial aid to and recruitment of student-athletes, cost containment and governmental arrangements. Additional legislation of consequence during the period — on championships, drug testing, women's issues, student-athlete welfare and coaches' compensation, for instance — and the more recent eligibility rules will be discussed later in the book. The heightened debate over football television and the court decisions that settled it will be covered here, but most of what developed in the wake of these decisions will be taken up in Chapter Seven. One way or another, enforcement considerations arise with respect to all of these matters. It may help to begin with some data on that knotty and persistent issue.

THE NUMBERS SPEAK

IN THE NINE years after the 1974 actions strengthening the Association's enforcement mandate (1975-83), the Committee on Infractions meted out punishments in 96 cases — 69 involved recruiting, 46 involved financial aid and 41 dealt with extra benefits. There were breaches of the regulations on tryouts (25 cases) and excessive visits of prospective student-athletes (22), academic fraud (11), institutional control (20) and unethical conduct (32). Tied usually to recruitment activities were infractions involving transportation (64 cases), entertainment (55), inducements (54) and lodging (43). Fifty-four of the 96 cases related to football and 54 to men's basketball; 16 of them involved both. No other sport had more than six cases of violations.

Among the major conferences, the Pacific-10 had six member institutions placed on probation during this period. There were probation punishments involving five institutions in the nine-member Southwest Conference, five in the Big Eight (and three public reprimands) and four in the Southeastern Conference, while two Big Ten members were involved in five cases. Fourteen institutions had repeat violations, including three with three separate cases.

THE ADAMS STATE CROSS COUNTRY TEAM FOLLOWING THE 2002
DIVISION II MEN'S AND WOMEN'S CROSS COUNTRY CHAMPIONSHIPS.

Institutional infractions typically were well publicized in the violator's local media, particularly when probation or other serious penalties resulted. A number of the cases became notable nationwide. Five of the Pacific-10 universities, for example, were caught up in academic-fraud scandals involving fake grades for student-athletes, either through extension courses taken (but not attended) from other colleges or, in one case, from courses offered on campus. The conference's presidents made all five ineligible for the Pacific-10 football championship for one year and prohibited their participation in that season's bowl games. Game forfeits, television bans and grant-in-aid reductions were also handed down by the conference and the NCAA. The negative publicity generated by such cases, together with an understanding that the NCAA's enforcement function had grown in strength and effectiveness, began to capture the attention and concern of institutional presidents around the country. Before this period, presidents in general did not prominently support Byers' emphasis on NCAA enforcement. Instead they followed the practice of the time, a strategy of, as John Thelin called it, "avoidance and accommodation." Beyond that, for three-quarters of a century presidents had shown relatively little interest in being part of the Association's governance structure. The NCAA's Long-Range Planning Committee began serious discussions of enhanced presidential participation in the late 1970s. And Long Beach State CEO Stephen Horn had for some years been a tireless and articulate advocate of that cause. Now, as the return on Byers' investment in enforcement became more evident, presidents awakened to a realization of their institutions' vulnerability. As a result, NCAA governance increasingly became a focus of presidential attention.

JAMES FRANK, NCAA PRESIDENT 1981-83

PHOTO FROM NCAA FILES

For three-quarters of a century, presidents had shown relatively little interest in being part of that structure. During Byers' early years, Association leaders came mostly from the academic side of campus life. In 1953, not long after he became executive director, 11 of the NCAA Council's 16 members were faculty representatives. The other five were athletics directors. Twenty-five years later, the Council (composed of district representatives, vice presidents at large and three divisional steering committees) still had a distinctly academic flavor. Only seven of the 22 members of the Division I and Division II steering committees were athletics directors. Six of the eight individuals from Division III carried that title, but most of them served also as faculty members. Of interest that year (1978) was the presence of five institutional presidents on the steering committees. One of them, James Frank of Lincoln University (Missouri), soon became the first campus CEO to serve as NCAA president. By 1987, Byers' last year, 70 percent of the Council members directly represented athletics interests (29 athletics directors and two conference commissioners) and dominated all three steering committees. Many, again, particularly in Division III, were also institutional faculty members. Of the 13 remaining members, six were in positions specifically set aside — two in each division — for campus presidents. The demography of Association leadership had clearly changed, in more ways than one.

PROPOSITION 48

THE BIGGEST CHANGE occurred with the establishment of the Presidents Commission in 1984. But a clear augury of that development came the year before when the Convention, meeting in San Diego, took up new academic-eligibility legislation. The American Council on Education which, it will be recalled, had moved forward substantial reform measures in 1952 and 1974, led both initiatives. Motivated now, as on those previous occasions, by the fallout from collegiate athletics scandals and questionable practices, the ACE formed a committee to examine eligibility standards. Acting on a suggestion previously put forward by the CFA, the committee recommended legislation establishing a specific high school core curriculum that a student would have to pass with a minimum 2.000 GPA. In addition, to be eligible as a freshman, a student-athlete would be required to have at least a 700 combined verbal and math score on the SAT or a 15 composite score on the ACT. These requirements were to apply in Division I only and would take effect in 1986. The proposed legislation — "Proposition 48" — was approved, along with companion legislation allowing student-athletes who could not meet these requirements but had an overall 2.000 high school GPA to receive financial aid, although they would still lose a year of athletics eligibility. Even though the ACE and the Council cosponsored this legislative package, the proceedings were contentious from the start. Indeed, along with successor legislation based on similar premises, Proposition 48 produced passionate controversy that persisted for two decades, summoning memories of the 1.600 rule and the arguments that killed it.

The fundamental issue raised by Proposition 48 opponents on the Convention floor in 1983 was race. They claimed that the requirements would disproportionally affect students from economically deprived backgrounds, particularly minority students and most particularly African-Americans. The National Association for Equal Opportunity (NAFEO), representing more than 100 predominantly black colleges and universities, presented a letter to the Convention raising the prospect of discrimination and suggesting that implicit in the legislation was a withdrawal of the commitment shared by NAFEO institutions to admit and nurture high-risk students. Fifteen presidents spoke on the proposal during the delegates' debate. Five were from historically black campuses. Delaware State President Luna Mishoe argued that the SAT "is a restraint that penalizes low-income students and does not indicate whether a student can perform college work." He asserted that "test scores have nothing to do with ability." Presidents Joe Johnson of Grambling and Frederick Humphries of Tennessee State said the legislation was bigoted and had the hidden agenda of assuring whiter teams for institutions with major athletics programs. The discussion proceeded for two hours. When it was over, the delegates passed the legislation with a 52 percent majority.

This vote represented an initial victory for what later became known as a major reform agenda instigated by presidents. The 1983 Convention featured a large attendance by campus CEOs. The ACE representatives were on hand and actively lobbying the legislation, and presidents took the lead in promoting it on the floor. For some, Proposition 48 spoke to a need to breathe new life into a founding principle of the Association, one that had lost much of its significance as intercollegiate athletics had grown so big in scope and so motivated by money. These proponents said a strong tie between athletics and the academic mission of colleges and universities was needed, a tie that the 1.600 legislation spoke to two decades earlier. Controversy aside, Proposition 48, establishing for students an academic basis for their eligibility to compete, was an effort to reassert the importance of that historic connection.

THE PRESIDENTS SPEAK

PERHAPS EMBOLDENED BY its triumph in San Diego, the ACE now set its sights on larger prey. The target for the 1984 Convention was presidential primacy in the NCAA. For many observers of and participants in the Association, this was an idea whose time had not come. Or perhaps it wasn't so much the idea as the bold language through which it was articulated. The proposal was developed by the same committee that had assembled the academic-eligibility legislation, which was chaired by President Derek Bok of Harvard. The NCAA's Special Committee on Governance Review studied the ACE recommendations and eventually responded. The committees dueled during the last six months of 1983, with several seconds supporting each side. The ACE committee had the expected overall support of its parent organization. In terms of the final legislative proposal, the ACE's supporters included NAFEO, the American Association of State Colleges and Universities (AASCU), the Association of American Universities (AAU), and the National Association of State Universities and Land Grant Colleges (NASULGC) — the acronymic cream of the country's presidentially guided higher education organizations. In the governance review committee's corner were the Council, much of the membership, a number of institutional presidents (including three who were members of the committee and veterans of the Association's decision-making processes) and, decisively, Walter Byers. Despite the opposing points of view, the tone of the exchanges was relatively cordial for the most part. There were presidents on the ACE side who understood the NCAA's position, had friends in the Association's leadership and were interested in achieving a mutually agreeable solution. Occasionally, though, antagonistic sentiments were expressed.

Byers sent a lengthy letter to the review committee in late August. The ACE proposal draft he had seen would be altered a number of times before the delegates' vote four months later. But the major points would not change: A Board of Presidents would be formed to act on

1973 (June 17-23) —Ben Crenshaw of the University of Texas at Austin becomes the only participant to win three straight individual titles in the Division I Men's Golf Championships (including a 1972 tie with teammate Tom Kite).

1973 (June 18-23) —Stanford University wins the first of 17 Division I Men's Tennis Championships team titles between 1973 and 2000 under coach Dick Gould.

1973 (August 6) —Membership votes in a Special Convention to reorganize into three divisions.

1973 (November 10) —First Division III championship is conducted in cross country at Wheaton College (Illinois).

1973 (November 23-24) —The University of California, Berkeley, wins the first of 11 National Collegiate Men's Water Polo Championship titles between 1973 and 1992 (eight under coach Pete Cutino and three under coach Steve Heaston).

matters affecting the "academic standards, financial integrity and reputation of the member institutions."

This entity could suspend any bylaws, resolutions or constitutional provisions enacted by Convention delegates and any interpretations thereof by other NCAA bodies. The board, in other words, would have a veto power. This did not set well at all. Assorted limiting language was added as the debate progressed. But the core provisions, not the limitations, caught the eye of opponents. Even more alarming to the NCAA leaders than the language of the proposal was the ACE committee's rationale. Bok and his colleagues, these leaders theorized, seemed to believe that the Association was unresponsive to members, controlled by the Council and staff, and intent on advancing or protecting policies favoring athletics interests voted for by institutional representatives who were not attentive to (or instructed to follow) the wishes of their presidents. The presidents, Bok suggested, had neither the time nor the inclination to work within a structure that so limited their potential to effect necessary changes. This was a different interpretation of presidential disinterest than the ACE's Hanford team — as discussed in Chapter Three — had offered 10 years before.

DISCUSSION AT THE 1984 NCAA CONVENTION

FROM NCAA FILES

Byers' August letter and the Governance Review Committee's October communication to Bok expressed something close to outrage at this harsh characterization of NCAA structure and process and, as Byers put it, at a set of changes that "reaches into the discredited past of governmental regimentation based upon the absolute authority of an elite oligarchy." In a December letter to Association President John Davis of Oregon State, the executive director assailed Bok's claim that presidents do not attend NCAA Conventions because "they have no reason to believe that their individual presence will make a difference." If that were true, Byers asked rhetorically, how could Bok explain "the proceedings which led to the adoption of Proposal No. 48 in San Diego less then a year ago?"

Bok and his committee argued that they had not intended to offend the Association, its work and its people, and that, in fact, the ACE proposal would create only a limited set of responsibilities and authorities for the Board of Presidents. Further, they amended certain provisions to lend credibility to that claim and to assure that any suspension of legislation or interpretation coming from the Board would only be temporary. As the 1984 Convention neared, the ACE heavily lobbied its presidential constituency. The NCAA responded in kind. The Governance Review Committee proposed legislation to create a "Presidents Commission" that would have important but considerably less threatening authority than the ACE's board of campus CEOs.

The ACE initiative at the Dallas Convention in January 1984 was Proposition 35. The Association's answer was Proposition 36. The ACE proposal produced a lively, sometimes provocative debate. It consumed two hours and 20 minutes and was dominated by presidents on each side of the issue. Bok, attending his first Convention, introduced the ACE legislation. Other supporting presidents joined the discussion, seeking to calm the fear of a presidential takeover, or to insist on the imperative of CEO authority over academic standards and financial matters, or, in one case, to defend Proposition 35 on the grounds that the NCAA structure was "one big mess" and its processes reminiscent of "Alice in Wonderland." A number of presidents, such as Boston College's Donald Monan, spoke in forceful opposition or pursued conciliatory themes. The Rev. Monan had been an ACE leader, but he strongly supported the NCAA position in the Convention debate. President Otis Singletary of the University of Kentucky was another CEO active in ACE affairs who sided with the Association. The involvement of these and other presidents was critical. In the end, No. 35, needing a two-thirds vote to pass, failed to gain even a majority. It carried in Division I, which was the focus of the proposal, but lost overall by a vote of 328-313. Proposition 36 was then taken up. No presidents opposed, and it passed easily without a roll call. By June 1984, the NCAA had a Presidents Commission up and running. It would have its rocky moments, but soon enough it would provide an expression of presidential influence and authority worthy of those whose hopes for reform had rested on the ACE legislation that had not passed muster in Dallas.

RISE AND FALL

THE PRESIDENTS COMMISSION held its first meeting five months after the 1984 Convention. A number of the members had served on the ACE reform committee or participated — on both sides — in the floor debates on Proposition 35. The Commission, like the NCAA Council, was organized by division and would conduct some of its business using the federated approach employed by the Council. From the outset, however, there was a strong sense of common purpose, of bringing into focus the cares, concerns and ideas of fellow campus CEOs. President John Ryan of Indiana University was chosen as Commission chair. Byers welcomed the group, emphasizing the Council's desire for a collaborative relationship. Indeed, the NCAA's updated organizational table showed an equal standing of the two bodies, which had the same staff and received all the same materials. The Commission established four subcommittees reflective of its principal priorities — academic affairs, financial issues, student life, and institutional control and system integrity. The group also passed a resolution affirming the value of intercollegiate athletics and amateur principles, its confidence in and support of the NCAA, its commitment to the precept that student-athletes must be bona fide students, and

> *The determination of college and university presidents to participate actively in the formulation of policies and in the NCAA process to assure that the spirit and conditions of amateurism and of appropriate educational standards are maintained.*

There were those in sporting circles around the country, and perhaps within the NCAA, who said that the Commission could not and would not live up to the standard of participation and performance it set for itself. Others thought of the new body as potentially revolutionary. It would take some time to tell if failure was to be the fate of the Presidents Commission or whether, on this day at the end of June 1984, the revolution really was just getting underway.

The first big test came in summer 1985 at a Special Convention of the NCAA in New Orleans. This gathering grew out of a survey of institutional presidents, which Byers proposed at the Commission's second meeting. The executive director suggested at the time that an "integrity crisis" in college athletics had risen from rules and enforcement concerns, financial aid problems, and assorted cost and revenue issues. The New Orleans assembly, known as the "integrity Convention," provided the Commission an opportunity to show its strength. The results of the survey of presidents were received in March and reviewed at the April Commission meeting. The members generated several proposals for reform to be cosponsored, in a symbolic reflection of unity, by the Commission and the Council. Chair Ryan suggested that the stakes were high regarding these proposals, which he thought of as representing "a complete new direction for intercollegiate athletics." The Commission, he said, "will demonstrate or fail to demonstrate in June that it is an effective vehicle for addressing policy-making and reform issues …"

Eight reform proposals with Council and Commission sponsorship appeared on the Special Convention agenda. Among them were requirements for an institutional self-study of athletics programs every five years and an annual academic report for Division I institutions. This report would cover entrance requirements, high school GPAs for football and men's basketball, information on satisfactory progress in relation to eligibility, and graduation rates for recruited student-athletes and the general student population. Two proposals were advanced under the heading of "Institutional Control and Responsibility," one mandating an annual outside audit and the other subjecting athletics budgeting to normal institutional budget procedures. There was a resolution on student-athlete eligibility and another limiting the number of contests. Proposition 4 would require that restrictions imposed on coaches as a result of infractions be applied even if the coaches took employment at other institutions. The most ambitious was Proposition 3, which drew dis-

IN THE ARENA
The NCAA's First Century

1973 (December 1) —College Athletics Publishing Service relocates to Mission, Kansas, and becomes NCAA Publishing Service.

1973 (December 8) —First Division III Football Championship is conducted (Amos Alonzo Stagg Bowl in Phenix City, Alabama).

1973 (December 15) —First Division II Football Championship is conducted (Camellia Bowl in Sacramento, California).

1974 (March 1-2) —First Division III Wrestling Championships are conducted at Wilkes College.

1974 (May 25) —First Division II Lacrosse Championship is conducted at State University College at Cortland.

1974 (May 29-31) —First Division III Outdoor Track Championships are conducted at Eastern Illinois University.

1974 (November 30) —First Division III Soccer Championship is conducted at Wheaton College (Illinois).

PHOTO FROM NCAA FILES

1975 (January 7) —**Gerald Ford** becomes second U.S. president honored with Theodore Roosevelt Award (presented by NCAA President Alan Chapman).

tinctions between major and secondary violations, addressed the issue of repeat violators, and presented a significant strengthening of penalties the NCAA could assess. One dealt with institutions committing two major violations within a five-year period. These cases could lead to the "prohibition of some or all 'outside' competition in the sport involved … for one or two sports seasons …," plus "the elimination of all initial grants-in-aid and all recruiting activities" in that sport for a two-year period and other stern punishments. Put another way, Proposition 3 provided for what came to be known as the "death penalty."

The Commission exercised its authority to require a roll-call vote on its eight proposals. All eight passed by handsome margins, the audit measure attracting the most "no" votes (14, in a voting population of more than 400). The "discipline of members" proposal, dealing with types of violations and punishments, received overwhelming support. Two years later, the "death penalty" for which it provided was imposed for the first and — thus far in Division I — only time.

INDIANA COACH BOB KNIGHT

PHOTO BY RICH CLARKSON / NCAA PHOTOS

The New Orleans Convention legislation was, as one Commission member suggested, a historic accomplishment. It clearly lent credibility to the Commission's standing and goals. Victories of smaller size and import were achieved at the 1986 Convention, and significant progress — replete with surprises — was made at the regular assembly in January 1987. The next major challenge for the Commission, a daunting one, materialized at the Special Convention held in Dallas in June of that year.

Meanwhile, the delegates approved some memorable measures that January, including reductions of initial grants-in-aid in I-A football (from 30 to 25) and total grants allowable in basketball (from 15 to 13). A part-time basketball assistant coaching position was eliminated. Boosters were banned from participation in recruitment. Proposals were passed requiring coaches to report all outside income to their athletics directors and CEOs, prohibiting their use of institutional names and logos without employer permission and mandating presidential approval before endorsing brands of sports equipment for pay. From a cost-cutting and institutional-control point of view, these actions seemed to translate as support for the Commission's ambitious agenda. NCAA President Davis said that the delegates sent "a message that there is a great deal of strength in what the … Commission plans to do … and that we are ready to make appropriate cuts in costs." Byers, coming from the last annual Convention of his long career, observed that "a change of attitude has taken place," the meeting having demonstrated "the most harmonious spirit we've seen in years" and "a certain goodwill that may have been missing" recently.

The Presidents Commission had requested that the key proposal passed by the delegates — on cost cutting, recruiting and coaches — be withdrawn from consideration in January so that it could be considered five months later at the Special Convention the Commission had scheduled. Surprisingly, the delegates disregarded the request and took supportive action anyway. Could some hidden meaning be read into this act of rejection? There might be an answer in July, but for the moment, that question was rhetorical.

Bobby Knight, then Indiana's men's basketball coach, did not speak rhetorically in addressing the Convention's decision to reduce basketball scholarships from 15 to 13. "I'm so sick and tired of the things the NCAA comes up with," he said. "You cannot operate a basketball program today with 13 scholarships. That's impossible … Anybody who would propose that or vote for it is an absolute idiot … The Division I people have to get the hell out of the NCAA and form an organization of people who want to play the game and play it right …"

The July Special Convention was preceded by a national forum on athletics issues sponsored by the Commission. It was intended to be the first of several, to be held over an 18-month period, though whether that intention would be realized would be up to the delegates. The next day, the delegates voted to support the forums. They approved a number of resolutions sponsored by the Commission, covering recruitment practices, freshman participation and several studies that needed to be done. The delegates also passed legislation for all three divisions establishing limits on playing and practice seasons in a range of sports and reducing the number of recruiting visits allowed in Division I football and basketball. However, the principal Commission agenda for this Convention was cost cutting, especially in football. With few exceptions, measures limiting or eliminating spring football practice and reducing the number of annual and total grants-in-aid were defeated, referred back to the Commission or postponed indefinitely. A complex proposal to reduce Division I football coaching staffs enjoyed little success. Some parts passed in I-AA but none (another referral to the Commission) in I-A. Football coaches, working through the American Football Coaches Association, worked for months to convince their athletics directors and presidents to oppose some of the proposals. Not for the first time, nor for the last, the question of "who's in charge?" was appropriate.

Various efforts to rationalize what went wrong were launched, but the general reaction was still negative. Roy Kramer, then athletics director at Vanderbilt, said, "I don't think we saved anything, and we may have raised our costs a little bit." Stanford's faculty athletics representative, Jack Friedenthal, expressed a low opinion of the work of the Commission: "They made fools of themselves. They shot themselves in the foot. This [Convention] weakened their ability to really do something." The president and athletics director at Loyola Marymount, writing in The NCAA News, blamed the letdown on the presidents in attendance who declined to support the Commission agenda. They said the Commission needed help with the studies soon to go forward and, in the longer term, with the intricate and contentious politics of reform.

And there was to be some salt for the wound: The January vote to reduce grants-in-aid in basketball was reversed in July. The item was not specifically part of the agenda, but, even so, the Special Convention restored this number to 15 scholarships. Coach Knight had apparently attracted some converts.

THREE STORIES

THE EDITION OF The NCAA News published shortly before the 1987 Special Convention provided helpful information for the delegates, including a Presidents Commission policy paper on the first national forum. The large number of CEOs who had pre-registered for the Special Convention — notably, 60 percent of all Division I presidents were to attend — was mentioned. The usual listing and description of proposals to be considered was included. The article on lobbying by football coaches was in this issue. Some other items were covered that, while not directly pertinent to the Convention, nevertheless offered context for the event. Two of the latter dealt with decisions by the Committee on Infractions. One noted that the University of Utah was placed on one year's probation for football violations. The other, much longer infractions article focused on Texas and its football program. A two-year probation was levied in this case, as were other penalties. But the Texas article was only part of a much bigger story.

Between August 1985 and December 1988, seven of the nine members of the Southwest Conference were placed on probation for up to four years. Recruiting and financial aid or extra-benefits improprieties were usually involved, and the familiar litany of entertainment, inducements, transportation and lodging violations was recited in most cases. The Dallas Morning News contacted conference presidents and reported their shared view that the ultimate responsibility lay with campus CEOs. "It seems we lost perspective," one president said. "We lost sight of what athletics should be within a university." In one institution, though, the responsibility went beyond the president. This was Southern Methodist, a repeat violator in this period (two infractions cases in 18 months). Extra benefits were the big problem — $61,000 worth to 21 football players. Coaches; boosters; members of the school's board of governors; and a famous alumnus, William Clements, governor of the state of Texas, were involved. Southern Methodist received the death penalty — there would be no football there in 1987. Numerous limitations were placed on grants, coaching staff numbers and official visits by recruits. Additionally, the institution was allowed only limited competition in 1988. Byers, then in the waning months of his NCAA tenure, observed that "the SMU case confirmed my growing conviction that the colleges could not get the job done under the old structure."

A second article of interest in the Special Convention edition of The NCAA News was a reprint of a Bill Lumkin column in the Birmingham Post-Herald. Lumkin criticized the

1975 (March 20-22) —First Division III Swimming and Diving Championships are conducted at Allegheny College.

1975 (June 10-13) —First Division III Golf Championships are conducted at the University of Tennessee, Martin.

1975 (June 1) —National Collegiate Sports Services moves from New York City to Mission, Kansas; renamed NCAA Statistics Service.

1975 (August 1) —NCAA marketing program initiated through agreement with Descente Ltd. to use NCAA mark in marketing sportswear and accessories in Japan.

1975 (August 14-15) —Second Special Convention addresses recruiting limitations, financial aid limits, and football and basketball staff and squad sizes.

1975 (November 15) —North Central College wins the first of 12 Division III Cross Country Championships titles between 1975 and 1999 under coach **Allen Carius**.

1976 (January 14-17) —70th Convention and third Special Convention stages first roll-call vote in Convention history (need-based aid is rejected in the vote).

1976 (March 29) —Indiana University, Bloomington, finishes an undefeated season with its victory in the Division I Basketball Championship (no Division I men's basketball team subsequently has gone undefeated).

1976 (May 19-23)—Kalamazoo College wins the first Division III Men's Tennis Championships, claiming the first of its seven titles between 1976 and 1993 under coach George Acker.

PHOTO COURTESY OF KALAMAZOO COLLEGE

1976 (May 25-28) — California State University, Stanislaus, wins the first of six straight Division III Men's Golf Championships team titles under coach Jim Hanny (the team repeated the feat with six more consecutive championships from 1984 to 1989).

1976 (June 4-6)—First Division III Baseball Championship is conducted at Marietta College.

1977 (June 22)—Home Box Office televises College World Series championship game.

1977 (August)—Volunteers for Youth program is established.

1978 (January 11-13)—Division I realigns into I-A and I-AA for football.

1978 (March 18)—First Division II Ice Hockey Championship is conducted at Springfield College.

Presidents Commission and the NCAA in general for the emphasis on cost cutting, which he appeared to believe was "another attempt by the have-nots to keep up with the Joneses by inducing further parity." If the NCAA seemed to be the villain of the piece, the hero, for Lumkin, was the CFA. The patience of that body, he said, was "being tested," and "somewhere down the line" it would say "enough is enough and bolt the NCAA." The column must have awakened unpleasant memories for Byers since he viewed the CFA as having declared war on the NCAA several years earlier. Much had happened in the interim to make matters worse. The worst offense, for sure, was the CFA's central role in ending the Association's control of football television.

"Greed was gnawing at the innards of college athletics," Byers wrote in recalling the situation in the late 1970s that gave birth to the CFA. The lure of additional revenue from televised football games brought on the gnawing. The CFA stood ready to deliver the dollars. Sixty-three universities joined, covering most of the major conferences — the Southwest, Southeastern, Atlantic Coast and Big Eight, for instance. Notre Dame, following the lead of sometime NCAA nemesis Father Joyce, was a formidable member. The Big Ten and the Pacific-10, however, did not sign on. The CFA decided to compete with the Association for TV agreements with the networks during contract discussions in 1981. The NCAA had already solidified its position in basketball. The CFA leadership apparently believed that basketball was another money plum ripe for the picking, but, for the time being, that organization concentrated its effort on football. Complicated negotiations followed. There was the opportunity, as noted in the previous chapter, for the CFA to take on a relationship with NBC, contingent on its ability to secure substantial participation from its members, all of whom also belonged to the NCAA. But since a separate contract would be interpreted by the Association as a violation of its rules and thus punishable at the campus level, the CFA could not provide the institutional support the network required. The NCAA won round one in the football television battle.

There was no knockout, though, and, in any case, no neutral corner to which to retreat. In 1982, the CFA went to court instead, and the result for the NCAA (and, some would argue, for college football) was big trouble.

The lawsuit was brought by the universities of Georgia and Oklahoma, in a federal district court in Oklahoma City. The plaintiffs argued that NCAA control of football television was monopolistic and thus in violation of the Sherman Antitrust Act. They claimed that because of the NCAA, they were losing potential profits earned by their football programs, and their property rights therefore were being infringed upon. The Association responded that maintaining competitive balance among member institutions was the objective, and a more encompassing distribution of resources and institutional visibility, which its television policy provided, was the way to attain it. The presidents of the two universities testified first. Byers noted their testimony's distinctly commercial flavor. Fred Davison, the Georgia president (and also president of the CFA), remarked that "our people would be better able to run our business than would be the NCAA." And William Banowsky of Oklahoma said his institution should be allowed to make its own "market and business judgments." The goal, of course, was to assure that the two universities and their peers among the college football elite could keep what, from their point of view, they fairly earned.

The business argument proved convincing. The district judge, Juan Burciaga, found for the plaintiffs, determining that the NCAA rules were "paradigmatic examples of restraints of trade that the Sherman Act was intended to prohibit." The Association, he wrote, was a "classic cartel [that] imposes production limits on its members and maintains mechanisms for punishing cartel members who seek to stray from these production quotas." After the NCAA's appeal to a federal circuit court failed, the Association went to the U.S Supreme Court. In June 1984, at about the same time the Presidents Commission was holding its initial meeting in Chicago, seven justices found the Association's argument unconvincing. The other two, Byron White, a former football all-American, and eventual Chief Justice William Rehnquist, disagreed. But the court's position was clear: The NCAA had behaved like a trust. It had restrained trade. It had violated the Sherman Act. It needed to get out of the football television business. The immediate cost of losing was $2.24 million in assorted bills and fees. One wonders whether Theodore Roosevelt, for whom busting trusts was a high priority, would have found it ironic that the Association he had fathered was now, almost 80 years later, placed in the same class as the J. Pierpont Morgan holding company Roosevelt had put out of business at the turn of the 20th century.

The Supreme Court, perhaps in an attempt to reach the better angels of the plaintiffs' nature, commented that its decision would not only bring greater freedom to football-playing institutions but, as well, would be good for amateur athletics. That logic was difficult to follow, and it is not at all clear from the subsequent history of televised college football that the free market has strengthened amateurism. Sports historian Allen Guttman concluded that it is "impossible to believe … the opportunity to harvest larger sums of money [would] be accompanied by a stricter observance of the NCAA's rules for recruiting and subsidizing …"

The CFA, which Byers came to view as "an insurgency designed to demolish the [NCAA] or at least to render it obsolete," ultimately found itself the target of the very process it had set in motion. It was able to secure television contracts for its members, but when the Southeastern Conference — the home of the University of Georgia — sensed it could derive benefits from independent discussions regarding football television, the CFA was forced to make a separate (and secret) arrangement with the conference. Trouble loomed when other CFA members discovered that arrangement. It loomed larger when Notre Dame, a founding CFA partner, negotiated a separate, individual and profitable contract with ABC in 1990. That same year, the Federal Trade Commission charged the CFA with violating antitrust law. Judge Burciaga had written in a memorandum related to his 1982 opinion that there would also be an antitrust problem if "today's victim of a price fixing conspiracy is tomorrow's price fixer." Petards are sometimes present, the CFA learned, for hoisting purposes.

In addition to these problems, the anticipated expansion of television dollars did not materialize. The bottom line from broadcast income did not quickly improve. As will be reported in detail in Chapter Seven, it got worse.

A third story appearing in that June 1987 edition of The NCAA News was a reprint of one that had recently been published in the Richmond Times-Dispatch. The subject of the story was Richard D. Schultz, who had recently been appointed to succeed Walter Byers and was soon to become the NCAA's second executive director. Schultz had been a student-athlete at Central (Iowa), a coach at the University of Iowa, and then athletics director at Cornell and Virginia. He had been selected over three other candidates, including a college president.

Schultz would not take office until after the Special Convention, but he understood at least some of what he needed to do. Byers had been mostly an in-house executive, available and responsive to the membership. Apart from Conventions and other major business meetings, he preferred to be at the office in suburban Kansas City, supporting, mentoring and monitoring the work of his staff. Unlike some of the Association presidents in earlier times, he did not give major Convention addresses. The membership leaders gave the speeches. Schultz would change that. He would bring the Association to campuses and conference meetings in person. He wanted to put the executive director's office on the NCAA's new airplane, he said, and pilot that plane himself "anywhere he perceives a problem or potential problem." He may not have known it yet, but he was to become a voice of reform in intercollegiate athletics. He would use the position's bully pulpit. And, in a significant departure, he would use his own speeches to take a stand on impending or needed legislation. Almost the first order of business was to get the Presidents Commission back in the game.

EXECUTIVE DIRECTOR RICHARD D. SCHULTZ

FROM NCAA FILES

1978 (March 18) —North Park College wins the first of five Division III Basketball Championship titles between 1978 and 1987 (three times under coach **Dan McCarrell** and two times under coach Bosko Djurickovic).

1978 (August 10-11) —Division I Basketball Championship is expanded to 40 teams.

1978 (September 27-28) —J. Neils Thompson, Edgar A. Sherman and Walter Byers testify before House Commerce Subcommittee on Oversight and Investigation about issues pertaining to the NCAA enforcement program.

1978 (November 8) —President Carter signs Amateur Sports Act of 1978.

1978 (December 16) —First Division I-AA Football Championship is conducted in Wichita Falls, Texas.

1979 (March) —First two-year agreement with ESPN is signed to televise selected championships; programming begins September 7.

1979 (March 24) — **Herb Brooks** claims the last of his three NCAA men's ice hockey championships as coach at the University of Minnesota, Twin Cities, less than one year before coaching the U.S. Olympic team to its "Miracle on Ice" at Lake Placid, New York.

THE ROAD TO REFORM

IT WOULD BE a while after its Dallas setback before the Commission was ready to return in a big way to its reform agenda. Ryan, the founding chair and a man familiar with the Association's sometimes perplexing processes, signed on as an advisor. When he left that post, Schultz asked Wil Bailey to serve. Bailey, former faculty representative and acting president at Auburn, was just completing his term as NCAA president, and he had been around the Association for many years. The Commission would benefit from his experience and expertise. The next regular Convention was scheduled for January 1988. Frustrations from the previous summer's failure were still fresh. This would be Schultz's first meeting as executive director and his first State of the Association address. It was also Byers' last Convention. He would be warmly recognized at the annual Honors Luncheon, where he gave a typically brief speech. This was not a propitious time for the Commission to take on major issues.

The meeting had its highlights. Another national forum was held, this one dealing mostly with finances. Mitchell Raiborn, author of an NCAA report on the subject, discussed his budget deficit projections for and within each division for 1987-88. The category with the highest percentage of institutions in financial difficulty, at 75 percent, was Division II football-playing members. The lowest such percentage was 35, in Division I-AA. Division I-A universities were forecast to have the highest average deficit (approximately $1 million). The operating costs of intercollegiate athletics programs, Raiborn said, had been exceeding the overall rate of inflation for a number of years.

Byers' luncheon speech was gracious, with flashes of sardonic wit. He was overwhelmed by the occasion, he said, and struggling to accommodate the diverse emotions he was experiencing: "excitement, disbelief, humility, and greater amounts of nostalgia and sentimentality." He had several points to make by way of saying goodbye. One was directed at the inhabitants of the Fourth Estate. College athletics, he suggested, "operate under extreme scrutiny. In that process, the favorite word of the headline writer is 'scandal.' " Further, for the modern media:

> There are more news outlets than there is news to fill the outlets. The reporters of yesterday have become the journalists of today, who create the story and after creating it they want to be a major player in the story … The headline writer has stretched 'scandal' and given it such elasticity that it covers [both] the varsity quarterback driving a car with an expired driver's license and [the current] multimillion dollar scandal on Wall Street.

Byers said that he was leaving the athletics world "totally convinced that it delivers on its promises to student-athletes really better … than higher education … delivers to the student body generally." Qualities such as commitment, dedication, perseverance and teamwork "make this world go." They are "part of the American fabric." They explain why "there is such profound support for intercollegiate athletics." Finally, addressing the young people in the audience, Byers spoke from the heart:

> I feel so privileged to have been a part of this scene for as long as I have. I hope you … continue your belief in this activity with all the passion that makes it so exciting. I can't begin to tell you how grateful I am that you have let me stay around for so long. Thank you for a rare privilege. I shall remember this day the rest of my life.

Byers would lose some of that belief in later years and turn his passion about intercollegiate athletics in a different direction. But on this day, concluding a long and, by any objective measure, remarkably successful career, he offered — and was given in return — a fitting farewell.

The Schultz address was hopeful. He spoke about the need for strong enforcement, greater federation, an enhanced role in the Association for student-athletes, and improved access for women and minorities. Mutual trust was the main message, though, and building it perhaps "the most important issue." The speech made clear that Schultz intended to be an agent of change. With the problems manifold and the challenge substantial, he said, a commitment to integrity would be necessary, and also a commitment to trust.

The Presidents Commission had not lost its interest in major change. Schultz's ideas and style seemed to fit the Commission's ambitious agenda. Eligibility legislation was still a primary (and contentious) theme, along with the requirement of solid research to support it. There was a mountain to climb on cost-cutting initiatives. A range of measures to protect and advance the interests of student-athletes needed to be examined, and there were also sure to be obstacles to surmount in that direction. A decision would have to be made on where next to take the discussion of an accreditation-type approach for member institution athletics programs. Presidents were of two minds on that question. There was the customary presidential dislike for the tendency of program accreditation organizations to place restrictions on institutional decision-making. The number of such organizations was growing, and the restrictions kept pace. There was as well an increasingly persuasive argument being made that such restrictions were precisely what the current situation in college athletics demanded. The Commission would have to make a choice in dealing with this dilemma. Off in the distance, there was more to be done in restructuring the way the Association governed itself. And, as always, there was enforcement. Tall orders abounded. The Commission's will and endurance would be tested. Schultz's leadership would be needed.

Given its 1987 setback in Dallas, the Commission intended to start the comeback with the time-tested strategy of winning relatively modest but meaningful victories. The work began at the 1989 Convention with a nagging issue about which there had been considerable debate since Proposition 48 passed six years earlier. That decision had brought the term "partial qualifier" into the athletics lexicon. The term referred to a prospective student-athlete who did not meet the standards imposed by No. 48 for test score or GPA minimums. Under the 1983 legislation, such a student, while ineligible to compete in the first year after admission, could still receive an athletics grant-in-aid. The Commission now sought to end that practice with Proposition 42. Arguments against this proposal, particularly from the historically black institutions, succeeded at first. However, in a second round of voting, the Commission prevailed. The vote was close, 163-154 in Division I, where the legislation would take effect, but in the familiar argot of athletics competition, this was a win. A related proposal would have given Proposition 48 nonqualifiers a fourth season of eligibility after their freshman year. The Commission opposed it, and it lost. But the possibility of a fourth year would return several times at later Conventions, encounter presidential opposition, engender contentious debate and then be voted down once more. Eventually, though in a somewhat different form, it passed. Proposition 42 would also be revisited and changed, but that happened the next year.

GEORGETOWN MEN'S BASKETBALL COACH JOHN THOMPSON

In the interim, the National Center for Fair and Open Testing challenged the legislation as invalid and discriminatory. Some men's basketball coaches joined the chorus of criticism and, heralding a much larger threat that presented itself five years later, coach John Thompson of Georgetown boycotted one of his team's games in protest. Seeking to calm the troubled waters, Schultz predicted that there would be efforts to alter the provisions of Proposition 42 at the 1989 Convention. As evidence of progress made at this one, he pointed to the creation of the Student-Athlete Advisory Committee (SAAC), the establishment of a special committee on cost reduction and a strengthening by Division III of its policy of not considering athletics ability in awarding financial aid to student-athletes. The Commission had re-entered the reform picture in 1989, with acceptable but unexceptional results. Schultz said he thought the 1990 Convention "might be a blockbuster."

TRIPLEHEADER

SCHULTZ'S FORECAST WAS close to the mark. Within the context of still-fresh memories of expectations thwarted in 1987, and the relatively modest record of accomplishment since that time, the Commission's achievements in 1990 were impressive. All of its major legislative items were approved. Spring football practice in Division I was shortened. The maximum number of regular-season basketball games was reduced from

28 to 25. The financial aid awards maximum for Division I-AA football was decreased from 70 to 65. An effort from the Convention floor to increase the number of initial awards in I-A football (from 25 to 30) was rejected. Legislation requiring Divisions I and II institutions to provide graduation-rates information to prospective student-athletes, their parents and coaches, and the general public was approved. The Commission urged the delegates to review Proposition 42 from the previous year and to make a constructive modification. As a result, partial qualifiers could compete again, but only if their first-year financial aid came from nonathletics sources. The fourth-year idea was again on the agenda and, after initially passing, was defeated on reconsideration. The highlight may have been the four hours and 42 minutes, 24 roll-call votes and assorted accommodations it took to pass Proposition 30. Ironically, this legislation dealt with mandated reductions in time demands on student-athletes during practice and playing seasons.

This Convention clearly represented a victory for the reform agenda. The NCAA News said it would be remembered as the meeting at which the Commission "finally exercised the muscle many had hoped it would flex from the time it was established six years ago." A USA Today editorial expressed appreciation for the work of the delegates:

> They didn't exactly wipe away the grime of corruption that has
> tarnished college sports for almost a century … But they did clear
> off enough ethical smudges to offer hope for the future.

Coach Knight was back in the news, weighing in on the reform effort. According to United Press International, he said he didn't think "the presidents have ever gotten together and told the chemistry department what the hell to teach or how to lecture. I don't know why they are any more qualified to tell the athletics department what the hell to do."

The second in this tripleheader of annual triumphs for reform came in 1991. Schultz, in his Convention-opening address, referred to a member of Congress who had recently declared that "the time has come for the power in intercollegiate athletics to be taken out of the hands of the NCAA …, an organization that answers to no one." The congressman claimed that there was ample support among his colleagues to limit the Association's authority if it did not enact major reforms at this Convention. Schultz also observed that recent polling supported the congressman's position — a large majority of the general public now believed that federal intervention would be necessary to solve the current problems. Within this framework, he urged the delegates to support the reform measures on the Convention agenda.

FROM LEFT: AL WITTE, JERRY HUGHES,
JUDITH SWEET, B.J. SKELTON AND AL VAN WIE.

PHOTO FROM NCAA FILE

The delegates did. The Commission's proposals, most of them backed by the Council, passed by substantial margins. Cost cutting was a principal focus, in grants-in-aid for all Division I sports (another 10 percent reduction) and in numbers of coaches in all sports. Additional time-demand reductions were approved. Recruiting activities were cut back; athletics dormitories, wings and floors were phased out; and the number of permissible training table meals was reduced. The Convention decided, with Presidents Commission urging, that the previous year's shortening of the basketball season had been hasty and voted to restore two of the three games it had eliminated. The delegates approved a resolution directing that the 1992 Convention receive a report on the Division I athletics certification (that is, accreditation) pilot program and that the program, if the Council so proposed, be made mandatory in 1993.

Another highlight was the passage of more restrictive criteria for Division I membership. The new rules involved scheduling, numbers of sports and the extent of financial aid commitment. This continued a process dating to 1957 and one that would still be under discussion when the NCAA's first century came to a close. Eighty-five years into that century, the delegates took another bold action, electing the organization's first female president, Judy Sweet. The new leader had been an athlete, coach, athletics director, vice president for Division III and secretary-treasurer of the Association. She would have a stern challenge to face. She would be ready for it.

Finally, it should be noted that part of the Commission's agenda in 1991 was the launching of a new type of position. It was called "restricted-earnings coach." It would turn out to be a problem, a trustbusting kind of problem. It could not have been anticipated at the time, but in the end, this piece of legislation would be worth more than $54 million.

Sperber remarked that the 1991 Convention results "will in no way change the present college sports system." Rather, he said, "if the reforms enacted are hailed as great, it will be because no one has read the fine print." Others expressed similar sentiments, not only about that Convention but the reform movement as a whole. The presidents and reform-minded members of the Council might have found solace at such times in the familiar message from Theodore Roosevelt regarding the relative importance of the contributions of critics to that of the men (and women) in the arena. Besides, plaudits from various quarters helped balance the criticism.

The Knight Foundation Commission on Intercollegiate Athletics issued its first report in March 1991, calling for large-scale changes. Many of the Knight commissioners had served or were serving on the Presidents Commission. Schultz was a member, too. The Knight model for athletics, set forth in that initial report, in some significant measure replicated the goals the presidents had set for the NCAA, with regard to which substantial progress had already been made. The Knight Foundation initiative captured widespread public interest, and as its work went forward on behalf of reform and its commissioners stayed on message, the NCAA was able in a sense to sail under the Knight flag. Father Hesburgh, former president of Notre Dame, and William Friday, who had gained nationwide regard as the long-time president at North Carolina, were the Knight co-chairs. Creed Black, president of the Knight Foundation, played a visible role in setting the direction and maintaining the momentum of the Commission. It was a sore point for some that this body was credited for an ambitious reform agenda on which the Association had already been working. Critics attacked the NCAA's contributions to reform while delivering encomiums to the Knight commissioners' efforts. No matter. Upon close examination, the reformers were working on the same objectives. Many people, as noted, were members of both groups. The wide publicity net the Knight Commission cast helped the Presidents Commission advance its agenda. Work on academic-eligibility issues remained. The 1992 Convention, the third in succession to feature critical reforms, was in the offing. The unfinished work would get attention there.

The Presidents Commission, again with the support of the Council, placed three key eligibility items on the legislative docket for 1992. One would raise the number of core courses required of a high school athlete from 11 to 13. This passed with little debate in Division I, 312-6. A second piece of legislation, approved in Divisions I and II, set degree-completion requirements for student-athletes by year: 25 percent of the required coursework was to be finished by the beginning of the third year, 50 percent by year four and 75 percent by the fifth year. Also, 95 percent of the GPA required for graduation was mandated for those entering the third year, and 100 percent for subsequent years.

The third item on the presidents' agenda would develop a notoriety almost equivalent to that of Proposition 48, and cause at least as much controversy. This was Proposition 16, which proposed to establish an initial-eligibility index relating GPA in core courses to test-score performance on a sliding scale. Higher GPAs offset lower test scores, and vice versa. For example, a 2.000 GPA required a minimum score of 900 on the SAT or 21 on the ACT for eligibility purposes. Or, a 2.300 GPA corresponded with a 780 SAT/19 ACT. The legislation proposed test-score linkages for 22 GPA levels. Arguments about the possible discriminatory impact of test scores as eligibility standards returned to the Convention floor. Additionally, No. 16 brought into question the validity of a sliding scale that, in effect, eventually stopped sliding. All GPAs above 2.500 corresponded with a 700/17 test-score performance, which meant that a high school student with, for example, a 4.000 GPA and a 680 SAT would be ineligible (as would, at the other end of the scale, a student with a 1.900 and a 1,000 SAT).

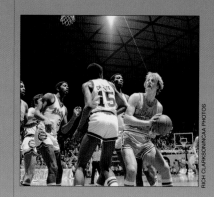

RICH CLARKSON/NCAA PHOTOS

1979 (March 26) —**Michigan State University** (and Magic Johnson) defeats Indiana State University (and Larry Bird) in the Division I Men's Basketball Championship final. The telecast on NBC attracts a rating of 24.1, the highest ever for the event.

1979 (August 13-14) —The Division I Men's Basketball Championship is expanded to 48 teams.

1980 (January 7-9) —Divisions II and III women's championships in basketball, field hockey, swimming, tennis and volleyball are established.

1980 (March 20-22) —Kenyon College, under coach **Jim Steen**, begins the longest streak of consecutive team championships in any NCAA division with its first victory in the Division III Men's Swimming and Diving Championships; the

PHOTO COURTESY OF KENYON COLLEGE

streak remains alive through the 2005 championships at 26 straight victories.

JOE CROWLEY ADDRESSES THE 1995 CONVENTION WHILE
LONG-TIME STENOGRAPHER JOHN BOWEN RECORDS THE SPEECH.

THE STUDENT-ATHLETE ADVISORY COMMITTEE (ABOVE) AT THE CONVENTION. COLORADO PRESIDENT JUDITH ALBINO (BELOW).

Decisions

The format has changed in recent years, but the purpose of the NCAA Convention remains the same. Athletics administrators from across the nation gather annually to identify ways to improve the student-athlete experience.

PETER VIDMAR, (ABOVE) OLYMPIC GOLD-MEDAL WINNER, ADDRESSES THE CONVENTION. A BUSINESS SESSION (LEFT) AT THE CONVENTION.

SOUTHEASTERN CONFERENCE COMMISSIONER ROY KRAMER

CONVENTION DELEGATES (LEFT) MEET IN THE HOTEL LOBBY.
PRENTICE GAUTT (ABOVE) OF THE BIG 12.

SOUTHERN CALIFORNIA ATHLETICS DIRECTOR MIKE GARRETT (ABOVE).
THE PRESS CORPS LEARNS DETAILS (BELOW) AT THE 1997 CONVENTION.

In 1985, the membership had authorized research examining the impact of new standards on prospective student-athletes, minorities in particular. The findings resulted in a decision to phase in the Proposition 48 standards over three years, instead of imposing them all at once. Later, the NCAA Research Committee embarked on a more extensive study of the effects of academic-eligibility legislation. Some of the data from this study were used as the basis for strengthening requirements in the form of Proposition 16 and related legislation at the 1992 Convention. As the debate continued on No.16, further research would be mandated. Eventually, the Association used the results of other studies to take a new tack in academic-eligibility legislation. For the time being, Proposition 16 was scheduled to become the determining set of rules in this area, and its opponents did not intend to give up the fight.

WINDS OF CHANGE

ALTHOUGH THE VICTORIES of the Commission at three consecutive Conventions solidified the understanding in college athletics circles that CEOs were now the overall leaders, important Association responsibilities over which the Commission had no jurisdiction remained. Some in the membership favored what the Commission called a "Draconian approach" — a complete "takeover" of power by the presidents along the lines of the old ACE idea of a Board of Presidents. The Council and the Commission, with frequent interaction and joint development of the reform agenda, enjoyed a generally harmonious relationship. The Association president, serving as Council chair, typically attended Commission meetings, and the Commission chair regularly visited Council meetings. Commission members did not wish to upset this useful balance. But unlike the Council, the Commission played no formal role in NCAA budget development, nor in hiring, evaluation and supervision of the executive director. Further, there was a need to formalize the process of legislative agenda development that had grown by this time into a workable informal arrangement.

Two ad hoc Association committees, one formed by the Council, the other by the Commission, had been engaged in separate efforts to examine an assortment of structure and procedure issues. Fortuitously, they decided on a joint meeting in spring 1991. That session produced a recommendation for a new entity, the Joint Policy Board. This board was to be composed of the officers of the Association (the president, secretary-treasurer and three division vice presidents), the officers of the Commission (the overall chair and three division chairs) and the executive director. This group would meet regularly to "review and concur" on budget, legislation, and other policies identified by the Council and the Commission. And it was to have a responsibility in personnel matters regarding the executive director. After approval, first by the two bodies, then by the delegates at the 1993 Convention, the Joint Policy Board's short — but full — life began.

The most important legislation at the 1993 Convention, which was attended by a record 248 chief executive officers, was a recommendation to initiate an athletics certification program for Division I institutions. This proposal, thought of by some as "a landmark on the road to reform," was several years in the making. It started with the self-study requirement in the mid-1980s, proceeding thence to a voluntary pilot program and a two-year effort to develop consensus around a set of standards that were both demanding and acceptable. Proposition 15 passed, 274-41. The standards dealt mostly with issues familiar to generations of reformers — academic integrity, fiscal integrity and institutional control (translated, in large part, as presidential authority). The Knight Commission viewed certification, along with financial and academic requirements, as a kind of holy trinity of standards, bound together by presidential supremacy in athletics matters. This was the Commission's well-known "one-plus-three" theme. There was still some distance to travel, from the Knight point of view, to assure the proper place for presidents. But certification solidified the trinity. It came with a process characterized by an institutional self-study, verified and evaluated by an external review team, and backed by an NCAA committee to make final certification decisions and assure consistency in the application of standards. However, a fourth standard was also recommended. Its essence was equity, related to gender and ethnicity and emphasizing student-athlete welfare as well. The Commission intended this program to be tough but not punitive, constructive rather than threatening. It was to allow complementarity with regional accreditation approaches and scheduling. The Knight Commission signified its pleasure that Convention approval "cements into place the athletics reform legislation raising academic standards and controlling costs …" With implementation to begin in fall 1993, the commission said, "the mechanism will be completed by which genuine reform of widely recognized abuses in college sports can be achieved."

Schultz had strongly endorsed the certification proposal in his State of the Association address. He also had supported legislation to establish an initial-eligibility clearinghouse to standardize such decisions, endorsed the creation of an infractions appeals committee to free the Council from that burdensome responsibility and favored the idea of developing student-athlete advisory committees on the member campuses. The speech's theme of reform was expected, but Schultz changed gears at the end, mentioning how personally and professionally challenging his life had been of late. He expressed the wish that "when my tour of duty is over … you will be able to say, he made a difference." Four months later, Schultz resigned.

In April 1992, a group appointed by the president at Virginia, Schultz's former employer, issued its report on allegations that student-athletes at the university had received loans from the Virginia Student Aid Foundation (VSAF) in violation of NCAA regulations. The VSAF had operated for some time with considerable independence to support the Virginia athletics program. Nevertheless, the NCAA expected member institutions to exercise responsibility over such organizations, which had been a challenge at Virginia. The VSAF head reported to Schultz during a portion of the six years before he assumed the Association's executive director position. The substance of the reporting relationship with VSAF and degree of control it afforded were in dispute, but not the fact that, during Schultz's tenure, illegal loans to student-athletes were provided by the foundation. This practice became public soon after the president's inquiry was launched. The NCAA's key concern was whether Schultz knew about the loans. If he did and if he had not reported the information, he would be party to an NCAA violation. He denied having such knowledge. The national office enforcement staff disqualified itself from the case as it related to the executive director. The Committee on Infractions hired James Park Jr., an attorney from Lexington, Kentucky, to investigate Schultz's possible involvement. At the end of December 1992, Park presented his findings, following with supplementary reports in January and February 1993. The information was not yet public at that time.

Park acknowledged credibility problems with some witnesses who claimed that Schultz was aware of the loans. He also said the sequence of events was murky and that "reasonable persons could reach different results in resolving conflicting evidence." Still, he determined that:

> The conclusions of this report are based upon information found
> to be credible, persuasive and of a kind on which reasonably prudent
> persons rely in the conduct of serious affairs. Applying these standards,
> one must conclude that Mr. Schultz had actual knowledge of at least
> some of the VSAF loans to student-athletes.

From the start of his NCAA service, Schultz had been viewed by the media and the public as a major spokesman for reform. His leadership had been applauded by members of the Council, the Presidents Commission and the Knight Commission. The allegations against him took on an importance and notoriety that threatened both the reform agenda and the NCAA's credibility as an agent of positive change. With the stakes obviously high, the media gave the controversy ample coverage. Schultz continued to insist he was innocent.

On May 6, 1993, Virginia having disclosed the violations, the infractions committee reported publicly on the case, except for the part tied to Schultz. Lack of institutional control was one of the findings. The university was placed on two years probation and given a public reprimand. The day before, the Executive Committee assembled in Monterey, California. This committee had responsibility for championships, budget and executive director evaluation. The president of the Association chaired the committee and, with other members, provided a link between the committee and the Council (which, as noted, the president also chaired). The May meeting was a regularly scheduled one, with a review of the Schultz situation on the agenda. Because a decision on Schultz's NCAA future was part of the review, the chair of the Presidents Commission was also on hand. It was understood that, at an appropriate point, the

IN THE ARENA
The NCAA's First Century

1980 (April 4-5) —Pilot National Collegiate Rifle Championships are conducted at East Tennessee State University.

1980 (April 4-5) —The Executive Committee votes to eliminate ski jumping as an event at the National Collegiate Skiing Championships after 1981.

1980 (May 25) — Hobart College wins the first of 12 straight titles (10 under coach **Dave Urick**, two under coach B.J. O'Hara) as host of the first Division III Men's Lacrosse Championship (the school added a 13th title in 1993).

1980 (October) —First NCAA women's sports committees formed; first NCAA women's sports committee meeting occurs (Divisions II and III Women's Basketball Committees).

1981 (January 13) —Governance plan including women's athletics programs and services within NCAA structure is approved.

1981 (January 14) —**James Frank** of Lincoln University (Missouri) elected first black NCAA president.

Joint Policy Board would be brought into the picture. All board members, and all Executive Committee members, had read the Park report.

The committee engaged in a lengthy discussion (14 hours, over two days) of the Park documents and findings, and of possible actions it could take with regard to the executive director. The fundamental question was whether Schultz, under the circumstances, could effectively discharge his duties. The committee — though concerned about the reaction of the media, membership and general public — determined that Schultz could remain in his NCAA position. The Joint Policy Board concurred. There was, as expected, an adverse reaction to the decision, in the media and elsewhere, and positive comments as well from prominent Schultz supporters. A few days later, after discussions with key staff members, the executive director stepped down. The decision, he said, was "in the best interest for all concerned." The Park report was made public the same day.

Schultz would stay on until a replacement was found. A broadly representative search committee that included a number of campus presidents and much of the Joint Policy Board was assembled. Cedric Dempsey, director of athletics at the University of Arizona and former secretary-treasurer of the Association, was selected to be the NCAA's third executive director. Schultz left office the following January; Dempsey then began a nine-year tenure as his successor.

Dempsey had been on the job for five days when an unexpected protest arose on the floor of the 1994 Convention. One proposal on the agenda, another No. 42, contained a recommendation to return one scholarship to Division I men's basketball, bringing the maximum from 13 to 14 players. At an earlier Convention, as mentioned, the allowable number had been cut from 15 to 13. In 1993, an attempt to restore the old maximum had been voted down. This vote yielded the same result, but only after a very angry debate. Some supporting delegates and observers claimed that the decision denied one more opportunity for a minority athlete, though that seemed a dubious assertion. The next day, the Black Coaches Association (BCA) declared that it was planning a boycott of Division I men's basketball games, possibly including the postseason tournament. The BCA's rationale appeared to be related as much to frustration over academic-eligibility legislation as to the 14th player issue.

Tensions had been building on Proposition 16, the new, more demanding academic-eligibility legislation. In part to ease hard feelings on the question of discriminatory impacts, the Council had requested, with Commission support, that a special committee be appointed to review No. 16's proposed standards, based on additional research on the impacts. The Convention agreed, and for the moment a modicum of peace prevailed. This committee's 1995 report renewed the discrimination debate but also added findings that would help in developing a different approach to eligibility in subsequent years. That report and the new approach are discussed in later chapters.

It might have been expected that additional tensions and more fierce debate would ensue from proposals presented to the 1994 Convention by the Gender-Equity Task Force, a group assembled by Schultz to examine a wide range of emotionally charged subjects. Consensus had been a rare commodity for the task force. Its two proposals, however, were modest enough. The main one recommended incorporating a gender-equity principle into the NCAA constitution. Although it passed, 804-1, there would be no shortage of equity issues to discuss down the line, particularly since two standing committees had been formed to represent the interests of women and minorities. In the more immediate future, the boycott question, which is covered in Chapter Six, would get serious. The more complex matter of large-scale governance changes was on the horizon as well.

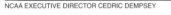

NCAA EXECUTIVE DIRECTOR CEDRIC DEMPSEY

PHOTO FROM NCAA FILES ©BETH GREEN STUDIOS, NEW YORK

NEW STRUCTURE, OLD CHALLENGES

FOR SOME YEARS, Conventions and committees had proposed various initiatives to smooth rough edges, tighten internal mechanisms, and balance the weights and measures of the NCAA governance structure. Viewed in the perspective of history, these initiatives — at least those that were implemented — seemed to follow an orderly progression. Much of the effort sprang from Division I concerns and, as we have seen, focused on greater federation. As a result, the divisions and subdivisions increasingly handled their own matters at the Conventions or within other Association decision-making bodies. Divisions II and III members made occasional rumblings about structure as their numbers grew and inter-institutional commonalities receded. After the 1994 Convention, the work got serious. Three years later, it would result in a major makeover of the Association. Proposition 13, recommended by both the Council and the Commission and adopted by the delegates in 1994, was one starting point. But a paper drafted by eight Division I-A conference commissioners and distributed at that Convention pre-empted discussion in the hallways. As later events demonstrated, this document showed the way to the future.

The commissioners made a case for equity, but their theme was neither gender nor ethnicity. The subject was money, and the authority they thought should go with it. They said the existing NCAA organization was "outmoded and ineffective." They claimed that a new structure ought to proceed from an understanding that the major conferences (described as "equity governance units") and their institutional members, contributing as they did the bulk of the Association's resources, should have the bulk of the say. Their proposal addressed Division I only. Chief executive officers chosen by those conferences were to be in charge there and, indeed, in command of the entire organization. Their responsibilities would include budget, bylaws and policies; criteria for determining equity-unit membership; and hiring and evaluation of the executive director. The Council, Commission and, at least in its present form, the Convention would become artifacts of history. There would be other components of this new structure. The commissioners' intention was that Divisions II and III would continue as members, but with no role in Division I matters and a subservient role in overall Association decision-making. Something close to total federation would be the operative objective for the future.

Proposition 13 grew out of a Joint Policy Board decision, supported by the Council and Commission, to invite interested entities to submit ideas about restructuring. A special committee was established to conduct a review on the subject. Eventually, each division appointed task forces, and an oversight committee was created to allow for some wider consideration and possible refinement of resultant recommendations. By December 1994, position papers had been developed and circulated to the membership. Of particular note was the working draft from Division I, which in several respects bore a strong resemblance to the paper prepared by the eight conference commissioners the previous January, including that division's role in budgeting and its exclusive authority over the executive director. In addition, the working draft proposed creation of an executive committee representing all divisions, but having very limited authority. Once Association "purposes, policies and principles" had been developed, this committee would monitor their application in each division. It could call for a membership vote on a division action it found to be problematic, with a two-thirds vote of all members in all divisions required to overturn such an action. The Executive Committee would have no other powers.

Not surprisingly, conflicts between the task forces flared as the restructuring efforts went forward. The oversight committee was one of the venues for resolving these conflicts and securing agreement on an overall proposal to bring to the 1996 Convention. The Commission also became a key vehicle for achieving compromise. There was initial anger over the Division I demands for virtually complete control of the Association's future, but once that dissipated, civil discourse ensued and consensus formed around key issues. Paramount for Divisions II and III were the financial entitlements they would have in the new structure. A broader constituency worried about what this structure would do to the concept of shared values and commitments that had from the beginning fundamentally bonded Association members. In other words, what would hold this new NCAA together?

Answers were forthcoming. Common meeting sites and times for the divisional governance bodies would help, as would the continuation of several Association-wide committees. The Convention would continue, though it would cease to be a legislating assembly for Division I. The new Executive Committee would become a considerably more consequential entity than the Division I task force had initially envisioned. CEOs would be in charge in all three divisions, organized into Presidents Councils in II and III and a Board of Directors in Division I, and the

The University of
Chicago, once a major
power in football and
now ensconced in
Division III, played at
Grinnell one Saturday
afternoon in 1978
before a crowd of about
200 spectators. There
was no admission fee
and there were no
bands or cheerleaders.
It was reported that one
of Chicago's yells, not
heard on this occasion,
goes like this:

*"Thermistocles, Thucydides,
the Peloponnesian Wars*

*X-squared, Y-squared,
H-2-S-O-4.*

*Who for, what for, who
we gonna yell for?*

O' Maroons!"

Executive Committee would be a presidential body also. That committee, and not the Division I Board, would be responsible for executive director hiring and evaluation.

The final proposal — with divisional Management Councils and other components, and built in part on the hopeful expectation that the large number of committees would diminish — was approved at the Association's 90th Convention in 1996. The dramatically reorganized NCAA became operational the next year. The problems, frustrations, grumbling and further adjustments that followed are discussed in Chapter Seven. The experiment that started in 1984, when the Commission drew its first uncertain breaths, had ended. The "one" — presidential control — that the Knight Commission had proposed six years earlier was in place, at least at the national level. Presidents now ruled the NCAA. That would not change. But many of the challenges remained the same.

Among them would be, as always, enforcement. Byers had understood the need for the NCAA to have a regulatory presence among the membership. That started, as we have seen, in the 1950s, with the passage of certain Convention mandates and the arrival of the first full-time enforcement staff member. Byers had seen to the growth of that staff, and the membership had periodically expanded its responsibilities. From time to time, its machinery was refined, as when the Council was relieved of its appeal duties in 1994 and when a number of due process recommendations took effect in 1992. If nothing else had mandated the enhancement of the function over the years, the growth of the NCAA Manual — concrete testimony to the eternal search for a level playing field — certainly did. As the Association grew, compliance became an increasingly important institutional responsibility. Correspondingly, compliance education for campus staff was established as a regular activity of the NCAA. Self-reporting of violations by members evolved into a common practice. The Association continued to add investigators from time to time. More of them have law degrees now, a perhaps inevitable development given the high stakes, but one that can make investigations more adversarial. Tips about possible violations frequently arrive via the Internet these days, and new technology contributes in other ways to improve the process.

Often enough, there is adverse reaction from the campuses, from coaches and athletics administrators, boosters and legislators, and local media when an institution is penalized. The NCAA is criticized, variously, for heavy-handedness, or favoritism, or rigid bureaucratic thinking and practice, or for being an organization whose rules are somehow separate from the member institutions that make them. It was ever thus. For whatever reason, the urge to experiment with those rules, or find ways through or around them, or, too often, to just disregard them, is still a fact of life. In 1984, Byers told the Associated Press he thought that "as many as 30 percent of major sports schools were cheating on the rules — 15 percent simply to win, another 15 percent because … they must fight fire with fire." His estimate may have been too high (or too low) and may or may not be applicable 20 years later. However, the problem remains substantial.

The number of punishment-producing infractions cases between 1975 and 1983, as stated earlier, was 96. Between 1995 and 2003, that number was an even 100. There are other similarities between the two periods. During the latter one, recruiting violations were reported in 65 cases, extra benefits in 62 and academic fraud in 13 instances. These figures are reasonably consistent with those of the earlier period. This time, though, academic-eligibility problems were significant (26 cases). Findings of a lack of institutional control were reported in 51 percent of the cases (as compared with 21 percent in the late 1970s and early 1980s). Unethical conduct penalties, unfortunately, were also on the rise. From 1975 to 1983, 33 percent of the institutions penalized had committed such infractions. Between 1995 and 2003, that percentage was 56. Six universities each from the Southeastern Conference, Big 12 and the Pacific-10, and five from the Big Ten, were placed on probation during this time. In all, 29 of the 63 institutions that initiated the Bowl Championship Series — until recently, the exclusive preserve of the six leading Division I conferences — spent a year or more on probation. Football (38 violations) and men's basketball (51) were still the sports with the most major offenders, but others, including women's basketball with 17 infractions, were significantly more involved than two or three decades ago.

The NCAA enforcement staff doubled between 1998 and 2004. President Myles Brand, Dempsey's successor, added eight new investigator positions (a 40 percent staffing increase) in 2003 alone. That would appear to have been a judicious decision. ●

IVAN LEE OF ST. JOHN'S (TOP) BATTLES WESLEY NEWKIRK OF NORTH CAROLINA
DURING THE MEN'S SABRE COMPETITION AT THE 2002 DIVISION I FENCING CHAMPIONSHIPS.

Ecstasy and Agony

Any contest can yield the highest of highs or the lowest of lows. Whatever the result, the goal remains the same: Win with class and lose with grace.

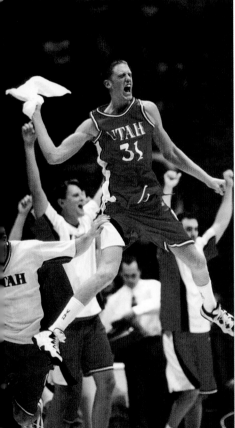

PHOTO BY RICH CLARKSON / NCAA PHOTOS

JOHNSON BRITTON OF UTAH JUMPS FOR JOY AFTER HIS TEAM'S WIN OVER NORTH CAROLINA IN THE SEMIFINAL GAME OF THE 1998 MEN'S FINAL FOUR.

ANDY UHL OF FINDLAY CELEBRATES AFTER PINNING CURRY PICKARD OF NORTH CAROLINA-PEMBROKE DURING THE 2005 DIVISION II WRESTLING CHAMPIONSHIPS.

ANNE SHADLE OF NEBRASKA (ABOVE) CELEBRATES
HER FIRST-PLACE FINISH IN THE WOMEN'S 1,500-METER
RUN DURING THE 2005 DIVISION I OUTDOOR TRACK
AND FIELD CHAMPIONSHIPS.

THE COLLEGE OF NEW JERSEY'S WOMEN'S LACROSSE
TEAM (LEFT) CELEBRATES AFTER WINNING THE 2005
DIVISION III CHAMPIONSHIP.

UCLA'S BRETT ORMSBY IS MOBBED
BY TEAMMATES AFTER BEING NAMED
THE MOST OUTSTANDING PLAYER OF
THE 2004 MEN'S NATIONAL COLLEGIATE
WATER POLO CHAMPIONSHIP.

NEBRASKA STUDENT-ATHLETES CHEER
A TEAMMATE'S STRIKE DURING THE 2005
WOMEN'S NATIONAL COLLEGIATE
BOWLING CHAMPIONSHIP.

UCLA CELEBRATES (ABOVE) ITS WIN OVER STANFORD AFTER THE 2001 INAUGURAL NATIONAL COLLEGIATE WOMEN'S WATER POLO CHAMPIONSHIP IN 2001.

RICHARD SCOTT (LEFT) OF GEORGIA HUGS TEAMMATE BRENDON TODD DURING THE 2005 DIVISION I MEN'S GOLF CHAMPIONSHIPS.

J. BRENT COX (FAR LEFT) OF TEXAS CELEBRATES THE LONGHORNS' VICTORY AGAINST FLORIDA DURING GAME TWO OF THE 2005 DIVISION I MEN'S COLLEGE WORLD SERIES.

STRONG SAFETY MICHAEL DOSS (ABOVE) OF OHIO STATE CELEBRATES THE BUCKEYES' VICTORY OVER MIAMI (FLORIDA) DURING THE 2003 FIESTA BOWL.

DENVER PLAYERS (LEFT) CELEBRATE THEIR VICTORY OVER NORTH DAKOTA DURING THE 2005 DIVISION I MEN'S ICE HOCKEY CHAMPIONSHIP.

JAMIE SCHWABEROW / NCAA PHOTOS (ALL THREE)

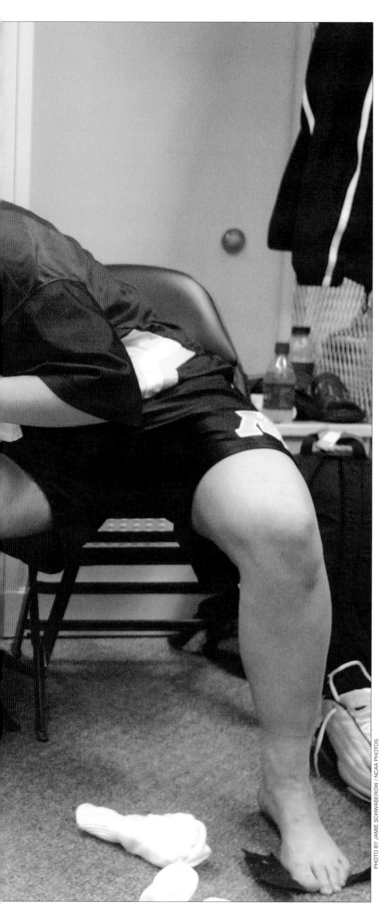

DAMION HAHN OF MINNESOTA (GOLD SINGLET) CELEBRATES HIS WIN OVER JON TRENGE OF LEHIGH IN THE 2003 197-POUND CHAMPIONSHIP COMPETITION.

TEAMMATES CONSOLE FORWARD KADIDJA ANDERSSON OF MINNESOTA (LEFT) AFTER THE GOPHERS LOST TO CONNECTICUT IN THE 2004 DIVISION I WOMEN'S FINAL FOUR SEMIFINAL GAME.

EMILY BREEDLOVE (BELOW) OF MARY HARDIN-BAYLOR REFLECTS DURING THE 2003 DIVISION III WOMEN'S GOLF CHAMPIONSHIPS.

THE CONNECTICUT TEAM STORMS THE COURT AT THE FINAL BUZZER
OF THE 1999 DIVISION I MEN'S BASKETBALL CHAMPIONSHIP.

CHAPTER FIVE

COURTS, CONGRESS AND CAPITOLS

BY THE CLOSING decades of the 20th century, the NCAA had become, manifestly and necessarily, a regulatory organization. It was much else, of course, but the media, the membership and the sporting public focused on the Association's responsibility to develop, issue, enforce and refine its regulations. This emphasis, in light of the prominence athletics had come to occupy in the American consciousness, also whetted the appetite of governmental entities — executive, legislative and judicial — on both state and national levels. The greater the NCAA's regulatory reach, it seemed, the more that appetite grew.

LAWS AND LOOPHOLES

AGAIN, THE SHEER numbers tell tales.

In 1952, the NCAA issued a 5 x 8-inch, 25-page pamphlet containing the organization's constitution, bylaws, executive regulations and resolutions. This document eventually became the NCAA Manual, which in 1989-90 was enlarged to an 8 x 11-inch format and included both an overall version and operating manuals for each of the three NCAA divisions. When the 1996/1997 restructuring legislation took effect, the Association abandoned the overall edition in favor of three separate divisional Manuals. The 2004-05 Division I Manual was 488 pages long. The numbers for Divisions II and III were 368 and 322, respectively. In all, 1,178 pages were needed that year to accommodate the Association's growing reach.

One tale, evident in the move to separate divisional publications, might be the final (or at least the latest) triumph of federation. That story is told in Chapter Seven. A second, more consequential, tale is the testimony the numbers offer to the NCAA's long-standing search for a level playing field.

That goal has represented a kind of Eldorado for the Association. There are several reasons for the ever-increasing sizes of NCAA Manuals, among them the growth of the Association itself, the need to adjust to changing circumstances and the practical refinements necessitated by defects in the original language. Another continuing and related reason ties back to what Amos A. Stagg insightfully observed is the American propensity (in both competitive sports and elsewhere in the national life) for finding ways to gain an edge. With regard to the Manuals, this character trait has translated into efforts to discover loopholes. Institutions may develop approaches that abide by the letter of legislation but damage its intent. Unwanted limitations can thus be eased, and loopholes thereby created. Plugging such holes with amendments adds pages to the Manuals, providing in the process more landfill for the level playing field. Eldorado still looms as a desired destination here, but the penchant for tilting the field keeps that goal on the far horizon.

A third tale revolves around the bench and the bar. Whatever the sources of growth in the Manuals may be, those multiplying pages have provided another of the many modern applications of what could be called the "law of litigative physics." That is to say, when there is additional NCAA legislation (or regulation), additional litigation is likely to follow. In particular, this law governs in a country — the United States — where, increasingly, the settlement of disputes has moved away from traditional internal or political processes and into the country's courthouses.

Higher education is familiar with this development. Federal and state statutes, administrative regulations, and judicial determinations in areas such as civil rights, faculty rights, employment discrimination, equity policies, student privacy, First Amendment entitlements and collective bargaining have brought the academy to court and attorneys to the academy. This has occurred on a scale not envisioned 50 years ago. As late as 1961, only 50 American colleges had legal counsel-related employees, and few had more than one per office. By 1981, the National Association of College and University Attorneys had in excess of 2,000 members. In 2004, more than 3,000 belonged. Some of the issues with which member campuses were dealing were also on the NCAA agenda, although the Association has been occupied by its own concerns as well. Challenges to eligibility legislation, questions about amateurism and due process issues in enforcement have been among the dominant

"The popular impression that there is a litigation frenzy in sports is fairly accurate. Sports is one of the two industries that are now most inundated with lawyers and lawsuits; the other is entertainment."
—PAUL WEILER, "LEVELING THE PLAYING FIELD," 2000

emphases of the last quarter-century.

While federal and state courtrooms have become arenas for a different kind of competition in recent decades, state legislatures have also joined the game, proposing and sometimes passing legislation that defied NCAA rules. Congress has periodically involved itself, through hearings and statutory action, both threatened and actual. The processes through which agencies of the national government promulgate administrative law have also factored into Association policy-making. Often enough, the threats did not materialize; the hearings, statutes and processes were beneficial; the states backed away from problematic initiatives; and court decisions favored the NCAA. But not always. Either way, external influences and interventions became important facts of life for the Association and the way it does its work. This chapter examines some of these involvements, changes and key court decisions, and assesses their contemporary and possible future impacts. We begin by recall-ing the turn toward antitrust law so painfully manifest in the football television case from the early 1980s. The decision in that case — Georgia's march through Sherman, as it were, with Oklahoma also in the vanguard — proved inviting to assorted plaintiffs in the years that followed.

THE NAKED TRUTH

ONE WONDERS: WOULD the result have been the same had the terminology been different? The establish-ment of restricted-earnings positions in Division I sports has a worthy provenance. The concept began life as an effort to remedy a problem that evolved under previous legislation covering entry-level coaching positions in bas-ketball. In addition to three full-time coaches, institutions were permitted to have two positions designated as either part-time, volunteer or graduate assistant coaches (plus an undergraduate assistant). The intent was to pro-vide experience to younger people interested in coaching careers. Some programs abused this intention by find-ing ways of using these positions to compensate older, more entrenched coaches. Further, there were uneven compensation levels between public and private colleges, and a number of institutions could not use graduate assistants because they had no graduate programs. Significant and demonstrable competitive inequities had developed. Then too, Division I men's basketball had come to be seen as a sport characterized by the large-scale expenditures of the most successful programs. For some observers, both on and off campus and within athletics departments, it was hard to understand why up to six coaches were necessary to handle 13 student-athletes.

This was a particularly difficult question to answer during a period of budgetary challenges for intercolle-giate athletics and academic institutions in general. For that reason, and because of the history of abuse associat-ed with the allowable entry-level positions, the special NCAA committee charged with examining possible areas where expenses could be reduced initially decided to recommend "that all entry-level positions … be abolished." Ultimately, the committee proposed to allow one such position, in the interest of maintaining opportunities for entering the coaching profession. Thus was born the restricted-earnings coach. This was a new name for an idea that had been around for a while, now with the objective of serving that idea with greater economy and equity. That's where terminology took over and, perhaps, the path to astonishing defeat began. The proposal was one of many offered by the special committee (officially, the Committee on Cost Reduction) and approved at the 1991 Convention. It is no small irony that a recommendation designed in part to cut institutional athletics expendi-tures ultimately cost those institutions, and the NCAA, tens of millions of dollars.

The legislation passed with an 85 percent-plus majority, despite serious concerns expressed by coaches and their advocacy groups. The new rule provided that, during the academic year, coaches in the restricted-earnings category could "receive compensation or remuneration from the institution's athletics department that is not in excess of either $12,000 or the actual cost of educational expenses incurred as a graduate student." In addition, restricted-earnings coaches could earn up to $4,000 during the summer from the department, camps, clinics and the like. Except for football, each sport covered by the legislation was limited to one such coach. Although the partisans of several of these sports expressed general unhappiness, coaches of men's basketball complained the longest and loudest. They were also the group that, paying implicit homage to Stagg's insight, was the most cre-ative in discovering the legislation's loopholes and how to maneuver through them.

Accordingly, various schemes were launched to get around the compensation constraints and assure that the extra coach the restricted-earnings legislation provided was not a young person seeking an inexpensive way into the profession but, instead, an extant and experienced member of the staff. For example, an assistant coach might serve one year making the allowable $16,000 and the next making more than $100,000. In other instances, institutions sought additional sources of funding support (paying a nice stipend to a spouse, for example) to assure that veteran coaches in the restricted position could enjoy comfortable compensation while waiting to return to their customary institutional recompense.

The Presidents Commission, a champion of the new coaching category from the outset, did not bend in its insistence that the intent of the legislation be upheld. Loopholes having been found, efforts went forward to close them. The Commission reported to the Council in April 1993 that "the legislation is not perfect and needs some modification." However, the report added that, for basketball, "there should be no fourth full-time coach under any circumstance …" The fourth coach "should be considered an entry-level position with limited earnings." While discussing proposed legislation in August of the previous year, the Council noted that vagueness in the 1991 legislation had led to "a proliferation of interpretations related to the types of activities for which the restricted-earnings coach could be compensated." Programs had found methods "to retain current experienced personnel by supplementing the allowable compensation." And these activities had "at times resulted in outside groups … arranging for and providing questionable employment" for these coaches. So the Council and Commission moved a proposal forward to remedy the situation. The proposal was approved, the room for interpretation narrowed and attempts to compromise went nowhere. The next step was litigation.

Eventually, a class-action suit, brought on behalf of an estimated 1,900 restricted-earnings coaches in various sports, went before a federal district court in Kansas. The touchstone of the suit was the Sherman Antitrust Act. The result was financially disastrous for the Association and its membership and, some might argue, not really a big monetary victory for the coaches.

There appears to have been very little (some say no) thought given to possible antitrust problems during the course of committee deliberations, Council and Commission review, and Convention discussion of the proposal. Though the outcry was loud and sustained from Division I head basketball coaches, their principal concern seemed to be not having available the services of a fourth fully compensated position. Soon enough, though, the conversation shifted to the courtroom. Plaintiffs' attorneys entered the dispute, and they proved themselves masters of truly disputatious language. The supporting material for their motion for summary judgment featured extensive use of the word "naked, as in "naked price fixing" or "a naked restriction on price or output" or "a naked horizontal combination of employers to fix the wages of their employees" or "the price fixing in this case is a naked restraint for which the law recognizes no justification." And there were other pungent declarations of the supposedly malign intent of the NCAA and its decision-makers, including:

> *The pernicious practice of price-fixing in the employment of their coaches.*
> *A price-fixing conspiracy of the most cruel and exploitative kind.*
> *An agreement among employers on the maximum compensation*
> *they will pay to their lowest-paid employees.*

As for the coaches, well, they were "relatively powerless individuals" who "do not command large salaries," holding "membership in the only class of Americans not allowed to negotiate for the best salary they can get …"

The intent of those who crafted the restricted-earnings coach legislation was to fix a problem, not a price. It beggars the imagination to think of them as "conspirators," as "cruel and exploitative," or as "pernicious" practitioners manipulating the powerless. It is equally difficult to look upon the coaches involved as something akin to the persecuted workers of a teeming 19th century Dickensian metropolis. But that was the picture painted at least inferentially by the plaintiffs' attorneys. Still, the district court judge was receptive. She concluded that it was not these attorneys but those who argued on behalf of the NCAA who were given to "alarming rhetoric," and she decided in favor of the people she called the "price-fixing victims." There would be no trial. She granted summary judgment to the plaintiffs.

1981 (November 23) —The University of Texas at El Paso wins the Division I Men's Cross Country Championships with a record low score of 17 points (claiming first, second, third, fifth and sixth places individually).

1981 (December) —First Divisions I, II and III Women's Volleyball Championships are conducted at the University of California, Los Angeles; the University of California, Riverside; and Maryville College (Tennessee).

PHOTO COURTESY OF UNIVERSITY OF TEXAS, EL PASO

1982 (March 12-13) —Suleiman Nyambui of the University of Texas at El Paso becomes the first participant to win seven career individual titles in the Division I Men's Indoor Track and Field Championships.

1982 (March) —First Divisions I, II and III women's swimming (University of Florida, Truman State University and the University of Massachusetts, Boston) and basketball (Norfolk, Virginia; Springfield College and Elizabethtown College) championships are conducted.

1982 (March 26-27) —First National Collegiate Women's Gymnastics Championships are conducted at the University of Utah, where the host team wins the first of nine team titles extending through 1995 under coach Greg Marsden.

The 10th Circuit Court affirmed her decision. The U.S. Supreme Court declined to accept an appeal. The case was referred back to the district court for a jury trial on damages. The judge refused to allow the NCAA to explain the context and rationale of the restricted-earnings legislation during this trial. She also would not permit the Association to present an alternative formula for determining damages. The jury awarded the plaintiffs $22.3 million. The amount was automatically trebled under the federal antitrust statute to $66,829,724. On appeal back to the 10th Circuit, a mediated settlement — agreed to by all parties — set the final number at $54.5 million. The Association, while continuing to assert that the legislation did not violate the Sherman Act, and conscious that the interest clock on damages was still running, reluctantly accepted the results of the mediation.

It remained, then, to figure out a way to pay the bill. After extensive study of possible alternatives, the NCAA Executive Committee gave final approval in April 1999 to a three-way allocation of the debt. This became known as the "one-third, one-third, one-third" solution. The first third would be handled by the use of NCAA reserves, the second through the existing revenue-distribution plan and the third by an equal payment from each of the 310 Division I institutions. The impact on campuses and conferences would be considerable. "Ironically," one observer wrote, "the monetary judgment may negatively impact the number of jobs and the amount of salaries within a school's athletics department."

Meantime, there was the business of distributing the spoils, no small matter given the complexities of the case and the number of people involved. After a lengthy effort to find a workable formula, the district court approved a final settlement in July 2000, six years after the litigation began. It was the NCAA's view that, of the 1,900 coaches thought to be part of the class action, only 59 could be identified as individuals whose salaries had been adversely affected by the legislation. The Association urged the court to consider, in deciding who would get how much, the effect of other compensation the coaches received "from summer camps, outside sources, under-the-table payments and benefits such as automobiles, medical insurance and retirement plans." The judge declined, because, she said, of likely added costs, delays, difficulties of data collection and fairness. She awarded attorneys fees exceeding $18.2 million and costs of more than $1.7 million. A complicated set of calculations was used to decide the amounts to be given to the various categories of coaches entitled to participate.

The judgments in the restricted-earnings case probably opened wider the gates of Sherman Act challenges to the NCAA. There is no doubt that the court decisions came as a great surprise to the Association — likely greater even than those in the football television cases of the early 1980s. In hindsight, it is easy to conclude that the legislation was a bad idea with an unfortunate title, crafted by experienced and well-intentioned people who had a serious issue to resolve and who would never have dreamed that in the act of resolving it they would become — in the eyes of the court — pernicious price fixers. For the NCAA, it was a lesson expensively learned about the unpredictability of judicial behavior, the perils inherent in a litigious culture and the strong lure of victimhood in modern America.

Was it the perceived "deep pockets" of the Association and its Division I members that moved the coaches from the court to the courtroom, in the company of legal counsel? It would be best to let this question reside in the rhetorical realm. It is fair, however, to inquire as to the depth of the coaches' (and their counsels') pockets once the litigation ended. As noted, attorneys' fees were a bit more than $18 million, plus costs. Interest accumulated in the settlement account until all the dollars were paid in March 2001. The cost of administering the account was approximately $669,000. When all expenses were covered, $32,575,955 remained for distribution to the plaintiffs. The 1,900 estimate proved to be high: The number of coaches receiving checks was 1,636. Although obviously some got more and some less, the average return per coach was $19,912.

GOLDFARB'S CHILDREN

THE REAL PRECEDENT for the restricted-earnings judgment was not the football television decision (often cited though it was by attorneys in the case) but a 1975 U.S. Supreme Court ruling, in *Goldfarb v. Virginia State Bar.* In that case, the court applied antitrust doctrine to nonprofit entities for the first time. Mr. Goldfarb and his wife, in purchasing a home, had been required to have a title examination performed by a member of the Virginia bar for a prescribed fee. The fee was established by the Fairfax County Bar Association and enforced by the state organization. The claim was that this practice was price-fixing and thus violated the Sherman Act. The court agreed, holding that Congress had not intended "any sweeping 'learned profession' exclusion" from the coverage of the act and that, accordingly, the county and state bar associations were not exempt from Sherman's reach.

The broadening of antitrust law stemming from the *Goldfarb* decree has brought diverse litigants to try this suit on for size in seeking relief from NCAA regulations. The *Oklahoma Regents* litigation is a prime example, of course. Remember, however, that even while issuing its negative order in this case, the Supreme Court gave the Association some legal ground to stand on. "It is reasonable to assume," the court observed, "that most of the regulatory controls of the NCAA are justifiable means of fostering competition …" A Washington Post story interpreted this to mean that the organization could still "set academic-eligibility standards and competitive restrictions." However, the tempered language did not provide blanket authority. The extent of flexibility involved would need to be determined on a case-by-case basis. The NCAA, as matters evolved, would usually be successful.

One of those successes, coincidentally, came at about the same time the Supreme Court issued its invalidating order on football television control. At issue was the legality of the Association's action in 1980 and 1981 to enter into women's athletics competition through the holding of championships in all three divisions. The context and impacts of these actions will be examined in Chapter Six. Here, the focus is on the antitrust suit brought by the Association of Intercollegiate Athletics for Women (AIAW) and the handling of the matter by the courts.

As early as 1971, legal counsel George Gangwere expressed to Walter Byers his view that the NCAA was obligated under the law to offer women an equal opportunity to participate in NCAA events. The AIAW was organized during the same year. Within a decade, the Association was in the women's championship business and the AIAW was ready to litigate. The resulting suit was filed with the U.S. District Court for the District of Columbia in late 1981, initially seeking to prevent the NCAA from proceeding with its women's championships plans. The court denied the request. An appeal followed and failed, as did an attempt at mediating the substance of the suit. The AIAW's case, as an entity based on a single-sex approach to athletics administration, was not helped by the circumstance that by the early 1980s the great majority of campuses had combined men's and women's programs into a unitary organization. The judge hearing the case noted that the AIAW's "separate but equal … guiding principle" ran counter to this development. But the plaintiff's biggest problem stemmed from its inability to demonstrate that the NCAA had monopoly on its mind, rather than competition. Borrowing from an earlier opinion, the judge wrote that the "purpose of antitrust laws is and always has been the protection of competition, not competitors."

Further, on the claim that the Association had used "anti-competitive economic incentives," the court heard testimony from female athletics leaders on both sides of the issue. Those testifying for the NCAA negated the AIAW claim. The judge concluded that the evidence was "imprecise and contradictory" and determined that the plaintiff had failed to prove an antitrust violation. The AIAW took its case to the U.S. Court of Appeals for the District of Columbia. This appeal was denied in May 1984. There was no further appeal. The NCAA won. But the next month the Supreme Court ruled against the Association in the football television case. Soon thereafter, the AIAW closed its doors. In terms of major Sherman Act litigation, a decade and more before the restricted-earnings case, the NCAA was batting .500.

This average improved later as diverse plaintiffs — influenced by *Goldfarb*, heartened by *Oklahoma Board of Regents* and apparently abjuring *AIAW* — laid their claims at the Association's doorstep. Among them were coaches; student-athletes; sports-equipment manufacturers and other commercial entities; and, eventually, other NCAA member institutions. Certain of the coaches were discussed previously, in the restricted-earnings litigation, and others returned to court later, taking different tortious paths. Student-athletes pursued eligibility, discrimination and contract concerns as well as antitrust complaints. Commercial enterprises have sought Sherman Act relief from regulations on topics as varied as logos, aluminum bats, webbed football gloves and a tournament exemption rule. As for universities, the antitrust focus arose from the impact of NCAA postseason basketball requirements on alternative participation opportunities and, possibly, on institutional treasuries.

Two cases stand out regarding student-athlete challenges based in significant part on antitrust claims. In one (*Tanaka v. University of Southern California*), a soccer player at the defendant institution wished to transfer to UCLA after her freshman year without losing a season of eligibility. Forfeiture of one season in such circumstances was required by both the Pacific-10 Conference and the NCAA. Both organizations were named in Tanaka's suit. Southern California denied her transfer request on the basis of the rule, an action she alleged was an unreasonable restraint on trade. Proving this claim meant that the plaintiff had to show the rule had an anticompetitive effect within an identified market. That market, for Rhiannon Tanaka, was the city of Los Angeles. The Ninth Circuit Court, acting on her appeal of a negative federal district court decision, found the market definition irrelevant and the claim to anticompetitive outcomes inadequate. Whether against the university or the NCAA, the court held, "Tanaka simply has no antitrust cause of action." In June 2001, the appeal was thus denied and the district court decision affirmed.

One of Tanaka's attorneys in this litigation was Renee M. Smith, a former volleyball player at St. Bonaventure who had been a plaintiff in an earlier, more complex antitrust case. That case also involved a Title IX discrimination claim and in that way raised the critical question of whether the NCAA is a "state actor" (that is, having the same legal status as a state) under the 14th Amendment to the U.S. Constitution. Smith had competed for two of the allowable four seasons before her graduation and wanted to use her remaining eligibility, first while pursuing a graduate degree at Hofstra, then when enrolled in law school at Pittsburgh. The NCAA rule permits post-baccalaureate students to play, but only at their undergraduate institutions. Both Hofstra and Pittsburgh requested waivers of the rule from the Association. These requests were denied. Smith sued. Noting that NCAA bylaws are jointly developed with and enforced by member institutions, including Hofstra and Pittsburgh, she claimed an antitrust violation had occurred because the Association had "engaged in a contract, combination and conspiracy to place unlawful restraints upon the trade and commerce of intercollegiate athletics between the several states." Smith's case, like Tanaka's, dealt with eligibility, and the court observed "it is clear that the Sherman Act is applicable to the NCAA with respect to those actions … related to its commercial or business activities." But eligibility was not a business or commercial matter. On this count, therefore, the court ruled against Smith. There would be other eligibility questions to answer in other lawsuits, but this decision effectively placed the Sherman Act out of bounds for those cases.

However, there was a second count in the Smith litigation. The suit claimed that the NCAA had violated Title IX by granting a disproportionate number of eligibility waivers to male student-athletes. The Association was subject to this statute, it was argued, because it is an educational entity and a recipient of federal financial assistance. Such assistance was admittedly indirect, in that its source was the NCAA's "limitations and regulations on the receipt of federal financial aid for student-athletes." In one breathless 206-word sentence, the court dismissed this count, too. The NCAA is a private organization, the judge held, and not subject to the mandates of Title IX. But, down the appellate road, exception would be taken to this conclusion.

Attorneys from the National Women's Law Center handled Smith's appeal before the Third Circuit Court in February 1998. By now there was widespread interest in the case. Supporting briefs came from a varied array of organizations, including the ACLU, YWCA, American Association of University Women, National Association for Girls and Women in Sport, National Coalition for Sex Equity in Education, and the Women's Law Project. The circuit court affirmed the district court's decision as to the Sherman Act's relevance. But, on Title IX, the court, in effect, divided the Solomonic baby. Claiming that the Supreme Court, in related cases, "did not distinguish between direct and indirect financial assistance," noting "the broad regulatory language under Title IX," and looking favorably on Smith's amended submission on federal funding, the appellate body ruled that the Association's receipt of dues from federally funded member institutions would suffice to bring the NCAA within the scope" of the statute. This holding, if it stood, would adversely affect other national higher education organizations as well. A dozen of them, led by the American Council on Education, filed as amici curiae, supporting the Association in its Supreme Court appeal of the Third Circuit's decision.

Smith had proposed in her amended complaint that the NCAA "is a recipient of federal funds because it … receives federal financial assistance through another recipient and operates an educational program or activity which receives or benefits from such assistance." The Supreme Court reversed the circuit court's acceptance of this complaint, pointing out that the latter's ruling was "inconsistent with the governing statute, regulation and this Court's decisions." Citing an earlier case, the court maintained that while "a college qualifies as a recipient … when it enrolls students who receive federal funds earmarked for educational expenses," it refused to make the NCAA also a fund recipient when the college potentially passed through a portion of its federal dollars to the NCAA for membership dues. In upholding its status as a non-federal fund recipient, the holding in *NCAA v. R.M. Smith* perforce meant that the Association is not subject to a large variety of federal regulations. Therefore, its actions could not be second-guessed by the courts in those areas. Had the court determined otherwise, the NCAA's path ahead, on eligibility and other litigation, would have been exceedingly thorny.

OTHER HEIRS

CONCERNED ABOUT THE growing role of sports apparel companies as yet another commercial influence on intercollegiate athletics, the NCAA passed legislation (Bylaw 12.5.5) limiting the size of manufacturers' brands on uniforms and equipment used in competition by student-athletes. Member institutions were required by this bylaw to restrict company marks and logos to a space "not to exceed 2 1/4 square inches in area …" Adidas, probably serving, in effect, as a representative of a very profitable industry, took the NCAA to court to try to get its signature three stripes spread over a larger area of its uniforms. The company had an arrangement with colleges and coaches typical of sports apparel manufacturers. In return for providing free or discounted merchandise to an institution's teams, coaches or athletics programs in general, adidas received certain promotional rights. These included, most notably, a commitment to dress in trademarked uniforms and footwear for games and practices. From the company's perspective, such relationships authenticated its brand and contributed to profitability. The NCAA bylaw, adidas claimed, operated as a restraint of trade and so was at cross-purposes with the Sherman Act. Adidas also claimed the Association was a direct competitor in the market because it asked member institutions to place its own logo on uniforms and other articles of apparel.

The case was filed in a federal district court in Kansas. Adidas requested injunctive relief from the enforcement of Bylaw 12.5.5, plus damages. The NCAA moved for "judgment on the pleadings." The court, observing that adidas had failed to define the "relevant market" in which it competed for sales of its merchandise (a requirement in Sherman Act litigation), accepted the Association's motion and, in August 1999, dismissed the case. A subsequent appeal to the 10th Circuit Court was withdrawn by the company. The bylaw remains in effect, as does the use of the NCAA logo.

At about the same time logo issues were being contested in one Kansas courtroom, a complex battle over baseball and softball bats was getting underway in another. NCAA regulations, injury risks for student-athletes, science and technology, capitalist competition, bat speeds, ball velocity, hitting machines, migrating sweet spots, wood versus aluminum, conspiracy accusations, and product indemnification were all involved. So were claims of antitrust violations by the NCAA — restraint of trade again — and several bat companies sought refuge in the Sherman Act, suing the Association in 1998. The threat of litigation quickly disappeared, or seemed to, when, in *Baum Research and Development Co., Inc., v Hillerich & Bradsby Co., Inc.*, a federal district court in Michigan ruled that the NCAA had the authority to regulate the rules for bats. Other companies dropped their claims and turned toward a strategy of participation instead of litigation in resolving the issues. Legal activity continued, however, through a tortious interference with a contract suit brought by the same individual whose 1998 antitrust case was unsuccessful. The Association, acting with other defendants, resolved the matter through settlement in March 2005.

Considering where jerseys, shoes and bats have gone in recent years — to court, that is — it comes as no surprise that gloves eventually would follow. In this instance, the gloves are webbed and designed for use in football. The manufacturer (Aculeus 5) sued the NCAA, the NFL and a

PHOTO COURTESY UNIVERSITY OF NORTH CAROLINA

1982 (May-June) —First Divisions I, II and III Women's Outdoor Track and Field Championships are conducted at Brigham Young University; California State University Sacramento; and North Central College.

1982 (May 24-29) —Abilene Christian University wins the first of 14 Division II Men's Outdoor Track and Field Championships titles between 1982 and 2004 (including seven in a row from 1982 to 1988 under coach Don Hood).

1982 (November 21) —Old Dominion University wins the first of nine Division I Field Hockey Championship titles between 1982 and 2000 under coach Beth Anders.

1982 (November 21) —The University of North Carolina, Chapel Hill, wins the first of 17 Division I Women's Soccer Championship titles between 1982 and 2003 under coach Anson Dorrance; 17 Tar Heel players win offensive or defensive most outstanding player honors during that period, including two-time honoree **Mia Hamm** (1992 and 1993).

1982 (November 28) —The University of North Carolina, Greensboro, wins the first of five Division III Men's Soccer Championship titles between 1982 and 1987 (two under coach Mike Berticelli, three under coach Michael Parker).

high school sports federation, claiming antitrust violations in the refusal of each organization to certify the glove for game competition. The court dismissed the suit. The glove, the court said, would change the nature of the game, and the Association had a right not to certify. The manufacturer appealed to the Ninth Circuit Court of Appeals in early 2005.

The nature of another type of game (games, actually) was changed appreciably by an NCAA initiative in 1999 that had nothing to do with equipment. That year, an amendment was approved preventing institutions from playing in more than two "exempt" preseason men's basketball tournaments every four years. Such tournaments, certified by the Association and often held outside the continental United States (in Alaska and Hawaii, notably), were multiple-game affairs. Teams competing in them were permitted to count the several contests as a single game, to stay within the seasonal number of contests allowance. The Association became concerned that institutions in the major conferences were disproportionately represented in these tournaments, which presented competitive-equity problems. Recruiting and other advantages for the institutions involved were inherent in the unequal distribution of competitive opportunities. That reasoning led to the "two in four" rule, another in the long line of efforts to maintain a level playing field.

Exempt tournaments had become a profitable business for those who promoted them. These individuals opposed the two-in-four legislation and, in keeping with the customary practice, sought to prevent the NCAA from implementing the rule. The promoters felt that some experience with "two-in-four" was necessary, however, to assess its impacts, so it was not until 2003 that Worldwide Basketball and Sports Tours, Inc., brought its antitrust suit, seeking a permanent injunction, to a federal district court in Ohio. The plaintiffs said the rule had a significant anticompetitive effect. Under a concept known as the "rule of reason," often applied by courts in such cases, the NCAA had to demonstrate that countervailing benefits justified this effect. And, of course, the Association had to meet the usual mandate for identifying a credible market in which competition was affected.

The court was not convinced by the benefits argument. The predicament was that, while the court did not accept the plaintiff's position regarding an adverse impact on competition, the NCAA still had to prove that the legislation it passed to create equitable competitive opportunities for its member institutions did in fact offset such an impact. In other words, greater equity inside the Association must be proven to sufficiently mitigate an external consequence that, in the NCAA's view, had not materialized. Obviously the "rule of reason" can produce some tough logic. The court, inferring from conflicting testimony that an appropriate market had been defined, and finding the benefits presentation inadequate to the purpose, granted the Worldwide group its injunction.

The Association appealed the decision to the Sixth Circuit and, in November 2004, that court reversed the district court's judgment. The reversal was not based on the question of whether the two-in-four legislation was anticompetitive, nor on the viability of the NCAA's rule of reason argument on mitigating benefits. The problem for the Worldwide promoters was that they "had failed to meet their duty to define the relevant market and submarket," and the district court judge had erred in concluding that they had.

Although it will probably not be the last of the antitrust cases, the ongoing litigation placing certain institutions in the position of bringing suit against the organization of which they are members offers an apt culminating point for the Association's experience with the Sherman Act. For the NCAA, the suit filed by the Metropolitan Intercollegiate Basketball Association (MIBA) is among the youngest of *Goldfarb's* heirs. The case provides an example of a family feud gone public and from a litigative perspective was the first one since Georgia and Oklahoma upset the NCAA's football television applecart 20 years before. Though the game was different this time, the motivation, again, was money.

MIBA is an organization comprising five institutions located in New York City: Fordham, Manhattan, St John's, Wagner and New York University. Their challenge was to both the aforementioned preseason participation limits and an NCAA requirement that institutions selected for the Association's postseason tournament must participate. This mandate meant that, if chosen by the NCAA, an institution could not take part in the National Invitation Tournament (NIT), an old, annual and still prestigious pre- and postseason competition that is closely identified with the city that is their home. The basis of the suit, as usual, was restraint of trade. The legislative home, once more, was Sherman. The case was settled in summer 2005 when the NCAA purchased the NIT and the rights to its preseason and postseason tournaments. The MIBA institutions received $40.5 million for those rights and $16 million in damages to be paid over a 10-year period. For at least five years, the customary games would continue to be played in the New York City area and televised by ESPN. The rule that led to the suit is to be given further consideration through the Association's normal governance process.

FULL-COURT PRESS

THE LAW OF litigative physics has also governed in eligibility matters. *Tanaka* and *Smith* had eligibility as well as antitrust implications, and, in terms of its Title IX component, *Smith* was one of several instances in which eligibility questions and federal legislation joined forces in the courtroom. There were precedents — in judgments like those in *Jones v. NCAA* (1975) and *Gaines v. NCAA* (1990) — that helped determine outcomes in the litigation that came forward in the later years of the last century. Although *Jones* and *Gaines* were also cases in which plaintiffs alleged Sherman Act violations, eligibility considerations supplied the impelling force. Jones had played hockey for several "amateur" teams and received compensation for doing so. Gaines had entered the NFL draft but had not been selected. Both subsequently wanted to participate in intercollegiate competition, despite their clearly ineligible standing under the rules. Federal district court decisions protected the Association's relative autonomy in setting eligibility standards in each case. In some of the more recent suits, however, the NCAA has faced sterner challenges to the traditionally wide latitude it has enjoyed in determining eligibility. Its emphasis on enhanced academic qualifications was contested in a class-action suit questioning the use of standardized-test scores. The impact of such a requirement on individuals with learning disabilities became the focus of several cases. And the arrival on American campuses of increasing numbers of international student-athletes began to have courtroom consequences as eligibility issues arose in connection with the principle of amateurism.

The *Cureton* suit gave the NCAA a victory on standardized-test use, but it was both hard won and narrow. Tai Kwan Cureton is an African-American who graduated from a Philadelphia high school ranking 37th in a class of 305. His fellow graduate, Leatrice Shaw, also an African-American, ranked fifth in that class. Their GPAs easily exceeded the minimum under Proposition 16. But neither student met the required test score. Both would need to sacrifice their initial year of college-level participation. Two other plaintiffs in similar situations joined the case later. The four were represented by attorneys from the National Women's Law Center and, along the way, supporting briefs were filed by organizations similar to those that joined in the *Smith* litigation. The ACE, a strong backer of academic reform, was again among the entities and individuals appearing as amici curiae in support of the Association. The suit was brought in a federal district court in Pennsylvania in 1997. It alleged that Proposition 16 — specifically, the test-score component — had an unintended but real disparate impact on African-American student-athletes and therefore violated Title VI of the Civil Rights Act of 1964.

Central to the plaintiffs' case was the assertion that the NCAA was — in one sense or another — a recipient of federal funds, which would make the organization susceptible to a Civil Rights Act Title VI claim. The Association had a relationship with the National Youth Sports Program (NYSP), which receives financial assistance from the U.S. Department of Health and Human Services to provide summer education programs on college campuses. Initially this assistance went to the NCAA and then was advanced to the NYSP Fund with no diversion of dollars for Association use. After 1991, the federal money went directly to the Fund. The NCAA regarded the program as having affiliate standing. The circuit court in *Smith* had noted the existence of this relationship but did not incorporate it into the appeal decision. The basic issue in *Smith* — whether the NCAA effectively became a federal funds recipient through its control over member institutions that indisputably did receive such funding — arose again (though under a somewhat different rationale) in the *Cureton* litigation.

The district court judge determined that, in fact, the Association was covered by the Civil Rights Act. It was, through the NYSP, an "indirect" recipient of federal dollars, and it exercised a controlling influence over its affiliate organization. And, the judge ruled, the NCAA's authority over its member colleges and universities brought it "sufficiently within the scope of Title VI irre-

1983 (January 10-12) —Division I approves Proposal No. 48, which requires prospective student-athletes to reach specified grade-point averages and standardized-test scores.

1983 (March 11-12) —First National Collegiate Women's Indoor Track Championships are conducted at Pontiac, Michigan.

PHOTO COURTESY WEST VIRGINIA UNIVERSITY

1983 (March 18-19) —**West Virginia University** wins the first of 13 National Collegiate Rifle Championships team titles between 1983 and 1998 (four under coach Edward Etzel, one under coach Greg Perrine and eight under coach Marsha Beasley).

1983 (June 11) —Roger Clemens pitches a complete game for the University of Texas at Austin as the Longhorns defeat the University of Alabama, Tuscaloosa, for the Division I Baseball Championship title in Omaha, Nebraska.

1983 (November 12) —Bloomsburg University of Pennsylvania wins the first of eight Division II Field Hockey Championship titles between 1983 and 2003 under coach Jan Hutchinson (in addition to Division III titles in 1984 and 1987, during an eight-year period when the Division II championship was discontinued).

PHOTO COURTESY NORTH DAKOTA STATE UNIVERSITY

1983 (December 10) —North Dakota State University wins the first of five Division II Football Championship titles between 1983 and 1990 (one under coach Don Morton, two under coach Earle Solomonson and two under coach Rocky Hager).

1984 (January 8) —Executive Committee approves 64-team Division I Men's Basketball Championship field.

1984 (January 9-11) — Creation of NCAA Presidents Commission approved.

FROM NCAA FILES

1984 (March 8-10) —Kenyon College wins the first of 17 straight Division III Women's Swimming and Diving Championships team titles under coach **Jim Steen** (the team added championships in 2002, 2003 and 2004).

1984 (March 9-10) —The University of Arkansas, Fayetteville, wins the first of 12 straight Division I Men's Indoor Track Championships team titles under coach John McDonnell (the team added another four consecutive titles from 1997 to 2000 and additional championships in 2003 and 2005).

spective of its receipt of federal funds." These conclusions led the court to enjoin the Association from employing the standardized-test score as a determinant of eligibility, although continued use of GPAs was to be permitted. The NCAA requested a stay of this order so that it could appeal the decision. The judge refused the request. The Third Circuit, however, agreed to the stay, and the case went to that court on appeal in late 1999.

The circuit court found fault with both of the district court's findings regarding the federal funds issue. The court held that the Title VI regulations include disparate impact provisions that are by their terms program specific. Thus, to the extent that the NCAA received federal financial assistance by way of grants to the NYSP, the plaintiff's action must fail because the NYSP's programs and activities were not at issue in the case. As for the NCAA's relationship to its member institutions, the court left little doubt about its opinion of the district court's conclusion:

> We cannot understand how the fact that the NCAA promulgates rules and regulations [on] intercollegiate athletics somehow means that the NCAA has controlling authority over its member programs or activities receiving federal financial assistance.

The Third Circuit, accordingly, reversed the district court's decision and later acted on an additional appeal in the case. This appeal came from the plaintiffs who, after the circuit court ruled against them, sought to amend their complaint. The disparate impact basis of the initial claim meant that the plaintiffs were alleging unintentional discrimination, which has a lower standard of proof. Now, the plaintiffs argued that the NCAA used Proposition 16 as an instrument of intentional discrimination. The district court denied the request, and the Third Circuit affirmed this judgment. There was no further appeal. Proposition 16, the heart of the Association's 20-year academic reform effort, survived its first fundamental challenge. It would not be the last.

No. 16 contained a core-course requirement as well as the GPA and test-score standards. This provision became the target of a complex, long-running suit filed by a learning-disabled student named Michael Bowers in 1997. Bowers sought relief under the Americans with Disabilities Act (ADA) of 1990. His high school curriculum had included a number of special education courses, leaving him short of Proposition 16's mandate of 13 core courses for initial eligibility. The NCAA Clearinghouse, which makes the decisions on freshman eligibility, determined that he did not meet that mandate. Bowers claimed that institutions that had been recruiting him stopped after learning of this determination. He had been a star football player at a New Jersey high school, but he did not receive an athletics grant-in-aid to attend college. He sued the NCAA on several counts, as well as ACT (which administers the Clearinghouse) and several universities and colleges. A wide array of thorny issues arose during the many hearings needed to surface all the claims and counterclaims and rule on the multitude of motions. "Difficult legal questions" were presented in this "hotly contested case," the district court judge said early on, in "an area of law that has become fertile for civil rights litigation." The judge issued numerous opinions over the course of his involvement in the case. By the time the litigation ended, nearly eight years after it began, Bowers was dead and his mother was carrying on in his stead.

A new judge was on the case by then, and new information was now belatedly available. Bowers had succumbed to a drug overdose in 2002, and, earlier, had attempted suicide. Evidence of his drug addiction, unsuccessful treatment and other medical problems had been kept from the defendants' attention until 2004. The judge determined, as a result, that sanctions would be imposed on Bowers' attorneys, "due to serious discovery misconduct." He granted the defendants' motion for summary judgment and dismissed the case in March 2005.

The Bowers litigation was one of many suits brought under the ADA in the late 1990s. Complaints about the initial-eligibility requirements had been lodged with the U.S. Department of Justice by learning-disabled student-athletes. The department concluded that the requirements violated the act, a contention disputed by the NCAA. The Association also said that it was not subject to the ADA anyway, because it was not "a place of public accommodation," a requirement for the Act to apply to the NCAA. Nevertheless, the two parties agreed to discuss possible modifications to the NCAA rules. The result was a 1998 consent decree that effectively eliminated the possibility of future ADA-based litigation against the Association. Under the terms of the decree, the NCAA proposed a number of wording and policy changes acceptable to the Department of Justice and easing the burden of eligibility qualification for learning-disabled students. The parties acknowledged the Association's continuing position on the public accommodation issue and its refusal to admit liability under the ADA.

Somewhere along the litigious way, amateurism was bound to rear its head. Critics have claimed for decades that the Association's amateur principle should be regarded as a historical artifact and that the NCAA and inter-collegiate athletics generally should remove their hypocritical heads from the sand and acknowledge as much. There is, of course, a worthy counter-argument. We will examine some of the particulars of this ongoing debate in the final chapter. At this point, it bears notice that complicated amateurism issues remain to be considered, that the prior activities of international student-athletes can provide a focus for this consideration and that the courts, unsurprisingly, are part of the dialogue. The case of *Lasege v. NCAA* provides an instructive example. It also allows for an understanding of why the celebrated "home-court advantage" is not solely a property of the world of sport.

Muhammed Lasege filed his suit in a Kentucky circuit court (the court of original jurisdiction in that state). Lasege, a Nigerian student-athlete, was found by the NCAA to be ineligible to play basketball at Louisville because of his experience as a professional in Russia. Specifically, he had signed contracts in that country to play on a professional team, had an agent there, received a salary (which Lasege denied), monetary incentives, a furnished apartment, meals, a driver, a cook, a clothing allowance, air travel tickets and a visa permitting him to fly to Canada. An individual in that country gave him lodging and meals for about eight months, plus automobile transportation and airline tickets for unofficial campus visits, and a one-way ticket to Louisville where he was to enroll for the 1999-2000 academic year.

The Kentucky state circuit court was not persuaded that there was a problem, finding instead that the Association had ignored "overwhelming and mitigating circumstances" and had made a determination that conflicted with its own amateurism guidelines and precedents. The clear weight of evidence, the court held, led to a conclusion that Lasege had signed contracts and received emoluments not because he wanted to be a professional player but simply to put himself in a position to obtain a visa so he could compete as a student-athlete in the U.S. The NCAA's behavior in the matter was "arbitrary and capricious," leading the court to order the Association "to immediately restore" the young man's eligibility. In addition, a certain NCAA bylaw was declared invalid. This was the rule of restitution, a level playing field provision whereby the Association — if it is enjoined per *Lasege*, but the student-athlete then becomes eligible to play and the injunction is later vacated or reversed — is empowered to take such action as may be necessary to ensure that the institution involved has not gotten an unfair advantage. This can mean, for example, that victories would be nullified. The circuit court decided that the bylaw "prevents parties from availing themselves of the protections of the courts." The court of appeals affirmed the lower court's decision on Lasege's eligibility. It did not address the rule of restitution.

In Kentucky, appellate courts can reverse circuit court rulings on temporary injunctions only for "extraordinary cause" (for example, abuses of discretion). The state Supreme Court found such cause in the circuit court's handling of the Lasege suit as well as in its invalidation of an NCAA bylaw. The court observed that the Association's decision on Lasege's eligibility had "strong evidentiary support" and that the trial court "simply disagreed with the NCAA as to the weight which should be assigned to this evidence." Disagreement was not a sufficient reason for issuing an injunction. Also, the lower court had erred in judging that the NCAA would "not suffer any potential harm" as a result of its finding in favor of Lasege. As for the determination that the rule of restitution "thwarts the judicial power," the Supreme Court held that this view "is simply without foundation." The court therefore vacated the circuit court's injunction on both counts. The NCAA had won another eligibility suit, but questions about the amateur standing of international student-athletes were not conclusively answered by the Kentucky decision. In this area, much work awaits.

This was another thin victory. Three of the Kentucky high court's seven justices dissented from the majority's opinion.

NAVIGATING THE POTOMAC
IT HELPS TO remember that the NCAA was conceived (though not born) in Washington, D.C. When

"The rules are designed with but a single purpose in mind: To implement the fundamental tenet of the NCAA constitution, that the student-athlete be a student first and an athlete second. If this principle cannot be maintained successfully, then colleges should not be sponsoring varsity athletic teams."
—NCAA PRESIDENT J. NEILS THOMPSON, IN HIS PRESENTATION TO A CONGRESSIONAL SUBCOMMITTEE, SEPTEMBER 27, 1978

1984 (March 15-17) —The University of Florida's **Tracy Caulkins** wins four events at the Division I Women's Swimming and Diving Championships to extend her record career total to 12 individual titles; the same year, the University of Texas at Austin wins the first of five straight team titles under coach Richard Quick (who then moves to Stanford University and wins a sixth straight championship).

1984 (March 24) —The Central Missouri State University men's and women's teams win the Division II Men's and Women's Basketball Championship titles, making Central Missouri State the first school in any division to accomplish the dual feat in basketball.

1984 (April 1) — The University of Southern California, led by **Cheryl Miller** and **Paula** and **Pam McGee**, wins its second straight Division I Women's Basketball Championship title.

President Theodore Roosevelt told the university representatives he summoned to his office in late autumn 1905 that it was time to reform football or kill it, he was saying in effect that there is a national stake in intercollegiate athletics. Although it did not necessarily follow from this implicit assertion that the federal government should protect such a stake, one can view Roosevelt's handling of an urgent problem as setting a kind of precedent. Over time, a need for federal intervention has been periodically suggested — by elected officials, generations of critics, or, as in its long struggle with the AAU, by the NCAA itself. As the discussion of court cases suggests, Congressional initiatives and judicial interpretations and decisions have further involved Washington in the shaping of college sports policy. Civil rights legislation, the ADA and initiatives such as Title IX have materially influenced the Association's priorities and structure, particularly during the last three decades. The NCAA's increasing focus on regulatory responsibilities has inevitably invited the attention of, and the possibility of intervention from, national decision-makers. Often enough, Washington's interest has been a product of legislators' displeasure with adverse infractions decisions involving their home institutions. A series of hearings in the House of Representatives, covering a 17-month period in 1978-79, confirms this point. The Congressional temper prevailing during these hearings could be described as approaching, if not surpassing, high dudgeon. The individual whose role in an infractions case was the launch pad for the process was men's basketball coach Jerry Tarkanian of UNLV.

The NCAA's contentious relationship with Tarkanian began in 1972 with an investigation of the Long Beach State football and men's basketball programs. Tarkanian was the institution's head basketball coach at the time, and, after he moved to UNLV in 1973, Long Beach State's basketball program was placed on probation for recruiting violations occurring during his tenure there. He denied the violations and stated that the findings had been made without his participation in the hearings (although it is the affected institution, not the NCAA, that decides on the hearing participants).

Three years later, the Association announced a two-year probation for UNLV men's basketball based on a finding of numerous rules violations from 1971 through 1975. Included in the charges were improper gifts to players, improper cash allowances, and free air travel tickets to players and members of their families. Among the university's penalties were probation and a ban on postseason competition and television appearances during the next two seasons. In addition, the institution was asked to suspend Tarkanian from involvement in athletics activities for those two years. UNLV complied, the coach sued and, in September 1977, a state district court judge issued a permanent injunction against the suspension, thus reinstating Tarkanian as coach. These events set the stage for the hearings and attendant investigation of the NCAA's enforcement program undertaken by a House of Representatives subcommittee — at the request of Nevada Congressman James Santini — in late February 1978.

The first witness was former NCAA investigator J. Brent Clark, just appointed to a staff position with the subcommittee. Clark was described by a committee member as a "breakthrough" witness and a "prize defector." A Sports Illustrated article said he "has passed on to his new employers an elaborate scenario of an NCAA enforcement/penalty system corrupted by 'vendettas' against schools and coaches. He has described a monolith that runs roughshod over due process and 'preys on the weak and vulnerable.'" His testimony produced major headlines around the country, and no wonder. He made charges of selective investigations, coercion and "flesh-peddling" by fellow investigators. He said Walter Byers meddled in cases. He observed that Association staff "routinely cajoled, even bribed, athletes into sacrificing their careers." Follow-up questioning by a subcommittee member, along with Clark's admission that he had no proof to offer, suggested that there could be a problem with these sensational claims. The subcommittee assigned three staff members to investigate Clark's accusations. After six weeks of inquiry, they reported that Clark's testimony had been "deficient," as well as "derelict and misleading." Clark resigned from his subcommittee job the same day. His claims were untrue, but this discovery did little to alleviate what writer John Underwood of Sports Illustrated characterized as the "threats and anger" and "bitter tone" that pervaded the hearings. Subcommittee chair John Moss, wrote Underwood, "never swayed from his antagonism toward … the NCAA." Byers, falsely charged with protecting "sacred cow" member institutions, described the proceedings as a "high-profile onslaught from Capitol Hill," and his treatment by Chairman Moss and Congressman Santini as something one might expect would be extended to an "unrepentant gangster."

So, the proceedings continued. Representatives of institutions recently penalized by the Committee on Infractions appeared and aired their complaints of unfair treatment. Mississippi State and Michigan State were among these institutions. The former's football program had been placed on two years' probation for providing assorted extra benefits, improper recruitment, failure to exercise necessary supervision over "representatives of its athletic interests" (a standard euphemistic description of boosters) and a lack of institutional control. Mississippi State also was denied television appearances and postseason competition and was required to sacrifice a number of football grants-in-aid during the probationary period. Michigan State's transgressions were similar and also involved football, but included improper financial aid and unethical conduct. The sanctions included three years' probation and accompanying prohibitions of television and postseason appearances. In June, Tarkanian testified, along with UNLV's president, and both took further exception to the putative unfairness of the Association's enforcement policies and procedures. Other penalized institutions and their spokesmen also had their day. As far as the NCAA was concerned, their purpose was not laudatory.

UNLV BASKETBALL COACH JERRY TARKANIAN

PHOTO BY RICH CLARKSON / NCAA PHOTOS

Meanwhile, Association officers wondered whether and when they would have an opportunity to defend the organization against what NCAA President J. Neils Thompson of the University of Texas called "a distorted view" arising from "a one-sided presentation of evidence." The opportunity was delayed twice, and finally, at the end of September, seven months after the hearings got underway, the officers got their chance.

Byers testified. So did Thompson and Charles Alan Wright, a professor of constitutional law and chair of the Committee on Infractions. The Association's president expressed his resentment at the previous testimony of a number of hostile participants, which had conveyed "the impression that in some fashion the members of the Committee on Infractions were engaged in the perpetration of a selective, vindictive or corrupt program of enforcement." He commented on the Association's interest in and history of continuing study and revision of enforcement procedures, took note of the criticisms directed at the size of the NCAA Manual ("… no one in touch with the reality of intercollegiate athletics would seriously suggest that equality of opportunity can be maintained by just 'a few simple rules'") and welcomed the suggestions for greater cooperation with institutions involved in enforcement cases. On this subject, though, he observed that:

> Those who complain most stridently of a lack of cooperation on the part of the
> NCAA enforcement staff are those who have evidenced their own unwillingness
> seriously to investigate the facts in an objective, as distinct from a defensive, manner.

Thompson found "ludicrous" the accusations made during earlier hearings that the infractions committee was merely a "rubber stamp" for decisions already taken by members of the enforcement staff. This was, he said, a "scurrilous charge," and he pointed out that in the cases of institutions that had testified previously, the committee often (approximately 40 percent of the time) eliminated allegations presented in the staff's official report of inquiry. Finally, he reminded the subcommittee members of the fundamental principle put in place by Palmer Pierce and colleagues at the beginning and fortified in Byers' time to address hard modern realities:

> It is the institution itself which is primarily responsible for policing its own
> affairs, and it is only when that institution fails to do so that the NCAA
> enforcement mechanisms come into play.

Wright had indicated what he intended to emphasize at the subcommittee hearing when he addressed a media seminar in May 1978. He saw problems, he told the gathering, when he heard "such experts on Constitutional law as basketball coaches [and] sportswriters lecturing on the requirements of due process." The model the average person understood is the one used in criminal proceedings. The U.S. Supreme Court had determined that "due process is a flexible concept. It calls for such procedures as a particular situation requires …" He pointed out that what is necessary in an NCAA procedure (when, for instance, witnesses cannot be subpoenaed) is not the same as what a criminal case demands. Wright's insights would become important at a future time, when due process and the NCAA became an object of considerable curiosity in state legislatures around the country. That development will be addressed later. Here it will suffice to take note of certain remarks he made to the Congressional subcommittee. If he were the attorney representing an institution or coach in an infractions matter, Wright said, he might argue that his client had been deprived of due process, especially if that client was guilty. He would insist on procedures, such as the right to cross-examine witnesses, since that would mean many of them — given the facts of life in intercollegiate athletics — simply would not appear. And, he concluded, if he lost his case anyway, "I would be telling my local sportswriters that the procedure is one-sided, the hearing was a farce, [and] that the penalty was far too severe …"

While there had been ample accusatory smoke emanating from the subcommittee hearing room for nearly a year and a half, there was in the end a paucity of evidentiary fire. The accusations simply were not accompanied by proof. That is not to say, however, that the enforcement process was without shortcomings or that the hearings served no useful purpose. The subcommittee turned over to the Association a list of suggestions offered by participants during the months of testimony. Many had already been on the table at previous, internal discussions of enforcement. The NCAA reviewed all of them anyway and recommended a half-dozen as reform measures to the delegates at the 1979 Convention. All six were approved. Perhaps of most importance was a proposal to remove the Committee on Infractions from the responsibility to review the scope of an infractions case before authorizing an official inquiry. The need to develop further separation between the committee and NCAA investigators would continue to be studied and acted on in subsequent years. In that sense, the subcommittee initiated a long-term process of review and refinement that was consequential in improving the enforcement function.

There were other lessons to be learned of life beside the Potomac from the lengthy subcommittee experience. The national river is navigable for the most part, but it has its turbidity, its rapids and floods and its share of pollution. A permanent presence in the area was beginning to seem a good idea. That would have been only a gleam in the eye (if that much) in 1979, but a decade and a half later, the idea became fact. Meantime, members found comfort in the words of subcommittee member Norman Lent of New York:

> I have always found it hard to justify this subcommittee's investigation of
> college athletics. During 1978, the Oversight and Investigations Subcommittee
> devoted more of its time and resources to the NCAA investigation than to any
> other single issue — including such vital questions as cancer-causing chemicals
> in foods and decontrol of crude oil and gasoline prices.

STATE ACTORS AND STATES' ACTIONS

BEFORE THE QUESTION of whether the NCAA was a state actor under the 14th Amendment surfaced in *Smith* and *Cureton*, it was the central issue in a case involving a men's basketball coach. The case had a long duration. The coach was Jerry Tarkanian. The state district court decision in 1977, enjoining UNLV from suspending him, reached the Nevada Supreme Court in 1979. This court reversed the district court's action. Tarkanian filed an amended suit, remained in his job and the state district court (this time with a different judge) took up the matter again in June 1984. Judge Paul Goldman, observing that the NCAA had behaved like "arrogant lords of the manor," doing "the same things the [Soviet] KGB and the Third Reich did," once more granted Tarkanian's request for a permanent injunction on grounds he had been denied due process. On appeal, the Nevada Supreme Court this time affirmed the decision, holding that Tarkanian had a "property interest in continued employment as basketball coach" and was entitled therefore to due process. He was an employee of the state of Nevada, and the discipline of such employees is "traditionally the exclusive preroga-

". . .Thankfully, the subcommittee did not conclude at the end of its series of hearings that there was a need for federal intervention into intercollegiate sports. Such a proposal would have been, in my opinion, a mistake of inestimable proportions."
—REPRESENTATIVE NORMAN LENT OF NEW YORK, SPEAKING OF THE 1978 CONGRESSIONAL HEARINGS

tive" of the state. The NCAA's requirement that UNLV suspend him therefore, "constituted 'state action' for purposes of due process analysis." In addition, since many of the Association's member institutions were public or received public money, its regulatory activities could also be construed as state action. The NCAA, the court effectively ruled, was indeed the kind of state actor to which the 14th Amendment referred. This was big news. It meant that, if the ruling held, major changes in the way the Association worked would be required. Unsurprisingly, the NCAA appealed to the U.S. Supreme Court, which did not take up the case until February 1988.

The ruling on the appeal 10 months later reversed the Nevada decision. The NCAA "cannot be deemed to be a state actor on the theory that it misused power it possessed by virtue of state law," the court held, and UNLV's determination as a member to accept NCAA rules "did not transform them into state rules." The university "delegated no power to the NCAA to take specific action against any" of its employees. The court's opinion was clear that the Association was, in fact, a private actor. It could not "directly discipline Tarkanian or any other state university employee." Further, "it had no power to subpoena witnesses, to impose contempt citations or to assert sovereign authority over any individual."

The decision was another major victory for the NCAA. Once again, however, it was a narrow one. The Supreme Court vote in the *Tarkanian* case was 5-4.

On the due process front, there was much more to come. Interest in finding a way to force the Association to move its enforcement procedures toward the criminal model described by Professor Wright had not subsided. The new approach, now that efforts at the Congressional and federal court levels had not borne fruit, was to turn to state legislatures to take up the cause. There were enough recently penalized athletics programs around to attract the necessary legislative attention. What then transpired was something of a replay of the 1978-79 hearings in Washington, D.C. — a series of replays, actually, as the old familiar charges of unfairness, pettiness, favoritism and serious process problems echoed through the corridors and hearing rooms of numerous state capitols. In the years immediately after the Tarkanian decision, down to spring 1992, legislation was proposed in 14 states to address due process by requiring the NCAA to submit to each state's own particular procedural requirements. By the time legislative activity concluded in 1991, four of the states (Nebraska, Illinois, Florida and Nevada) had put due process statutes on the books.

In three of these states, the Association had assessed serious sanctions against member institutions in the past three years. The University of Illinois had been placed on two years' probation in 1988 and received another three years in 1990. In the state of Florida, three institutions (the University of Florida, South Florida and Florida A&M) had suffered probationary penalties since 1986, two of which were levied in 1990. Nebraska's last sanction, resulting in a one-year probation, came in 1986. In Nevada, the NCAA had initiated an investigation of UNLV basketball in 1987 and, in July 1990, decided to prohibit UNLV from defending the national championship it had won three months previously. Of the other 10 states (Iowa, Kansas, Kentucky, Minnesota, Mississippi, Missouri, New York, Ohio, Rhode Island and South Carolina), seven had experienced probationary penalties against major local universities since 1988. The sanctions in Iowa and Mississippi went back to 1986. Rhode Island had been free of infractions cases. As in the related state actor controversy, Nevada played the lead role on due process. Life had been difficult for the Association in that state for a number of years, but on this occasion the timing was terrible.

The state of Nevada's 1991 legislative session was but a few days old when Assembly Bill 204 was introduced. Six months earlier, the postseason ban on UNLV basketball had been announced, and only one month had passed since the NCAA had issued an official letter of inquiry alleging 29 infractions, again involving the university's men's basketball program. Anti-Association fever was running high in Las Vegas and environs, the home of nearly two-thirds of the members of the

1984 (April 2) — **John Thompson** becomes first Black to coach a team (Georgetown University) to the Division I Men's Basketball Championship title.

1984 (June 27) — Supreme Court upholds ruling that NCAA Football Television Plan violates Sherman Antitrust Act.

1984 (December 8) —Portland State University wins the first of four Division II Women's Volleyball Championship titles between 1984 and 1992 under coach Jeff Mozzochi.

1985 (March) —First Divisions II and III Women's Indoor Track Championships are conducted at North Dakota State University and Bates College.

1985 (May 19) —**The College of New Jersey** (then known as Trenton State College) wins the first Division III Women's Lacrosse Championship, claiming the first of its 10 titles between 1985 and 2000.

state legislature. That feeling was reflected in comments made when the bill was introduced and during the hearings that ensued. The chief sponsor, Assemblyman James McGaughey, observed that "the NCAA is probably the number one intimidator in the history of athletics." He said the Association functioned "as a dictatorship with power … to lock a person up or take away their property." For "the last 40 years," he told his colleagues, the organization has had "a reign of terror over the universities of this country." He cited the accusations made a dozen years earlier by Brent Clark before the House subcommittee, though by this time that testimony had long since been discredited. The sponsor reiterated the long-held, if inaccurate, view that "small schools were singled out for sanctions that were not applied to larger schools." Other legislators referred to the Association's "McCarthy behavior," pointed to "sanctions placed against [UNLV] for actions considered to be rather minimal in their severity [while] the sanctions have been severe," and commented on what they regarded as discriminatory penalties at other institutions. The final bill, with a few amendments, passed both houses of the legislature unanimously.

On an earlier reading of the bill, in the Assembly, there had been one nay vote. This came from Robert Sader, an attorney who, noting that other states were also considering due process legislation, suggested that there could be "10, 20, 50 different standards for the NCAA to have to deal with in the 50 different states." That, he said, would produce "an untenable situation." Although it was true that the Nevada bill was modeled on the one that had passed in Nebraska a year earlier, there clearly were variations in the proposals under consideration around the country. They dealt in differing ways with matters of notice, records-keeping, legal representation in the investigative process, the cross examination of witnesses and the appeals process. The bills typically proposed that the states' own civil rules of evidence be used, different though they were from one state to another. The Nevada legislation had such a requirement, as well as a mandate that the presiding official at hearings "must be impartial." If the procedural dictates were not followed, a "national collegiate athletic association" would not be allowed to "impose a sanction on a Nevada institution, or anyone associated with it …" Monetary penalties against such an association would be permitted if the bill's imperatives were not honored. The NCAA decided that this was the legislation to contest and took its case to a federal district court in Nevada.

One year later, in June 1992, the court granted the Association's request to enjoin the application of the new statute to the UNLV infractions case. The court also issued a declaratory judgment voiding the statute. It "imposes a direct burden on interstate commerce," the judge wrote, and "impairs existing contractual rights and obligations … between the NCAA and its members." The statute therefore violated two clauses of the U.S. Constitution. In addition, it deprived the Association and its members "of the right to freely associate with each other" and in that way violated the First Amendment. Finally, the court ruled that the Nevada law "contains provisions which are vague and overbroad in violation of the due process clause of the 14th Amendment." The state did not appeal.

The district court decision represented a resounding defeat not only for the Nevada legislation but also for the companion bills that had been either passed or proposed in the 14 other states noted earlier. The actions of these states to bring a substantially enhanced standard of due process to bear in NCAA enforcement cases were nullified by this decision. The principal defect in all these efforts Constitutional problems aside, was the one pointed out by the legislator casting the only negative vote against Assembly Bill 204. No national regulatory body could operate effectively, if at all, when required to observe different process requirements and different rules of evidence from one state to the next. Such a situation, as that lone legislator insisted, would be "untenable."

UNFINISHED BUSINESS

AT THE 1992 Convention, Richard Schultz had expressed great concern about the near-blizzard of state due process legislation. He reported in his State of the Association address a year later that the problem had been resolved. Schultz also told the delegates in 1992 of talk in Congress on NCAA enforcement procedures. The Nevada delegation introduced federal due process measures relating to the NCAA in 1992. New York Congressman Ed Towns presented a bill in 1991 that would require the Association to provide institutions, coaches and student-athletes due process protection in infractions cases. Towns was apparently aware of similar proposals at the state level, including the one in his home state.

For the NCAA, 1991 was a busy year in Washington. Congressman Tom McMillen, a former Maryland basketball player and a member of the Knight Commission, announced a so-called "omnibus bill" — the

"Collegiate Athletics Reform Act" — that would mandate major changes for the Association in a number of areas. Included was a revenue-distribution plan favoring institutions that were working to comply with Title IX and forbidding any allocation of dollars on the basis of win/loss records. The McMillen bill would require comprehensive annual reporting to Congress and the Secretary of Education, establish an NCAA board of presidents with certain control responsibilities, and decrease expenditures on revenue-producing sports and on athletics administration. The bill also included a due process component. Moving along a narrower track, Congressman Mervyn Dymally of California introduced a bill that year to establish a National Commission on Athletics. None of these proposals — neither the one from the Nevada delegation nor the three from Towns, McMillen and Dymally — traveled far in the legislative process. However, another set of hearings on intercollegiate athletics in 1991 brought the Association to the nation's capital on several matters of significant interest. This time, a subcommittee of the House Energy and Commerce Committee scheduled the hearings.

Congresswoman Cardiss Collins of Illinois chaired the hearings, which reflected the issues that, during the 1990s, she frequently and forcefully discussed with NCAA representatives. Among them were gender equity, academic standards, graduation rates, Proposition 48, the Knight Commission report, athletics programs at historically black institutions, minority representation on Association committees and — an oft-visited issue that year, both in and out of Washington — due process under NCAA enforcement procedures. Later, Collins would involve herself substantively in the development of NCAA gender-equity policy (including another hearing in 1993) and Association research on the impacts of Proposition 16. These matters will be taken up in the next chapter.

The continuing debate on due process led Schultz to propose to the Executive Committee that a group be formed to study the matter, then make suggestions for change. The Special Committee to Review the Enforcement and Infractions Process that was appointed in April 1991 included Rex Lee (chair), president of Brigham Young and previously U.S. solicitor general; Warren Burger, former chief justice of the Supreme Court; Benjamin Civiletti, former U.S. attorney general; two individuals who had served as federal district or circuit court judges; and a one-time state supreme court justice. Also appointed were members with law school faculty experience, a campus attorney and two Council representatives. This was clearly a blue-ribbon committee, in a way picking up on a recommendation of the Moss subcommittee from 12 years earlier. It was charged with reviewing the investigative process, the function of the Committee on Infractions, hearing procedures and other matters of consequence, with a view toward maximizing fairness while preserving effectiveness.

Within six months, the committee completed the review and forwarded 11 recommendations. Following discussions by the Presidents Commission, Council and the Committee on Infractions, nine of the recommendations, most in modified form, were favorably acted on by the 1992 Convention. A number of procedures were strengthened to build greater confidence in the process. Also, the infractions committee would add distinguished members from the general public and an appellate body, also with membership from the external community, would be created. The Association drew the line, however, on opening the hearings to the public and on providing independent hearing officers in major violations cases.

Only the naïve expected that the Supreme Court decision in the Tarkanian "state actor" case, the federal district court judgment nullifying the Nevada statute and the acceptance by the NCAA of most of the Lee committee reforms would end the argument over due process. Complaints continued to be aired during the 1990s, often following the assessment of major sanctions against prominent member institutions. A recent case in point — another Congressional hearing — came in September 2004. Earlier that year, Auburn had received a two-year probation for infractions in its men's basketball program, and in 2002 Alabama began serving a five-year probationary period connected to a series of football violations. The hearing was set by the House

1985 (December 21) — Georgia Southern University wins the first of six Division I-AA Football Championship titles between 1985 and 2000 (three under coach **Erk Russell**, one under coach **Tim Stowers** and two under coach **Paul Johnson**).

1986 (January 13) — George H.W. Bush honored with Theodore Roosevelt Award during his vice presidency (he was elected to presidency in 1988, making him third president to receive the award).

1986 (January 13-15) —NCAA drug-testing program approved. (First testing was conducted at Division I Men's and Women's Cross Country Championships in November 1986.)

1986 (March 12-15) —**California State University, Bakersfield**, wins the first of 13 Division II Men's Swimming and Diving Championships team titles between 1986 and 2004 (eight under coach Ernie Maglischo and five under coach Bob Steele).

Judiciary Committee's Subcommittee on the Constitution. It was requested by Congressman Spencer Baccus of Alabama, who said he did not want to discuss the particulars of those two home-state cases but the NCAA's enforcement procedures in general. He called for public hearings of such cases and for "an independent trier of the facts." Josephine Potuto, vice chair of the Committee on Infractions and a professor of law at Nebraska, described and defended the NCAA process.

Professor Potuto pointed out that, after initially rejecting the Lee committee's recommendation on the matter, the Association had adopted a bylaw permitting institutions and individuals to request the use of hearing officers, instead of the infractions committee, in violations cases. During the 10-plus years this alternative was available, she said, only one request had been made to exercise the option. That request came from an individual; the institution in that instance wanted the committee to conduct the hearings. Given this record, the NCAA eliminated the bylaw. As for holding hearings in public, she offered the long-standing and still persuasive explanation of the impracticality of this idea: Confidentiality is imperative. The cooperation of witnesses is often critical and much less likely to be forthcoming in a context of full public disclosure. The likelihood of extreme public interest in major cases makes open hearings problematic.

In the Association's long experience with Congressional hearings, this one — although indulging an ample supply of angry language — was not particularly burdensome. It was brief and equitably open to all sides. It did not lead to legislative activity or a long list of suggested changes. It did not produce a succession of dramatic headlines. Even so, it was unlikely to be the last of the legislative and other inquiries on due process. As long as the temptation to cheat persists, and the will as well to punish the cheaters, strong interest in enhancing procedural protections will live on. But that path can also lead to greater temptation and a weakening of will. Gary Roberts, a professor of sports law and faculty athletics representative at Tulane, submitted written testimony on this point at the September hearing:

> I do not recommend that Congress impose any "due process"-type requirements on the NCAA. Giving accused schools and individuals more procedural protections … would do little to enhance justice, yet it might well enable many violators to escape based on technicalities, which would in turn cause more rule-breaking … Furthermore, a legal due process right would give those found guilty a guaranteed avenue of appeal to the courts, which would burden both the enforcement process and the judicial system.

Roberts proposed instead an expansion of the enforcement staff, a policy of placing only "paid, respected jurists" on the Committee on Infractions and Infractions Appeals Committees, and Congressional action to provide the NCAA with the capability "to obtain search warrants and subpoenas from federal courts …"

PAST, PRESENT, FUTURE

THERE WILL PROBABLY be business yet to transact in the due process marketplace — reforms to consider, hearings to attend, perhaps more lawsuits to defend. And from all the external forums, including legislatures, agencies, courtrooms and others, additional challenges will come to Association policies and practices in areas unrelated to due process. The future is visible in the demands at hand and, as always, the past can be a guide both as to what to expect and how to handle what actually arrives. Consider, for example, some current litigation and initiatives that may bode ill or well once the results are in:

▶ A possible class-action suit in a federal district court (in Seattle) seeks to have walk-on players identified, and duly compensated, as "victims" under the Sherman Antitrust Act. The numbers in this instance, of both walk-ons and dollars, could be immense and the impact devastating.

▶ State courts in Texas have supported the claim of an international student — denied eligibility under NCAA rules because she transferred from one Division I school to another without sitting out the requisite number of terms — that she has a right, as distinct from a privilege, to participate in intercollegiate athletics competition. She competed successfully for Texas while her suit moved slowly through the state judicial system and completed her senior season. At stake for her would be her victories and championships, which could be voided if she loses.

On the other hand, in 2001, the West Virginia Supreme Court affirmed the long-held understanding that participation in intercollegiate athletics is a privilege, not a right. In this case, a college wrestler sued the NCAA, his university and the university's conference because of his ineligibility to compete at a lower weight class than he had been in previously because of a change in NCAA rules designed to prevent dangerous weight-loss practices. The change was put in place after three college wrestlers died as a result of rapid weight-loss programs. The plaintiff sued for an additional year of eligibility and won a preliminary injunction from a lower court in West Virginia, a decision overturned at the state Supreme Court level.

Jackie Sherrill, former football coach at Mississippi State, sued the Association in a federal district court in 2004. He became one of a number of litigating coaches whose contracts had been terminated after NCAA infractions penalties. The claims customarily asserted in these lawsuits are defamation, negligence, interference with a contract or business relationship and the tort of "outrage" (intentional infliction of emotional distress). Sherrill has requested damages totaling $15 million.

In another case, where defamation and contract interference claims were also made, the NCAA and the University of Washington reached a settlement with the university's former football coach after it was determined that Association staff used an outdated bylaw (on disclosing the purpose of an interview) in its initial meeting with the coach, Rick Neuheisel. Editorial changes had been made to the bylaw six weeks before the meeting. Complex questions of interpretation were involved. The decision to settle was a result of "restrictions placed on the NCAA by the court about how the Association could explain the bylaw and defend its rightful interpretation."

In California, state Sen. Kevin Murray introduced the Student-Athletes' Bill of Rights in February 2003. The measure would have prohibited colleges and universities in that state from adhering to a variety of NCAA rules, meaning that 47 institutions there would lose their membership in the Association. These institutions would be unable to compete in NCAA championships, bowl games and contests with members in all other states, and be ineligible to receive the millions of dollars in revenues channeled through the Association, the Pacific-10 and other conferences. The bill was introduced by Murray at the behest of the Collegiate Athletes Coalition, an organization that views student-athletes as employees and is supported by the United Auto Workers. The bill passed the California State Senate by a margin of 36-10. A large coalition of interested organizations (the NCAA, athletics conferences, higher education systems, and California colleges and universities) expended a good bit of time and energy to defeat the proposed legislation. The proposal died without a vote in the California State Assembly in 2004.

In 2003, the Nebraska legislature passed a bill, signed by the governor, allowing the payment of a stipend to football players at the University of Nebraska. Four of the other six states in the Big 12 Conference would need to pass similar bills for this legislation to take effect. This did not happen.

In recent years, the NCAA has taken the offensive in the courts, especially to protect its trademarks that have been infringed upon by Internet sites, including those associated with sports gambling. The effort has succeeded in shutting down such sites, getting domain names containing Association trademarks transferred to the NCAA, and winning a cyberpiracy lawsuit against an online ticket broker who used NCAA trademarks and domain names, and resold championship tickets at increased prices.

The Association has collaborated with Congress in the implementation of federal legislation on sports agents. The Uniform Athletic Agent Act provides a state model for agent registration and the imposition of criminal, civil and administrative penalties against unscrupulous practitioners. By January 2005, 31 states, plus the District of Columbia and the U.S. Virgin Islands, had passed this model legislation. The NCAA also provided support for the Sports Agent Responsibility

IN THE ARENA
The NCAA's First Century

1986 (April) —Men's Basketball Rules Committee adopts three-point shot in basketball for 1986-87 season.

1986 (November 16) —First Division III Women's Soccer Championship is conducted at State University College at Cortland.

1987 (February 25) —Southern Methodist University football program suspended for one year in Division I's first (and to date only) application of the "death penalty" for assorted and ongoing rules violations.

1987 (March 13-14) —Louisiana State University wins the first of 11 Division I Women's Indoor Track and Field Championship team titles between 1987 and 2004 (one under coach Billy Maxwell and 10 under coach Pat Henry); in May, the school claims the first of 11 straight outdoor team titles.

1987 (March 16) —New York University's **Michael Lofton** becomes the only man to win four titles in the same event (sabre) at the National Collegiate Fencing Championships.

1987 (April 2-4) —Stanford University's Pablo Morales surpasses the University of Southern California's John Naber as the most victorious individual titlist in the history of the Division I Men's Swimming and Diving Championships, claiming his 11th championship.

and Trust Act (SPARTA), which was passed by Congress and became law in September 2004.

▶ In 1995, under the leadership of new Executive Director Cedric Dempsey, the Association established that "permanent presence" near the Potomac by opening an office in the nation's capital. The objectives were (and are) to facilitate efforts to work with the Congress and federal agencies and, of symbolic as well as substantive importance, to build strong relationships with the other higher education organizations housed in Washington.

How might Palmer Pierce and his colleagues and successors during the Association's founding era view these developments? What would their attitude be toward the growing influence of the courtroom and legislative chamber on the NCAA's programs and priorities? That group was at pains, certainly, to ensure that the work of regulation would follow the home-rule principle: The responsibility would be exercised by the member institutions and conferences. If that understanding had survived into the 21st century, a very different history would need to be written. But it did not, and the organization's 50-plus year experience instead as the major regulatory presence in college sports is the main reason courts and legislatures and other external entities have become so much a part of the picture. Pierce and his compatriots would be hard put to recognize this picture. They probably would be puzzled to learn that the Sherman Act they thought of in relation to mighty corporations has taken root in intercollegiate athletics and that the organization they started and extended is now seen in some circles as just another big cartel. They would be challenged to comprehend the concept of a restricted-earnings coach; or how that concept could somehow cost the NCAA and its member institutions more than $54 million; or, in that debacle's aftermath, why today it takes a head coach, three full-time assistants, one or more undergraduate assistants, an academic advisor or two, and a director of basketball operations to get 13 players to perform on the court and in the classroom. They would likely be dismayed to learn that, these days, torts are almost as much a part of the athletics lexicon as teamwork. Demands for 14th Amendment protections would mystify them, as would the knowledge that the Association they built on a foundation of what they considered to be noble principles is often reviled in the hearing rooms of Congress and state capitols.

For the modern NCAA, however, as it ends its first century, this is all part of the real world. It's often an adversarial world, which helps account for the accusations of pernicious and conspiratorial behavior, of arrogance and favoritism, and of functioning as a dictatorship and conducting a reign of terror. In a way, this world is like an arena, a place of wins and losses and, sometimes, close games. In the football television case, the Association lost — to another athletics organization — at every level. Against another such organization, the AIAW, it won at both levels at which the game was played, as it did also in the *Tanaka* and *adidas* litigation. In *Smith*, with two separate issues being contested, there were two victories at the district court, a split at the circuit level and then a concluding win in a U.S. Supreme Court decision. The *Cureton* and *Worldwide Basketball* cases both featured district defeats and circuit court victories. The NCAA lost in two Kentucky lower courts in *Lasege*, then prevailed in the state Supreme Court. A losing streak in the state due process debate, in the Nevada legislature and two local courts ended with a major triumph in a federal district court. Regarding litigation over the ADA, the record could show that, with the consent decree, the result was a tie. The margins, from time to time, were thin: a 2-1 loss at the circuit level in *Oklahoma Board of Regents* and a 4-3 win in the Kentucky Supreme Court. And of course there was that very large (and very narrow) victory in the 5-4 U.S. Supreme Court judgment on the Tarkanian state-actor litigation.

The Tarkanian-NCAA competition became a season in itself, one that lasted 26 years. From the first investigation at Long Beach State in 1972, through suits and countersuits and courts at every level, a veritable trail of torts leading to Congress and a state legislature as well, this season finally ended, in another case and another court, in 1998. Acting at that point on a suggestion from the Ninth Circuit, the two parties agreed to mediation. Neither admitted liability. Tarkanian's claims were dismissed, as were the NCAA's. As part of the settlement, the Association paid Tarkanian (and his wife) $2.5 million. By then, he had gone on to coach men's basketball at Fresno State. An infractions case there — one in which the university cooperated with the NCAA and imposed significant sanctions on itself — led to a four-year probation based mostly on violations in the men's basketball program. The Association announced this decision in September 2003. Tarkanian had retired by this time and was not named in the infractions report. ●

ATTACKER CAITLIN BANKS OF VIRGINIA AND MIDFIELDER MARY BETH HOGAN OF PRINCETON
BATTLE FOR THE BALL DURING THE 2004 DIVISION I WOMEN'S LACROSSE CHAMPIONSHIP.

Net Result

Women's volleyball is among the Association's most popular sports. A total of 990 institutions sponsor women's volleyball, the third-highest among all NCAA sports (trailing only men's and women's basketball).

CLOCKWISE FROM TOP: THE SOUTHERN CALIFORNIA TEAM ERUPTS IN CELEBRATION AFTER DEFEATING STANFORD DURING THE 2002 DIVISION I WOMEN'S VOLLEYBALL CHAMPIONSHIP.

KATIE LAUCKS OF JUNIATA SERVES AGAINST WASHINGTON (MISSOURI) DURING THE 2004 DIVISION III WOMEN'S VOLLEYBALL CHAMPIONSHIP.

OGONNA NNAMANI (1) AND NJIDEKA NNAMANI OF STANFORD UNIVERSITY CELEBRATE WITH COACH JOHN DUNNING AFTER DEFEATING MINNESOTA DURING THE 2004 DIVISION I WOMEN'S VOLLEYBALL CHAMPIONSHIP.

ALLISON ERICKSON OF WISCONSIN-WHITEWATER MAKES A DIG AGAINST CENTRAL (IOWA) DURING THE 2000 DIVISION III WOMEN'S VOLLEYBALL CHAMPIONSHIP.

PHOTO BY MATT BROWN/NCAA PHOTOS

PHOTO BY BILL INGRAM/NCAA PHOTOS

CANDACE WILSON (FAR LEFT) OF CENTRAL (IOWA) RECORDS ONE OF HER GAME-HIGH 22 KILLS AGAINST WISCONSIN-WHITEWATER DURING THE 2000 DIVISION III WOMEN'S VOLLEYBALL CHAMPIONSHIP.

KELLY BOWMAN (ABOVE) OF MINNESOTA HITS A BUMP AGAINST STANFORD DURING THE 2004 DIVISION I WOMEN'S VOLLEYBALL CHAMPIONSHIP

KELLY DANTAS (10) (LEFT) AND MELISSA LEHMAN OF BARRY CELEBRATE THEIR VICTORY OVER TRUMAN STATE DURING THE 2004 DIVISION II WOMEN'S VOLLEYBALL CHAMPIONSHIP.

Growing Success

In 2005, 44,920 fans attended the Division I Men's Lacrosse Championship final in Philadelphia. It was the second-largest crowd for any Association championship, surpassed only by the Men's Final Four.

KYLE BARRIE (5) OF JOHNS HOPKINS TAKES A SHOT ON GOAL DURING THE 2005 DIVISION I MEN'S LACROSSE CHAMPIONSHIP.

PHOTO BY LARRY FRENCH / NCAA PHOTOS (ALL THREE)

BRIAN SOLLIDAY (ABOVE) OF SYRACUSE HUGS TEAMMATE MICHAEL POWELL (22) AFTER A GOAL AGAINST PRINCETON DURING THE 2002 DIVISION I MEN'S LACROSSE CHAMPIONSHIP.

A PACKED STADIUM (LEFT) WATCHES AS VIRGINIA AND JOHNS HOPKINS FACE OFF DURING THE 2005 DIVISION I MEN'S LACROSSE CHAMPIONSHIP SEMIFINAL GAME IN PHILADELPHIA.

CHAPTER SIX

THE ROAD TO INCLUSION

OBERLIN IS SAID to have admitted both Blacks and women before any other college in the U.S. Given its progressive history, that should come as no surprise. The private Ohio institution was involved in the movement to abolish slavery before the Civil War. After that conflict, Oberlin was apparently the country's first predominantly white institution of higher education to have Blacks on its baseball team. Moses Fleetwood Walker and his brother Welday played there in the late 1870s. They went on to the professional game, signing on for one year (1884) with the major-league club in Toledo not long before segregation closed the door to black participation at that level.

Baseball was introduced at Vassar in 1866, one year after the institution opened. It was played there, "in spite of a censorious public," with match games on Saturday afternoons, and at Smith College as an "after supper fad." A Smith alumna, recalling those days on the diamond a half-century later, noted that the players donned "long dresses and on one occasion at least the pitcher wore a ruffled white muslin with a train for good measure."

Eventually, baseball disappeared from women's colleges, and for that matter as a women's sport, just as it did (but much earlier) for the likes of the Walker brothers. By the time the NCAA started in 1906, few African-Americans competed on the fields and courts of the Association's member institutions and most of the public regarded intercollegiate competition as something females ought to disavow. The journeys to acceptance at overwhelmingly white NCAA colleges and universities were long for most minority athletes, and longer for women. An appreciation of the nature of those journeys is essential to understanding the challenges and opportunities encountered by women and minorities in today's Association. This chapter examines the history of that long march, reviews the milestones along the way, and charts the related progress and problems of the last 25 years.

MOSES FLEETWOOD WALKER (SEATED, LEFT) AND WELDAY WALKER (STANDING) WERE THE FIRST BLACKS TO PLAY COLLEGE BASEBALL (1870s).

PHOTO COURTESY OF OBERLIN COLLEGE

DRESS AND DELICACY

IN THE VICTORIAN era, it was a bold step to put women in college, let alone have them compete in sports while they were there. It was a matter of conviction in some influential circles that the mental strain of academic life could do serious damage, emotionally and otherwise, to females, who were then considered to be generally less intelligent than males. Add to that the risks of rigorous activity on the playing fields, and physical impairment would likely follow, or so many believed. The Victorian ideal for women — emphasizing the procreative role, house and home, motherhood, femininity, fragile beauty, and innate moral superiority — left little room for campus life of any kind.

A countervailing view emanated from the women's movement of the 1840s and '50s and from the important contributions women made to the abolitionist cause. Suffrage and other rights and freedoms were paramount concerns in those years. One can draw a line from these weighty beginnings to the coeducational initiatives of the post-Civil war period and the contemporaneous establishment of women's colleges. The latter development represented a substantial advance on the female seminaries founded earlier in that century. These colleges were reform oriented with regard to athletics participation from the outset, although the image of female fragility continued to impose constraints. Among them, though it gave way inch by inch as time went on, was a dress code.

The main challenge was balancing the necessary activity of games and exercises with that era's demand that exposure of arms and legs be strictly limited, or, better yet, avoided altogether. The presence of gymnasiums on

MONIQUE HENDERSON OF UCLA RACES TOWARD A FIRST-PLACE FINISH IN THE WOMEN'S 400-METER SEMIFINAL RACE DURING THE 2005 DIVISION I TRACK AND FIELD CHAMPIONSHIPS.

women's college campuses supplied a partial answer. Typically, the founders and early leaders of these institutions — males who had come by a measure of enlightenment — decreed that physical exercise was essential. They built appropriate facilities and hired gymnasium directors (and directresses). Bloomers became the customary gymnastics attire, gradually rising from ankle length to a cutoff point below the knee. Women wore stockings to protect against any display of bare flesh. Men usually were not allowed in the gyms.

The controversy stirred by the appearance of bloomers in the 1850s had eased by the time gymnastics exercise became standard in the women's college curriculum, but it had not eased enough to allow for such apparel to be worn on outdoor playing fields. This explains the prescribed attire for baseball, with or without the muslin train, at Smith in the 1890s. At about the same time, tennis wear provided another challenge:

> *No girl would appear unless upholstered with a corset, a starched petticoat,*
> *a starched skirt, heavily button-trimmed blouse, a starched shirtwaist with*
> *long sleeves and cuff links, a high collar and four-in-hand necktie, a belt*
> *with silver buckle, and sneakers with large bows.*

Still, as the number of sports played on women's campuses increased, concerns about the presumed delicacy of the female constitution receded. Liberalization of the dress rules lagged behind, but, little by little, modifications were made.

DIVIDING BY THREES

BY 1890, 14 SPORTS for females had found a home, both on women's college campuses and at coeducational institutions. Croquet and walking were among them, as were swimming, fencing, bicycling, crew, track and field, and — at California in 1877 — a form of football. These were recreational or club endeavors, or were offered for instruction. Soon, a new game swept the country and, despite efforts to contain it, became the first women's sport to be widely played on the intercollegiate level. The sport was basketball. The year was 1893. The location was the Smith gymnasium, where, with baskets worth one point each, the Class of '96 beat the Class of '95, 5-4. The next year, with a thousand Smith girls in the galleries, banners flying, class colors on display, the college president (but probably no other man) in attendance and "wild enthusiasm" coming from the crowd, the sophomores took the measure of the first-year players, 13-7. "At the close of the game," the Boston Sunday Globe reported, "amid a waving of handkerchiefs, flags and ribbons … the captain of the winning team was hoisted on the shoulders" of her teammates. Afterward, the students "flocked into the city and until supper time the streets presented a lively spectacle …" The girls of Smith — both spectators and players — were demonstrating a zest for competitive sport similar to that which boys at other colleges were showing for football. Not everyone was pleased.

The enterprising inventor of women's basketball, borrowing and reshaping the idea from James Naismith, was a young director of physical education named Senda Berenson. She must have wondered later what she had wrought. Within two years of that second interclass contest at Smith, the first intercollegiate game was played 3,000 miles to the west, between Stanford and California. Again, males were not allowed to watch. Stanford won, 2-1. By the turn of the century, the women's game was established on many college campuses. Their yearbooks and archives attested to its presence with photographs of uniformed young women — the year of their exploits emblazoned on their blouses — arrayed around a basketball. This is not what Berenson had intended.

After that first game in the Smith gymnasium, she began to substantially change the rules. One of her players had dislocated her shoulder at tipoff. Other physical challenges presented themselves. Berenson did not want to replicate the men's game. She certainly did not want the sport to become the intercollegiate nonpareil. She was concerned about the risks to female health. So she devised a game that modified those risks and limited the requisite exertion. She divided the court into three sections. Three players occupied each section, and they had to remain there. No one could hold the ball for more than three seconds, nor dribble it more than three times. Players were not to grab the ball from an opponent because that could lead to roughness. And, as the above arithmetic suggests, they played the game nine to a side. That's the way it was when Stanford beat California in April 1896.

With the instant success the game enjoyed came variations in the rules from one locale to another. Standardization was needed. Berenson was the logical choice to lead the effort. Beginning in 1901 and continuing for 17 years, she edited the Basketball Guide for Women. She served thus as a principal arbiter of the rules for the country's most popular sport for females, as Walter Camp did at that time for football. Camp's sport, however, was filling large new stadiums; that was not Berenson's goal, and she had plenty of company from the women's physical education community in that regard.

In spite of the standardization efforts and the attendant focus on developing a distinctively different game for women, many institutions decided to play under men's rules. A women's basketball committee was formed at the end of the century, in part to build the sport in accord with a philosophy that stressed participation more than winning. The philosophy — "sports for all" as it was often called — was not limited to basketball. The objective among physical educators was to have it encompass all sports and to forestall any tendency toward making stars out of talented players. At its core, the sports-for-all movement was similar to the approach the founders of the NCAA had in mind for men's athletics, but there were significant differences. On the men's side, the intercollegiate model was already firmly in place, and the stress on winning had grown deep roots. However much they may have shared a philosophical core and its Greek origins, women leaders were determined to put the brakes on intercollegiate competition and get winning into a proper, low-priority perspective.

Even if Palmer Pierce and his colleagues had to some degree espoused the sports-for-all philosophy, women were more successful in implementing it. Pierce and other NCAA leaders of his time strongly supported the principle that athletics should be a department of the university, aligned with and guided by physical education faculty. However, they faced serious — and, for some sports, insurmountable — obstacles in making this principle work. By the 1920s, when college football became part of that decade's spectacle, the female physical education leadership firmly controlled women's sports and was moving them in a decidedly separate direction. Berenson was no longer at Smith by then, nor involved in higher education, but she must have wondered about what she had set in motion. The competitive urge had been manifest in other women's games certainly, but basketball gave it national prominence. Intercollegiate women's competition took a back seat for decades to come, though it was never completely abandoned. Other ways for college women to compete in athletics were developed. When the Women's Division of the National Amateur Athletic Federation (NAAF) was founded in 1923, its platform made clear that growth in intercollegiate competition opportunities was not near the top of the women's sports agenda; women's health was. Berenson had to be pleased. There was no specific reference to it, but an implicit affirmation was given that year to her health-preserving rule of threes.

JIM CROW IN THE ARENA

MOST AFRICAN-AMERICAN athletes also went their separate way in the 1920s, as they had been doing for a long time. The 1896 Supreme Court decision in the case of *Plessy v. Ferguson*, establishing the Constitutionality of the "separate but equal" doctrine, provided the imprimatur to a practice that evolved from the aftermath of the Tilden-Hayes presidential election of 1876. Rutherford B. Hayes owed his victory in that election to the commitment his supporters had made to end post-Civil War Reconstruction and remove federal troops from the South. At that point, the "separate" component of what later evolved into the *Plessy* formula became a fact of life. The "equal" part of that equation never did.

The year *Plessy v. Ferguson* was decided, Preston Eagleson graduated from Indiana. He was one of two black undergraduates (the first two in the university's history) to receive degrees that year. He had been the first African-American to play football for the Hoosiers. Eagleson was a halfback and, according to a university historian, a "valuable player" who in the 1893 Wabash game was "the victim of unnecessarily rough treatment which bore a strong racial overtone …" His solitary presence as a black man on the team was generally the way things stood at the major colleges and universities of the time, both public and private. That would be case for many years thereafter.

1988 (March 11-12) —Abilene Christian University and Saint Augustine's College, which combined have won all but one team title in the 21-year history of the Division II Men's Indoor Track and Field Championships, tie for the 1988 team crown; Abilene Christian's women also win the first of 12 team titles extending through 2000.

1988 (March 11-12) —Christopher Newport University wins the first of six Division III Women's Indoor Track Championship team titles between 1988 and 1998 under coach Vince Brown.

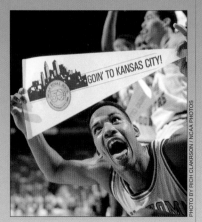

PHOTO BY RICH CLARKSON / NCAA PHOTOS

1988 (April 4) —50th Men's Final Four is conducted in Kansas City (the University of Kansas defeats the University of Oklahoma for title).

1988 (November 12) —First Division II Women's Soccer Championship is conducted at Barry University.

1988 (December 12) —U.S. Supreme Court rules NCAA did not violate the Constitutional rights of basketball coach Jerry Tarkanian in infractions case involving the University of Nevada, Las Vegas.

1989 (January 8-12) —Proposal No. 42, withholding athletically related aid from partial academic qualifiers, is approved.

There are other informative examples.

While Eagleson was playing at Indiana, William Henry Lewis, a law school student, was the football captain at Harvard. Lewis was the star center there, having played that position previously at Amherst, where he was also team captain his senior year. In this era, no real limitations were placed on length of eligibility. Continuing varsity participation during graduate or professional school was not unusual, especially for someone as talented as Lewis. He graduated from Amherst with Calvin Coolidge in the Class of 1892 and attended Harvard when his friend W.E.B. Dubois was a graduate student at the institution. Dubois, of course, became a major national spokesman on behalf of civil rights for Blacks and a founder of the National Association for the Advancement of Colored People (NAACP). Lewis became a noted attorney, among the first African-Americans to argue a case before the U S. Supreme Court. President William H. Taft, likely taking some risk for doing so given the temper of the time, appointed him as an assistant attorney general in the U.S. Department of Justice.

A decade later, Bobby "Rube" Marshall played end for Minnesota's football team, becoming the first Black to play in the Big Nine (later Big Ten). He was also an infielder on the baseball team, ran track, and starred in hockey and boxing. During his three years at Minnesota (1904-06), the football teams won 27 games and lost only two. He later played professionally in the National Football League, which accepted black players in those early years, and competed until he was 44. In 1971, he was posthumously inducted into the College Football Hall of Fame, an honor that fell as well to Frederick "Fritz" Pollard. Pollard played at Brown during the years just before World War I. He led his team to the Rose Bowl against Washington State (as the first Black to play in that bowl) and was named to Camp's All-America first team, becoming the first black running back to be selected. He qualified for the Olympic team as a low hurdler, had a lengthy career in the NFL (where he also served as the first African-American head coach) and later — when segregation took hold in that league — coached an all-Black team in New York. Pollard was to African-American football fans what Red Grange was to their Caucasian counterparts. Shortly after Grange signed a professional contract with Chicago, the Bears played Pollard's Providence club in December 1925. Pollard was his team's primary gate attraction. Many years and numerous honors later, he received an honorary doctor of letters degree from his alma mater. That was in 1981, five years before his death at age 92.

Then there was Paul Robeson, the son of a runaway slave who married a woman from an abolitionist Quaker family. He received a four-year academic scholarship from Rutgers. Robeson won 15 varsity letters in football (as a star player), basketball, baseball and track and learned on the football field (initially from teammates) how racism could assert itself physically. He received the Phi Beta Kappa key as a junior and was valedictorian of his senior class. Although he was the football team's most honored player, he was unable to participate — except in his freshman year — in the city of New Brunswick's annual banquet for the team because the event was at a downtown hotel that did not allow Blacks as guests. During his sophomore year, in 1916, Rutgers had a home game with Washington and Lee, a Virginia institution. The visitors said they would not play against a black man, so Rutgers agreed to hold Robeson out.

After graduation, Robeson completed Columbia Law School and then practiced for a brief time as an attorney. The bulk of his career, however, was spent as an internationally renowned singer and actor, on stage and in film. He also gained fame for his outspoken advocacy of civil rights and other causes. He was accused by the House Unamerican Activities Committee of being a Communist during the Red Scare of the late 1940s, had his passport revoked for eight years in the 1950s and retired from public life in 1963. In 1995, nearly two decades after he died at age 78, Robeson was inducted into the College Football Hall of Fame.

These examples illustrate the rare opportunities African-American student-athletes had at predominantly white Northern universities. Life was hard for the relatively small number who made the grade, but fame was nevertheless a frequent outcome. Well down the road, the notable accomplishments of these pioneers would inspire other young men (and, later, young women) of color. The hurdles would continue to be high, though, and alternative opportunities needed to be found. Separation of the races remained national policy. Jim Crow laws affected college playing fields and courts for much of the 20th century. Harvard President Charles Eliot offered a sense of the future of the race question toward the end of his 40 years of service, in 1909, noting that his thoughts were not newly formed. He set them down in two letters, written soon after returning from a trip to the South. "The Whites and Negroes," he wrote, "had better live beside each other in entire amity, but separate, under equal laws, equally applied ..." Blacks should have access to "all trades and all professions," and to the franchise if educationally qualified. As for inter-marriage, "all the best evidence seems ... to show that it is inexpedient." He did not believe that "complete seg-regation" of Blacks was necessary in the Northern states, but wherever "the proportion of Negroes should become large ...separate schools for Negro children" would be appropriate. As for the treatment of those "who are removed by four or five generations from Africa or slavery," Eliot observed that he was "in favor of leaving that problem to the people of a hundred years hence." In fact, Harvard alumnus W.E.B. Dubois — that friend and contemporary of William Henry Lewis — was already working on that. He and seven white colleagues founded the NAACP the year after Eliot retired.

The racial divide in athletics in the early 20th century was not confined to Blacks. American Indians expe-rienced it too. However, for a decade and a half during that era, a small Indian school in Pennsylvania demon-strated that its football teams could compete at the collegiate level with anybody. That was the Carlisle Indian Industrial School, established at a former army barracks, under direction of the U.S. Department of the Interior, in 1879. Carlisle hired the fabled coach Glenn "Pop" Warner in 1899. From that first year through 1913 (12 of these 15 seasons under Warner), Carlisle won 75 percent of its games, beating major competition and ranking highly among the football powers. Jim Thorpe, generally regarded as one of the greatest American athletes of the century, played at Carlisle, won two gold medals (for the pentathlon and decathlon) at the 1912 Olympics, played major-league baseball for six seasons and professional football until he was 41. Thorpe's Olympic medals were taken away at the insistence of the American Amateur Union because he had played baseball one summer for a minor-league team in North Carolina. Another Carlisle athlete of this period, a distance runner named Tewanima, won the silver medal for the 10,000-meter race in that same Olympics. Joe Guyon played with Thorpe at Carlisle and also had a notable professional career. Both Thorpe and Guyon are enshrined in the College Football Hall of Fame. Thorpe's Olympic medals were returned in 1982, 29 years after his death.

The Carlisle Indian School was closed in 1918. Its founder, Richard Henry Pratt, had earlier been involved in sending Native American youth to Hampton Normal and Agricultural Institute in Virginia. Hampton opened in 1868, in the wake of the Civil War, as an institution where Blacks could receive "indus-trial education." In effect, this was a practical learning venture, with a goal of producing graduates who could then impart their learning and skills to the large population of people recently freed from slavery. Hampton's program for American Indians (which continued for 45 years) began in 1878, one year before Carlisle accept-ed its first students. One of the former slaves studying there at that time was Booker T. Washington, who at age 25 would found a black college himself. That was Tuskegee Institute, which Washington started in 1881 in "a little old shanty and [an] abandoned church" and for which he served as president until his death in 1915.

The last three decades of the 19th century — that "Golden Age" of higher education alluded to in Chapter One — gave birth to numerous institutions for African-Americans, meeting an obvious and growing need. The exclusively black status of these institutions testified to the strong grip of Jim Crow. By the 1890s, when Carlisle launched its athletics program, these institutions were doing the same. Initially, this was an offering of sorts at the altar of "separate but equal." For much of the 20th century, the Historically Black Colleges and Universities (HBCUs) were where the great majority of black student-athletes went to play the game.

DEGREES OF SEPARATION

LINCOLN UNIVERSITY OF Pennsylvania was chartered as Ashmun Institute in 1854, becoming the first his-torically black institution to offer a college education. The institution produced graduates such as poet Langston Hughes; Kwame Nkrumah, the founding president of the Republic of Ghana; and Thurgood Marshall, America's first black Supreme Court Justice. Ohio's Wilberforce College followed in 1856, although it did not offer a high-er education curriculum until 1863. Howard was established in Washington, D.C., in 1865. Fisk opened in 1867, the year that Morehouse did the same in Atlanta. That city gave birth to two other African-American colleges

The retrospective football power ratings on the NCAA Web site show the Carlisle Indian School ranked in the top ten eight times between 1899 and 1913. The rankings include two number one finishes (1908 and 1911), and one second place season (1913). Carlisle was ranked third in 1907, fourth in 1912, and fifth in 1899. The school's record for these 15 seasons was 138 victories, 42 losses, and five ties.

— Clark and Atlanta — during the 1860s. They ultimately came together as a single institution. Morris Brown, another Atlanta college, arrived on the scene in 1881. And so it went, year to year and decade to decade. The first football game between black colleges — involving Livingston College and Biddle Memorial Institute (now

AN OKLAHOMA A&M FOOTBALL PLAYER PUNCHES JOHNNY BRIGHT OF DRAKE SHOWN IN THIS 1951 PULITZER PRIZE-WINNING PHOTO SEQUENCE. PHOTOS BY JOHN ROBINSON AND DON ULTANG ©1951, THE DES MOINES REGISTER AND TRIBUNE COMPANY. REPRINTED WITH PERMISSION.

Johnson C. Smith) — was played in 1892. Two years earlier, Congress passed the second Morrill Act, awarding land-grant status to a number of historically black institutions. Tuskegee benefited from the act and was playing football by 1894. In 1902, Tuskegee and Morehouse kicked off the oldest black college gridiron rivalry. Ten years later, the first sports conference for black institutions, the Central Intercollegiate Athletic Association (CIAA), was established. A year after that (1913), the Southern Intercollegiate Athletic Conference (SIAC) was formed. Tuskegee, Morehouse, Clark, Atlanta and Morris Brown were founding members. The Southwestern Athletic Conference (SWAC) was born in 1920, its makeup coming primarily from small denominational colleges in Texas, and Prairie View A&M, a Texas land-grant school. The SWAC would evolve into a major HBCU conference, comprising public universities such as Grambling, Southern University and Jackson State.

As the century progressed, great African-American athletes and coaches found a home in one or another of the HBCUs. Eddie Robinson's 56-year, 408-victory career as Grambling's football coach got underway in 1941. He sent hundreds of his players to the NFL. At Florida A&M, a charter SIAC member and, over time, a consistently strong force among black colleges and universities in the Southeast, the intercollegiate athletics program was inaugurated in 1901, 14 years after the institution's founding. The first black college bowl game, the Orange Blossom Classic, originated at Florida A&M in 1933. Later, Jake Gaither coached football there for 25 seasons and won six national black college titles. Benedict College, a private church-related school in South Carolina, started life in a run-down former slave owner's antebellum mansion in 1870. Its first seven presidents, down to 1930, were Northern white ministers. The Benedict athletics program started in 1907. Its first football coach, Ralph Bates, also served two seasons as the team's quarterback. Football became the big game at Benedict, with two undefeated and unscored-upon years in 1923 and 1924 and then a golden era in the late 1930s when the college dominated the SIAC with the help of All-American Leroy Walker. Walker's career took him to the chancellorship of North Carolina Central, head coach of the U.S. Olympic track and field team, presidency of the U.S. Olympic Committee, and, in the 1990s, service as a member of the Knight Foundation Commission on Intercollegiate Athletics.

In 1937, while Walker was setting records at Benedict, Dr. Naismith (then coaching at Baker in Kansas) helped develop the first small-college basketball tournament. The tournament was held in Kansas City, Missouri, which became its long-time home. The National Association of Intercollegiate Basketball (NAIB) was formed out of this initiative in 1940 and began to act as tournament sponsor. In 1948 the NAIB opened the games to black players. In 1953, its successor organization — the National Association of Intercollegiate Athletics (NAIA) — voted HBCUs into membership. Times were changing.

At the NCAA, there had been no specific prohibition of black college membership. Howard University had joined in 1924, Tuskegee in 1940 and Xavier (Louisiana), for a relatively limited period, in 1937. From 1949 to 1958, however, 40 HBCUs signed on, and over the years more than 60 such institutions became members. For a time, the historically black colleges retained allegiance to both the NCAA and the NAIA, though eventually they had to choose between the two. Initially, the Association seemed uncertain how to deal with the presence of black member institutions in a national environment just beginning to turn away from the separate but equal tradition of *Plessy v. Ferguson*. Four HBCU teams — Tuskegee, Florida A&M, North Carolina A&T and Lincoln (Missouri) — qualified for the small-college basketball postseason championships in 1959. The NCAA scheduled a four-team first round at Tuskegee and moved Lincoln well outside its assigned district to join the other three HBCUs in Alabama. Questions were raised regarding this arrangement. History did not repeat itself thereafter. The landmark school desegregation decision in *Brown v. Board of Education* had been handed down four years earlier. For higher education and intercollegiate athletics, the era of almost total separation was ending.

While HBCU sports programs grew in stature during the first half of the century, small numbers of African-American student-athletes continued seeking entry to Northern, traditionally white colleges and universities. As had been the case with their forebears in the Lewis-Robeson years, they often confronted a different kind and degree of separation. Jesse Owens, given that he, like Jim Thorpe, competed in the international arena, was perhaps the most famous example. He ran track at Ohio State in the mid-1930s and turned in an incredible performance at the 1935 Big Ten championships. In the space of an hour, he won the 100-yard dash (tying the world record), the long jump and the 220-yard dash (breaking world records in both events) and then set another world record for the 220-yard low hurdles. He nearly duplicated this showing at the 1936 Berlin Olympics, only to be scorned by the German chancellor. Adolf Hitler had in mind a much more terrifying answer to the question of racial separation.

Other black athletes in the post-Owens decades often faced something more than scorn. The University of Nevada, for example, had a star running back from Ohio in 1940. He described a situation he encountered at a road game that season when the Nevada football coach was advised by opposing team officials that the lone black member of his team would not be allowed to play. A compromise was reached limiting the player to participation for only half of the game. Seven years later, Nevada had two African-Americans on its football team and, before a game at Tulsa, the team was again informed that it would be best if no Blacks appeared on the field on game day. This time, Nevada held firm, announcing that either the players in question would be eligible to compete or the team would cancel and return to Reno. The teams — and the black athletes — played the game, without incident. Nevada won, 65-14. By then, that star player from 1940 was on his way to leading the Cleveland Browns to five consecutive All-America Football Conference and NFL championships. His name was Marion Motley.

More racial news came from Oklahoma in the 1950s. That decade began with a U.S. Supreme Court decision that represented a major, and successful, assault on the wall of separation constructed by the *Plessy* doctrine. In this case (*McLaurin v. Oklahoma State Regents*), a black Oklahoma graduate student — previously denied admission to doctoral study under state law — brought suit because, although he was subsequently admitted, his program of instruction under revisions in that law was to be "given ... on a segregated basis." That meant that McLaurin had to sit at a designated desk in a separate room adjoining the main classroom. He was to use a designated desk on a separate floor in the university library. He was to eat at a different time than other students and sit at a specific table in the school cafeteria. McLaurin argued that these arrangements violated his entitlement to equal protection of the law under the 14th Amendment to the U.S. Constitution. The Supreme Court agreed, reversing a judgment from federal district court. McLaurin could now sit with his fellow students in the classroom, library and cafeteria. The political leadership in the state was unhappy at this turn of events, as were other Oklahoma citizens accustomed to a different understanding of the equal-protection clause. That was the situation confronting Johnny Bright when he stepped onto the football field for a game at Oklahoma A&M (now Oklahoma State) one year later.

Bright was a senior tailback at Drake. He led the nation in total offense in 1949 and 1950, and was doing so again entering the game. He also was Black, and he was a marked man. Early in the game at Stillwater, after his part in a play ended and he looked downfield, he was slugged by a defensive lineman who left his feet to give momentum to his fist. Bright was caught unaware, the blow fracturing his jaw. He threw a 60-yard touchdown pass on the next play, and in the subsequent offensive series he was slugged again and carried from the field. As it happened, photographers from the Des Moines Register took a sequence of photos that ran next day on the front page

PHOTO COURTESY UNIVERSITY OF CALIFORNIA, SAN DIEGO

IN THE ARENA
The NCAA's First Century

1989 (January 8-12) —Creation of Student-Athlete Advisory Committee is approved.

1989 (January) —Georgetown University basketball coach John Thompson walks off court twice in protest of NCAA adoption of Proposal No. 42.

1989 (May 25-27) —Saint Augustine's University wins the first of seven straight Division II Men's Outdoor Track and Field Championships team titles under coach George Williams (the school added titles in 1998 and 2001).

1989 (September 27) —Knight Foundation Commission on Intercollegiate Athletics formed.

1989 (November 12) —The University of California, San Diego, wins the first of five Division III Women's Soccer Championship titles between 1989 and 1999 under coach **Brian McManus** (the team also later won two Division II women's soccer titles).

1989 (November 18) —State University College at Cortland wins the first of seven Division III Women's Cross Country Championships between 1989 and 1997 under coach Jack Daniels.

1989 (November 22) —NCAA and CBS sign $1 billion television agreement for 1991 through 1997; Executive Director Richard Schultz moves to examine equitable distribution of revenue.

of the paper's Sunday sports section. The photographs won a Pulitzer Prize. Drake protested the outrage in Stillwater to the Missouri Valley Conference, which took no action. The university withdrew from the conference in protest. Bright refused to play professionally in the U.S., fearing more racial antagonism. Instead, he had a successful career in the Canadian Football League. Later, Drake recognized him as the greatest football player in the institution's history.

Restrictions on the undergraduate enrollment of African-Americans remained in place in the state of Oklahoma until May 1955. The next year, coach Bud Wilkinson recruited the Sooners' first black football player, a young man who had starred in the state's annual high school all-star game that year (and was the first Black to play in that game). The player, Prentice Gautt, proved to be a three-year starter at running back, an All-Big Eight selection, an academic All-American and the MVP of the 1959 Orange Bowl. He endured numerous racial slights during his collegiate playing days, took them in painful stride, then went on to a seven-year career in the NFL, a Ph.D., and an associate commissioner's position in the Big Eight and Big 12 Conferences. In 1994, he began a term as NCAA secretary-treasurer. In 1999, the Dr. Prentice Gautt Academic Center opened its doors on the Oklahoma campus.

Gautt shared something with Owens, Motley, Robinson, Gaither, Eagleson, Lewis, Walker, Robeson, Pollard, Marshall — McLaurin as well — and a host of others who played at the HBCUs unnoticed by the national media, or often noticed too much at white institutions. Gautt was a pioneer. Like the others, he demonstrated the power of sport to make a difference, to put a spotlight on serious social problems and help solve them as well. Big challenges remained, but these individuals overcame many in their time and eased the burden on those who followed. Even in Georgia, in 1955, as Gautt emerged as the hero of that high school all-star game, the state's governor, Marvin Griffin, was admonishing Georgia Tech to boycott the 1956 Sugar Bowl. He was concerned because Pittsburgh, Tech's opponent in that game, had a black player. This, in his view, was not tolerable. His language explored the upper limits of hyperbole:

> *The South stands at Armageddon. The battle is joined. There is no more difference in compromising the integrity of race on the playing field than in doing so in the classroom. One break in the dike and the relentless seas will rush in and destroy us.*

Georgia Tech students responded quickly, picketing the governor and parading in protest in Atlanta. Notwithstanding the governor's heated opposition, their team played the game. Still, the Georgia Board of Regents, feeling the heat, voted to prohibit any future such competition. When Alabama was scheduled to play Penn State, which had five black players, in the 1959 Liberty Bowl, the Georgia Tech precedent stood the Alabama coach in good stead. Bear Bryant was the powerful coach of what would become a storied program. He heard the angry attacks of Alabama fans and politicians. He ignored them. Bryant's team played in the Liberty Bowl that year.

For the South, perhaps the biggest moment arrived off the football field in September 1962 when James Meredith attempted to register for classes at the University of Mississippi. He made the effort several times over the course of 11 days and was turned away each time. He was involved in this effort because of an order from the Fifth Circuit Court of Appeals, in New Orleans. Gov. Ross Barnett had claimed that Mississippi would "not surrender to the evil and illegal forces of tyranny," but the Fifth Circuit held him in contempt. Finally, under the protection of U.S. marshals, and later the U.S. Army and a federalized Mississippi National Guard, Meredith took "his lonely walk into the maw of Ole Miss" in early October. A 15-hour riot ensued, with both students and adults participating. Bottles and bricks were thrown. Tear gas filled the air. Gunfire erupted. Two people were killed and 160 marshals were wounded. On the day after Meredith's arrival, 3,000 army troops and guardsmen patrolled the campus. The university, reported the New York Times, was "under military occupation." Despite all the sound and fury, Meredith became an Ole Miss student. That meant something. The previous spring, the same institution had declined an invitation to the NCAA basketball tournament because it could mean competing against black players. Now, the 114-year-old university in the old Confederate heartland was integrated. However, one more casualty was yet to come. Medgar Evers, head of the Mississippi NAACP and an advisor to Meredith, was assassinated the following June.

JAMES MEREDITH

In 1963, Gov. George Wallace threatened to block the admission of two black students to Alabama. When they reported for their first day of classes, also accompanied by U.S. marshals, Wallace was there as promised, to "stand in the schoolhouse door." Thinking maybe of what had happened at Ole Miss the year before, he did not stand there long. He moved out of the way, and the students proceeded to integrate the institution. The university's athletic program took a while to follow suit. By 1971, other Southern universities had begun to bring in black student-athletes, though in relatively small numbers. That year, Bryant, who had successfully recruited Alabama's first black player in 1970, started the season with a number of African-Americans in camp. A half-decade earlier, the NCAA had arranged for an integrated regional basketball tournament in North Carolina, the first of its kind in the South. A few weeks later, Kentucky's all-white basketball team had been beaten by Texas Western (now UTEP) in the Final Four's championship game. All the members of Texas Western's starting five were black. This was a signal victory after which, as Walter Byers put it, "the walls tumbled." Excellent black athletes, including those who might otherwise have gone to HBCUs, now headed to institutions where their presence had previously been discouraged, if not forbidden.

Benedict dropped football in 1966 after 55 seasons. Although increased costs were one reason, the "draining of top black talent to white colleges," the college said, was another. As Bryant recruited those African-American players to Alabama in spring 1971, Samuel Barnes began a two-year term as NCAA secretary-treasurer. Barnes was from Howard University. He became the Association's first black officer.

THE CREED

WHILE BLACK STUDENT-athletes made their gradual way toward integrated intercollegiate competition, female athletes continued to be governed by determinedly different rules and practices. The NAAF Women's Division platform mentioned earlier was approved at a national conference on women's athletics in April 1923. The support of physical education professionals was key to its passage. The planks in this platform — a "creed," as one author observed — contained governing principles that guided the evolution of campus sports for women for the next 50 years. NAAF leaders saw intercollegiate competition as undesirable, particularly if it involved travel. If any other type of competition put "emphasis upon individual accomplishment and winning" instead of enjoyment and sportsmanship, it should be eliminated, as should gate receipts. Sports undertaken for the pleasure of spectators, or reputation, or publicity, or commercial advantage were to be avoided. Protecting health was a major priority, and, harkening back to the Victorian ideal, "the adoption of appropriate costumes" should be protected. Seven of the eight Women's Division committee members were physical educators. Their views represented those of their colleagues around the country, 93 percent of whom, in a 1923 study, opposed intercollegiate competition.

Chapter Two described the NCAA's post-World War I campaign to make physical education mandatory in the schools and colleges of the country. This effort was motivated by unhappiness over the questionable fitness of many young men who reported for military service during the war. The campaign offered the Association a chance to extend its influence and propagate its aims of exercise for the many and of athletics control by the faculty. Both males and females were to be included. The success of the endeavor in establishing required physical training nationwide was particularly helpful to female physical educators. The large football stadiums and admissions receipts from the fans that filled them might be justified, as Pierce suggested, by the need for financial assistance to mount the mandated training programs. But on the women's side, there were no stadiums to construct and little desire to attract spectators, paid or otherwise, to facilities where female sports were played. The campaign helped build for women's athletics an assurance that physical educators would be in charge. The 1923 platform was developed and implemented from that strong position. The creed and its devout adherents were in control.

The NCAA was already in the championship business by the early 1920s. The official position of the NAAF Women's Division was to minimize such competition. Many would have been

1990 (January 8) —Ronald Reagan becomes fourth president honored with Theodore Roosevelt Award.

1990 (January 10) —Proposal No. 42 rescinded; Convention also features lengthy debate over time demands on student-athletes.

1990 (February 26) —NCAA moves into new headquarters facility in Overland Park, Kansas.

1990 (May 30-June 2) —Suzy Favor of the University of Wisconsin, Madison, wins her fourth straight 1,500-meter run title at the Division I Women's Outdoor Track and Field Championships.

1990 —Edward Steitz dies suddenly in his 25th year as secretary-rules editor of the Men's Basketball Rules Committee.

1990 (September 18) —Sara Lee Corporation pledges minimum of $6 million to promote women's intercollegiate athletics, including first Woman of the Year award.

1990 (September 22 and December 2) —The University of Illinois, Champaign's, Howard Griffith sets a Division I-A single-game scoring record with 48 points against Southern Illinois University, and the University of Houston's David Klingler passes for a record 716 yards in a game against Arizona State University.

1991 (January 10) —Judith Sweet of University of California, San Diego, elected as first woman NCAA president.

1991 (March 2) — **Laura Wilson** of the University of Vermont becomes the first woman to win four career individual titles in the National Collegiate Men's and Women's Skiing Championships.

1991 (March 2) — Augsburg College wins the first of nine Division III Wrestling Championships team titles between 1991 and 2005 under coach Jeff Swenson.

1991 (March 2) — Portland State University's Dan Russell becomes the only participant honored three times as most outstanding wrestler at the Division II Men's Wrestling Championships, competing in a different weight class each of those years.

1991 (March 8-9) — Carlette Guidry of the University of Texas at Austin becomes the only participant to win six career individual titles at the Division I Women's Indoor Track Championships.

1991 (March 19) — The Knight Foundation Commission on Intercollegiate Athletics issues report concluding that chief executive officer control of intercollegiate athletics is essential.

1991 (April 18-20) — Mark Sohn of Pennsylvania State University joins the University of New Mexico's Chad Fox as the only gymnasts to win an event four straight years at the National Collegiate Men's Gymnastics Championships.

PHOTO COURTESY UNIVERSITY OF VERMONT

pleased if it disappeared altogether. The two entities were traveling down very different roads. This was hardly surprising given that, from the start, women's athletics leaders sought to avoid what they saw as the highly suspect practices endorsed by their male counterparts. Mabel Lee, the first female president of the American Physical Education Association (APEA), was clear on that point. She said in 1931 "how absolutely determined are the women of the physical education profession … and the women college students of today not to follow in the steps of men's athletics."

The creed did not end competition because by this time competition could not be ended. The horse had long since bid goodbye to the barn — the Smith basketball players and students had seen to that 29 years earlier — and there was neither a valid way nor reason to try to lock the door now. The leadership's main idea was to channel and contain the competitive energies, and steer them away from further kinship with the intercollegiate alternative. This strategy was successful at first. At the time the platform was approved, approximately 20 percent of American colleges and universities sponsored some type of "varsity" competition for females. It would be a while before that number would grow.

Until recently, no accepted method existed for gauging women's intercollegiate activity across the nation. There was no overarching organization, such as the NCAA, to act as a collector and distributor of complete and credible information. Institutions involved in varsity competition did so unevenly, in terms of sports sponsored, length of seasons and number of contests. It is clear, even so, that for almost a half-century after 1923, the intercollegiate model was relatively inconsequential. It was equally clear, however, that the competitive urge of female students persisted. It was not the stuff of newspaper headlines, or sports journals or campus sports information coverage. But it found ways of expressing itself and forced the physical education professionals to discover alternative competitive outlets for their students.

These leaders had used a telegraphic approach to competition for a number of years. This strategy continued to be reasonably popular after 1923. No travel was necessary. The students involved simply performed at or near their home campuses, in sports such as archery and rifle, and telegraphed their scores to a neutral official who determined the winners, minus the intensity and emotion of face-to-face contests.

The play-day program was a second approach, one strongly supported in both high schools and colleges. Young women from several institutions would gather at one location for basketball, volleyball, racing, exercises and other recreation. Skill level was not a matter of great importance. The basic concept of "a game for every girl and every girl in a game" still governed. (In California, the slogan was "a team for everyone and everyone on a team.") Teams of players from several schools banded together and were assigned to squads for competition purposes. Winning was not paramount. No institutional honor was at stake, No team preparation or practice was allowed. The socializing opportunities were more important than the competition. A 1930s survey showed that about 70 percent of the institutions responding preferred play days as their top athletics format for females.

Some still wanted to play strictly for their own institutions rather than for the mixed teams favored by the play-day approach. This desire led to the compromise of sports days, at which players competed for their colleges, but with certain constraints. Pickup teams might be used, for example, along with modified rules. Game times could be shortened and the element of victory downgraded. Over time, sports days edged closer to real intercollegiate competition. All the while, some colleges and universities still played their contests at the varsity level.

The number of schools reporting women's intercollegiate athletics activities was 28 percent by 1951. Ten years earlier, Ohio State held an intercollegiate women's golf tournament, despite strong opposition from the national physical education leadership. The turnout was small, perhaps because of this opposition, but the venture was successful. It was a step toward greater recognition of the varsity model and of championship play. World War II interrupted further scheduling of this event, but Ohio State renewed and expanded it after the war. Even so, as late as 1957 the principal organization for women's sports continued to regard play days, sports days and telegraphic meets as the best forms of athletics competition. By then, approximately one-third of the country's colleges and universities had intercollegiate women's programs. The next milestone came in 1963 when varsity play received a kind of official acceptance as a fourth "standard form" of competition for "highly skilled" women and girls. This acknowledgment came from the Division for Girls and Women's Sports (DGWS), a national organization with a strong presence in the physical education community.

TRANSFORMATION

THE DGWS TRACED its origins to the NAAF Women's Division of the early 1920s and, beyond that, to the women's basketball committee founded at the turn of the 20th century to bring order to Berenson's brainchild. Over the decades, a confusing array of organizations — some new, some renamed, some remodeled — played important roles in the evolution of women's athletics, creating an alphabet soup of acronyms. The APEA provided some continuity through these organizational changes, but by the 1960s had modified its name too, becoming the American Association for Health, Physical Education and Recreation (AAHPER). Through the years, a number of the bodies involved were divisions or sections of AAHPER. That was the case with the DGWS, a direct descendant of the National Section on Women's Athletics (NSWA).

The NSWA was established in 1936. It was extended to secondary-school girls in 1953, and then, having been upgraded to divisional status, received its DGWS nomenclature in 1957. The success of the Ohio State golf tournament after the war fed the growing interest in intercollegiate competition, which led the DGWS to create the Commission on Intercollegiate Sports for Women (CISW) in 1965. Among the CISW's purposes was to "develop and publish guidelines and standards for the conduct of intercollegiate events" and to make available a procedure for sanctioning such competition. Once the commission's name was changed, subtly but consequentially, to substitute "Athletics" for "Sports" (and thus become the CIAW in 1967), sponsorship of a series of national championships — gymnastics, track and field, swimming, badminton, volleyball — came next. Basketball was added in 1972. Another AAHPER section, the Athletics and Recreation Federation of College Women (ARFCW) was established in the mid-1960s to give a voice to female students in the evolution of sports for women. The ARFCW held annual Conventions at which student leaders from campus athletics and recreation organizations met together to discuss possibilities and, over the course of a decade, to place the emphasis increasingly on athletics and less on recreation. The participants were mainly young women who preceded Title IX and who were in many cases without opportunities to play intercollegiate sports. But they could influentially talk about them. Some went on to become coaches and athletics administrators after Title IX began to open up such opportunities.

As the scope of championship competition expanded, women's collegiate athletics needed a national organization that would recognize the value of the intercollegiate model and be based on institutional membership. To be effective, this entity would require the authority to administer regional and national tournaments, and the power to enforce its policies. This is what the Association for Intercollegiate Athletics for Women (AIAW) was intended to be. Although perhaps merely coincidental, there was at least symbolic significance in the AIAW's birth occurring the same year (1972) that the standing of Berenson's popular sport was acknowledged with the creation of a women's national basketball championship.

The other development of consequence for women's athletics that year was the passage of a piece of federal legislation known to history as Title IX. Under the sponsorship of Congresswoman Edith Green of Tennessee and Sen. Birch Bayh of Indiana, the legislation was passed during a time of Congressional concern about civil rights. The Civil Rights Act of 1964, proposed and approved in the wake of the assassination of John F. Kennedy and the 1963 march on Washington and the demonstrations and violence in Birmingham that year, was the progenitor. This law required extensive and angry debate, and a 75-day filibuster by Senate segregationists, before passage. The bill that became Title IX, evolving with less bitterness and no filibuster over a two-year period, focused on gender discrimination and involved only occasional discussion of college sports. Bayh, still a staunch

BIRCH BAYH

1991 (May 9) —NCAA Presidents Commission holds hearings directed at developing stronger academic standards.

1991 (May 25) —Annika Sorenstam from the perennially powerful University of Arizona team wins an individual title at the Division I Women's Golf Championships.

1991 (October 30) —Mary Beth Riley of Canisius College honored as first NCAA Woman of the Year.

1991 (November 25) — Villanova University's **Sonia O'Sullivan** wins her second straight Division I Women's Cross Country Championships individual title, a highlight of Villanova's streak of six consecutive team titles between 1989 and 1994.

1992 (January 10) — Council approves recommendations from the Special Committee to Review the NCAA Enforcement and Infractions Process.

1992 (January 10) — Proposal No. 16, establishing an initial-eligibility index based on standardized-test scores and grade-point averages, is approved in Division I.

1992 (January 23) —Five Division I-A conferences and Notre Dame strike agreement with group of postseason bowl games to increase likelihood of national-championship football game (predecessor of Bowl Championship Series).

PHOTO COURTESY VILLANOVA UNIVERSITY

supporter of the legislation more than three decades removed from its enactment, has said that he intended Title IX to cover campus extracurricular activities, sports included. In any case, women's intercollegiate athletics soon became the law's most prominent beneficiary. The AIAW thus began its work with the advantage of a new law that, despite delays, lawsuits, changing interpretations and an almost constant chafing at the bit, dramatically altered the world of college sports. For the AIAW, which shared some of Title IX's early aspirations and travail, life would be hopeful, productive, exciting, uncertain, contentious and short. For Title IX, life would be a chronicle of seemingly forever unfinished business, but nonetheless a business big enough to attract intense attention from the NCAA and its member institutions.

Although one finds occasional references to women's sports in NCAA Convention and committee discussions down through the decades, the members seemed generally content to focus on the men's game, where both the promise and the problems of intercollegiate athletics were more familiar to the general public. Attitudes began to change in the early 1960s, leading to cordial exchanges between Association representatives and women's sports leaders. At the request of the latter, the Executive Committee agreed in April 1964 to prohibit female student-athletes at member institutions from competing in NCAA championships. At the same time, the Council established a special committee to act as a liaison with interested women's groups. Within a year, however, a committee on women's sports was appointed, and among its charges was a delineation of the Association's possible roles in such sports. In late 1967, with member interest growing, the NCAA created another committee, this one "to study the feasibility of establishing appropriate machinery to provide for the control and supervision of women's intercollegiate athletics." The Association assured organizations involved with women's programs that this was intended as a study group that would be in discussions with them. Concern among these organizations about the NCAA's intentions grew at a pace matching that of the varsity model during the 1960s. These worries intensified after the enactment of Title IX.

By this time, there was ample reason for such concern. The new law bred anxiety for Association members regarding possible liability, a feeling, as reported in the previous chapter, that was shared by NCAA attorneys. The basic question was whether the Association, under the gender-neutral language of its constitution, could legally restrict its "services and programs" to male student-athletes. Further, could the members assure equitable opportunities while operating athletics programs under the differing rules of separate organizations? Another committee had been assembled in 1971. This one had a longer tenure to examine the issues, answer the key questions, meet with female leaders, listen to the continued concern from attorneys, observe the rapid growth of the AIAW, present a report to the Council and, finally, advocate passage of a controversial resolution at the 1975 Convention.

Actually, there were two related resolutions. The first one, noting that the Association "must move to … meet the demands of today's society and today's law," called for a comprehensive report to be completed by the Council during the next four months. The report would be sent to the membership, with a view toward preparing legislation for the 1976 Convention. It had Council support, but was defeated. The second resolution was similar but extended the opportunity to comment to the AIAW. This one passed. Supporters felt that providing equitable opportunities to female student-athletes was not simply a legal matter but also involved both an economic rationale and a moral obligation. Similar views were expressed in the discussion on which the 1976 report was based. This report, mailed to the presidents of NCAA and AIAW member institutions, concluded that the Association "should offer the same meaningful services and high-quality championship competition" to female student-athletes as it does to males. The fact that 46 percent of the NCAA membership (mainly in Divisions II and III) did not belong to the AIAW became particularly important. The AIAW strongly opposed the report. One of the resolutions presented to the 1976 Convention recommending that the NCAA apply its rules equally to men's and women's programs by September 1, 1977, was debated and returned to the Council for additional study. The delegates were not ready to take this stressful step. A second resolution dealt in part with eventual NCAA responsibility for women's championships. The Association was willing. Nevertheless, the resolution was tabled.

The Council decided to sponsor no additional proposals on women's athletics until and unless the membership directed. The next message came in 1978 from six Division III institutions seeking to initiate championships in three women's sports. The Convention delegates defeated the proposal. Division II members offered similar legislation in 1979, with the same result. In 1980, the two divisions proposed that the NCAA sanction championships in five sports (basketball, field hockey, swimming, tennis and volleyball). This time, the proposals passed by substantial margins. Sensing that change was coming, the Council created yet another group in October 1979 to examine the range of issues associated with the possible incorporation of women's programs. The Special Committee on NCAA Governance, Organization and Services was chaired by James Frank, who was soon to be elected NCAA secretary-treasurer. Frank was president of Lincoln (Missouri). When decision time came, at the 1981 Convention, he was about to be elected to the NCAA presidency. This made him the first campus CEO, and the first African-American, to serve in that position.

The Frank committee included four presidents, four faculty representatives, four athletics directors and one conference commissioner. Two of the members were women. In January 1980, a summary of committee deliberations was mailed to member chief executive officers for review and comment. Numerous responses were received. The contemplated actions, involving not only services and championships but major governance changes as well, presented a dilemma for many CEOs. Some counseled further consultation with the AIAW, even though previous discussions had not been fruitful. Others expressed concern about costs to the Association. The College Football Association, in particular, raised this issue. Some respondents expressed strong support. The legal problem engendered by operating men's and women's programs under different rules — specifically, the possibility or even likelihood of discriminatory consequences — was raised once more by Association attorneys. Campus presidents were worried about this possibility. The trend toward integrated athletics departments, and away from the old system of separate entities based on gender, had been accelerating. Most member institutions by this time had moved into a single-department approach. The fundamental question was whether the time had arrived for the NCAA to adopt this approach.

The AIAW had launched a major effort to oppose the work of the Frank committee and was lobbying its members to engage the attention of campus decision makers. However, the AIAW was itself a divided organization. Some of its leaders, including past presidents, were enthusiastic about having the option of NCAA rules and championship opportunities available. Almost from its establishment, there had been concern about the AIAW position on athletics scholarships (originally prohibited and subsequently permitted with limitations) and recruitment restrictions (no paid visits). The scholarship situation produced negative reactions — for different reasons — in two NCAA divisions. What was allowed under AIAW rules was not enough for Division I but was too much for Division III. In addition, funding was not available from the organization to pay for expenses accrued by members in championship competition. These issues had legal implications under Title IX. Nevertheless, a number of institutional responses to the committee's January mailing argued for the continuation of separate national associations for men and women. This argument was offered, too, at the forums held by the committee in the spring and fall of 1980. Frank's view on this matter was emphatic. It was in part a product of his own experience: "I think it is fallacious thinking … that 'separate but equal' is the answer," he said. "I, for one, know that 'separate but equal' does not lead to equality."

The Council extensively reviewed, then revised, the initial plan for governance and championships and sent it to the membership in November 1980. The plan provided for significant structural change to accommodate participation by female professionals in the governance process — membership on the Council and Executive Committee and service opportunities on an array of Association committees. It guaranteed the availability of approximately 215 positions on these bodies to women from member institutions. Women's championships would be added to those already approved for Divisions II and III, and inaugurated for Division I. Nineteen new championships would be started across the three divisions. Institutions could opt to keep their women's programs in the AIAW or other organizations. The proposals emphasized institutional autonomy and flexibility. These changes would be presented to the delegates at the 1981 Convention, which would be described

1992 (March) —Gender-Equity Task Force formed in response to first NCAA gender-equity study showing disparities in treatment of male and female student-athletes.

PHOTO FROM NCAA FILES

1992 (March 19-21) —**Stanford University** wins the first of five straight Division I Women's Swimming and Diving Championships team titles under coach **Richard Quick**.

1992 (November 21) —Adams State University scores a perfect 15 points in winning the Division II Men's Cross Country Championships; meanwhile, Adams State's women win the first of eight straight team titles between 1992 and 1999 under coach Damon Martin.

1992 (November 21) —Washington University of St. Louis beats the University of California, San Diego, for the second straight year in the last of three straight championship matches pairing the two teams at the Division III Women's Volleyball Championships; the two schools each won seven titles (including six in a row by Washington) between 1981 and 1996.

later as "one of the most significant events in the history of intercollegiate athletics."

The governance amendments, one requiring a two-thirds majority, passed easily. The championship proposals, however, stirred the passions, led to tense and lengthy debates, and, at one point, produced a real quandary. When the debate ended and the vote was taken on whether to establish women's championships in Division I, the result was a tie (124-124). The proposal failed in a recount, 128-127. Enter the quandary, which presented a serious threat to harmony among the divisions. Championships were already approved for Divisions II and III. Did it make sense, therefore, to deny them in Division I, or should the approval to hold them in the other two divisions be rescinded? A motion to rescind was defeated. A motion to reconsider the Division I vote was approved. The reconsidered motion, allowing Division I championships, then passed, 137-117. The AIAW, as reported in Chapter Five, took the battle to court and lost. The organization's brief but consequential history was over. The NCAA, however, became a new entity at the end of its first 75 years. Another era could be said to have ended at that Convention, the one stretching back to 1866, when the women of Vassar took up baseball.

Frank began his two-year term as NCAA president at the conclusion of the Convention. He had played basketball at Lincoln (Missouri), a historically black institution, and returned to coach the sport in the late 1950s. He coached the team that the NCAA removed from its normal geography and sent to Tuskegee with three other HBCUs for the 1959 regional tournament. He attended the 1962 Men's Final Four in Louisville and stayed with other black coaches in a segregated hotel. He was a vice president at the City University of New York's Medgar Evers College (named for Mississippi's slain black leader) in the early 1970s and returned to his alma mater as president in 1973. He had argued long and hard for the advancement of women's intercollegiate athletics within the NCAA. Frank supported the legislation guaranteeing certain numbers of positions for females. But he asked to have a statement about another under-represented group included in the 1981 Convention program. It read, in part: "The Association should commit itself to a concerted effort to continue to provide opportunities for blacks and other minorities to hold viable roles in [its] administrative structure." Plenty of work remained to be done in honoring that commitment.

TITLE IX

ELIZABETH CADY STANTON and Lucretia Mott were a major presence at the 1848 women's rights convention — the first of its kind — in Seneca Falls, New York. The bill of rights that issued from that meeting included a shocking claim that females were entitled to the franchise. The claim was shocking, along with others asserted in the Seneca Falls Declaration, because it ran so far beyond and so strongly against the accepted wisdom of the time regarding the place and role of women in America. Stanton and Mott, joined later by Susan B. Anthony and others, spent much of their durable and dedicated lives pursuing the right to vote. It would still be a long time coming after they went to their respective graves. The 19th Amendment to the U.S. Constitution finally recognized that right in 1920, 72 years after the demand for women's suffrage enlivened the proceedings in Seneca Falls.

Title IX, particularly its athletics component, produced a similar reaction once its broad language was interpreted by the implementing agency. Some people present at the law's creation probably still wonder whether, like the right to vote, Title IX will take generations to be fully realized. Some say (indeed, have said) that the law's biggest obstacle has been the NCAA. The truth, however, is rather more complicated. Whatever one's position may be on the matter, there is no denying that Title IX's impact in providing athletics opportunities for women has been enormous.

A lot of hopes, much meaning and frequent controversy have been attached to the 37 words that got the revolution underway:

No person in the United States shall, on the basis of sex, be excluded
from participation in, be denied the benefits of, or be subjected to

*discrimination under any education program or activity receiving
federal financial assistance.*

Putting the words to work has required policy interpretations, hearings, further legislation, court decisions, studies and reports, reams of commentary, changes in the NCAA Manual, and at least one task force. The NCAA has been involved virtually from the beginning, expressing immediate concern when the first draft of regulations was put out for comment by the Department of Health, Education and Welfare (HEW) in 1974. The Council's report to HEW said the draft's language was "unreasonably vague, ambitious and lacking in specific standards;" therefore, it would be almost impossible for institutions to know how to comply. HEW received nearly 10,000 responses. Consequently, the agency made significant changes in the final version, the first of the federal government's official policy interpretations, published in 1975. From the Association's perspective, the modifications were neither adequate nor reflective of Congressional actions taken following the circulation of the first draft.

After failing to convince HEW and its Office for Civil Rights (OCR) that athletics should not be part of Title IX implementation, the NCAA launched a major effort to ensure that revenue generated by individual sports (especially football and men's basketball) would be exempted from the proposed requirement that equal athletic programs be offered to each gender. The result was a legislative initiative known as the "Tower Amendment," which stated that Title IX would not apply to "athletic activity insofar as such activity provides to the institution gross receipts or donations required by such institutions to support that activity." The amendment, named for Texas Sen. John Tower, passed the Senate, but not the House of Representatives. A compromise was reached in more general wording proposed by Sen. Jacob Javits of New York. The "Javits Amendment" required that regulations include "reasonable provisions considering the nature of the particular sports." The NCAA believed this language would protect the big revenue-producing sports, but the language of the 1975 Policy Interpretation did not offer such protection. This concern, among others, was further registered during Congressional review of the interpretation; however, Congress made no changes. The regulations that became law in July 1975 notably included a mandate that institutions awarding athletics scholarships or grants-in-aid "must provide reasonable opportunities … for members of each sex in proportion to the number of students of each sex participating in … intercollegiate athletics." The NCAA went to court.

In the case of *NCAA v. Califano*, brought in 1976, the Association asserted that HEW had exceeded its authority in issuing the Title IX implementation mandates on athletics. The U.S. District Court in Kansas dismissed the case because, in its view, the Association lacked standing to sue. The NCAA filed an amended complaint and eventually appealed to the 10th Circuit, which in 1980 reversed the lower jurisdiction and awarded standing. By then, the situation had changed. The NCAA decided not to pursue the case but to search elsewhere for answers and assistance. In the interim, the OCR issued additional interpretations. That office moved in 1980, along with HEW's education portfolio, to the new Department of Education. Ronald Reagan was elected president that year. What looked so bad to the Association and its members in 1976 looked better in a new decade, with a new administration in Washington.

The 1979 Convention was held on the heels of a proposed interpretation issued by the OCR in December 1978. Discussion with HEW officials in recent years had led the NCAA to conclude that what the Association viewed as the sense of the Javits Amendment (that is, protecting football and exempting its revenue) now might be recognized in new regulations. That didn't happen in 1978. Also, testimony from these officials indicated that HEW did not view Title IX as requiring equal per capita athletics expenditures for men and women. But the proposed interpretation failed to reflect this understanding. Instead, the new language prescribed such expenditures — in financial aid, recruitment and other measurable benefits. Together, these two features of the interpretation suggested to the NCAA and its membership that the burden of a massive increase in funding for women's sports, and an indefinite growth in such expenditures, lay ahead. The prospect was alarming.

Title IX was the main attraction at the 1979 Convention, and the alarm bells were ringing. The subject dominated roundtable discussions, pervaded hallway conversations and was a significant component of the legislative sessions. Title IX was the front-page story in The NCAA News both in advance of and after the Convention. The delegates passed a lengthy resolution challenging the HEW's authority, the per capita expenditure test imposed in the latest interpretation, the absence of Javits Amendment intentions in that document,

"Much can be done by law towards putting women on a footing of complete and equal rights with man – including the right to vote, the right to hold and use property, and the right to enter any profession she desires on the same terms as the man. … Women should have free access to every field of labor which they care to enter, and when their work is as valuable as that of a man it should be paid as highly."
—THEODORE ROOSEVELT, FROM HIS AUTBIOGRAPHY, 1913

federal intervention in general, and the "excessive and unreasonable financial obligations" now demanded. Speakers articulated doomsday scenarios. CEOs, faculty representatives and athletics directors alerted in advance by the NCAA president were primed to take action. Attorneys' analyses were widely distributed. A coalition of institutions mobilized to enter the fray. For a time, at least, the proposed Policy Interpretation was Seneca Falls redux and became something like what the sage had to say about the prospect of hanging: It concentrated the mind wonderfully.

The Association sent to HEW a 49-page set of comments on the interpretation, plus the resolution passed at the Convention and numerous other appendixes. When the final interpretation was published in December 1979, important concessions had been made. The per capita expenditure test in all areas other than financial aid was eliminated. The "proportionate equivalency" concept was back, requiring institutions to distribute financial aid according to the percentages of male and female athletes participating. This idea had troubled the members five years earlier, but now, in view of what might have been, it seemed tolerable.

The interpretation contained two other parts. One added 11 athletics-program elements institutions needed to meet the equivalency test (recruitment, equipment, travel allowances, et al.). The other dealt with the accommodation of athletics interests requirement, but with guidelines that eventually became challenging alternative paths to meeting Title IX mandates. Overall, the membership reacted negatively, in part because the interpretation had been promulgated with no subsequent opportunity for public comment and no review by Congress. That meant it would not have the force of law. On the other hand, the interpretation would have (as a number of institutions learned later) "substantial practical significance."

The 1980s were mostly free of the frenetic punching and counterpunching that had characterized the previous six or seven years. The OCR was fairly quiet, in light of the proportional opportunity standard the 1979 final interpretation required. The Reagan Administration seemed content to allow for a more gradual approach to implementation. In 1984, the Supreme Court decision in *Grove City v. Bell* virtually nullified the impact of Title IX on athletics. In this case, the court held that the legislation was program-specific in its coverage, meaning that the program (rather than the institution) determined Title IX's applicability. In other words if the program received federal funds, it was covered. Simply because the institution received such funds did not mean its athletics department (which in almost all instances did not receive federal dollars) would be accountable. The reverse also was true, according to the court. But in 1988, when Congress passed the Civil Rights Restoration Act, this immunity vanished. The legislation, which survived Reagan's veto, held that if an institution was a federal funds recipient, its programs, emphatically including athletics, must meet Title IX. Four years later, another Supreme Court decision produced instant interest from the NCAA and its member institutions. This was *Franklin v. Gwinnet County Public Schools*. In this case the court ruled that plaintiffs who won Title IX suits were entitled to punitive damages. This decision returned the fat to the fire.

The NCAA's role in the Title IX developments of the 1970s and '80s was prominent and usually oppositional. For these reasons, the 1981 absorption of women's programs — an action ironically made almost inevitable in light of the Title IX rules — became more difficult. The AIAW and other strong supporters of the policy interpretations often viewed the Association as the villain of the piece. In fact, the NCAA was doing what its rules bound it to do, which was (and is) to represent the views of its members. Most institutions needed time to adjust to the new vision for women's intercollegiate athletics, especially to deal with the resulting financial demands. Abiding concern emanated from campus officers, and not just athletics directors and coaches. The Title IX mandates were much on the minds of presidents as well, and on the agendas of booster organizations, governing boards and other national higher education associations. Finding the necessary dollars to comply would be difficult, and painful decisions appeared unavoidable. Moreover, Title IX added to a long, growing list of unfunded, often expensive, federal mandates for educational institutions. For presidents, it looked at times like another invitation to take up residency in those uncomfortable quarters wedged between rocks and hard places.

In this complicated situation, the NCAA played the lightning-rod role that Byers saw as a necessary responsibility. The executive director was frequently in the forefront in implementing the will of the membership. He wrote later that "to decree that football and women's field hockey deserved the same per capita expenditures was financial lunacy." He believed revenue sports should be exempted. Leaders of other national higher education associations may have shared those feelings, but not the obligation to serve as lightning rod.

The guidelines on accommodating athletics interests imbedded in the 1979 interpretation ultimately became OCR policy under the label of the three-prong test for compliance with Title IX. One prong is providing opportunities for participation substantially proportionate to undergraduate enrollment percentages. Demonstrating a history and continuing practice of program expansion for the underrepresented gender is another. The third looks toward full and effective accommodation of the athletics interests of that gender. Brown University was challenged on the basis of this test in 1992, in the U.S. District Court for Rhode Island. Brown had cut two women's and two men's teams. The women successfully sought injunctive relief at the district level and then from the First U.S. Circuit Court of Appeals. Later, they prevailed on the merits of the case in both courts, the First Circuit rendering a detailed opinion in 1993. *Cohen v. Brown University* was appealed to the Supreme Court, which refused to grant Brown a writ of certiorari, meaning the First Circuit's ruling would stand.

The American Council on Education (ACE) presented an amici curiae brief at the Supreme Court proceeding, in support of Brown's appeal. This brief was filed on behalf of four other prominent higher education organizations. Together, these entities represented the great majority of the country's public and private institutions of higher education, excluding community colleges. The ACE brief, and the extent of representation behind it, spoke materially to the level of campus concern about the OCR's policy interpretations. For years, the NCAA had served as the principal voice of such concern. It is fair to criticize this opposition but important to understand how widespread it was, and why.

GETTING BEYOND BEYONDISM

WITH OR WITHOUT the Brown University decision and the other cases vindicating the OCR's handling of Title IX, a kind of peace was settling in for women's intercollegiate athletics and the NCAA's understanding of its related responsibilities in the 1990s. Together with the 1981 action that brought women's programs into the Association, Title IX stimulated many changes in NCAA governance and policy, and in the provision of expanded opportunities for women. Somewhat similar changes, also coming after bruising controversy, were put into effect for (and by) ethnic minorities. Diversity became a major NCAA message during the 20th century's final decade. But some hard challenges came first.

Proposition 48 lit the fuse for ethnic minorities. This legislation came soon after the walls of segregation in intercollegiate sport had crumbled. Black student-athletes were matriculating at campuses, North and South, in comparatively large numbers. Some of the angry reaction to Proposition 48 arose from black leaders' sense that this influx worried the white establishment. Grambling President Joseph Johnson spoke from that point of reference when the proposition was debated at the 1983 Convention. Race, as was noted in Chapter Four, was the fundamental issue on the floor that year. The anger had not abated by 1986 when HBCUs proposed a different method of determining initial academic eligibility. This was Proposition 14, which recommended a 2.000 GPA in the core curriculum and the elimination of standardized-test scores. Johnson spoke again at this Convention, on behalf of No. 14 and in frustration over what he believed to be the attitude of the institutions that had given life to Proposition 48:

> Black student-athletes at these institutions have never been considered educational entities; they have been an industrial commodity. Some of these institutions … have built their programs and launched their stadiums and field houses and built large athletics endowments on the backs of these black athletes. Now, they are saying to them, "We don't need you anymore. There are too many of you on our campuses."

Johnson added that "if there is any integrity, any morality and any shame left in this organization," the delegates should show it by approving Proposition 14. The measure was voted down, 289-47.

Similar defeats at later Conventions sustained the resentment felt by HBCU presidents and those who shared their concerns. For example, their efforts to add a fourth year of eligibility for partial or nonqualifiers failed, and an interest in strengthening the requirements of Proposition 48 gained support in Presidents Commission discussions. This interest took legislative form in Proposition 16, which the membership approved at the 1992 Convention for 1994 implementation. The grant-in-aid reductions passed in 1991, particularly the loss of two such grants in Division I men's basketball, gained entrée to the debate at this juncture. The change took the scholarships number from 15 to 13, upsetting the coaches. The Black Coaches Association (BCA) viewed the move as a loss of opportunities for black athletes. The accumulation of defeats and disappointments reached a critical point in fall 1993. That October, the BCA announced it would boycott the annual issues forum of the National Association of Basketball Coaches (NABC), not because of hostility toward the NABC but to dramatize BCA concern about cost reductions and academic eligibility. At the time of the forum, BCA representatives met in Washington, D.C., with members of the Congressional Black Caucus to discuss these and additional grievances. Association officers offered to confer with BCA leaders, who hinted at the possibility of more serious actions. No dialogue ensued. There matters stood until December when a member of the Black Caucus placed a distressing new item on an already crowded and contentious agenda.

Rep. Cardiss Collins of Illinois chaired the Caucus Task Force on Intercollegiate Athletics. That month the frequent commentator on NCAA issues, particularly gender equity and minority access, wrote to the NCAA president claiming that racial bias conceivably had tainted the research and conclusions of the Association's Data Analysis Working Group. Since 1985, that group had conducted inquiries measuring the impact of Proposition 48 and informed the process of consideration leading to the Proposition 16 legislation. Collins said she had information indicating that the chair of the working group and two associates were involved with psychologist Raymond Cattell. Cattell's research, on occasion, had dealt with eugenics, and his views on the subject — a kind of "religion," as he described it — were known as "Beyondism." While these views, collectively, were complex, putatively scientific and often abstract, one could draw from them an imputation of racial superiority. Scholars and others have sometimes associated eugenics with the idea of building a better race or class of people through genetic manipulation, Hitler's master-race philosophy being the most infamous example. Collins' letter resulted in the BCA's immediate call for an external investigation and a suspension of both research activities and "all NCAA rules dealing with eligibility standards."

John McArdle, a professor of psychology at Virginia, chaired the working group. One of McArdle's graduate students supplied the information on which Collins' charges and the BCA's demands were based. At the time, the student was angry with his mentor. Collins enclosed with her letter two chapters of Cattell's book, "Beyondism: Religion from Science," published in 1987, and several documents describing a Beyondism Foundation and a Cattell Research Institute. McArdle had been a graduate student under Cattell and, along with other participants in the working group's research activities, had subsequent professional associations with him. The material from McArdle's graduate student was sketchy in places and in part based on hearsay. Although there was enough for the NCAA to initiate a serious inquiry, the information proved inconclusive. McArdle and his associates denied any adherence to a eugenic or super-race philosophy. McArdle pointed out that Cattell had published 550 articles and 57 books over the course of a long career and that only five of these publications dealt with his Beyondism beliefs.

McArdle and the working group had long since made clear their conviction that an equally weighted index of GPAs and standardized-test scores was the best predictor of college-level performance. The NCAA's Academic Requirements Committee agreed, and recommended as much, but the Presidents Commission opted for a cut-score on the standardized-test measure. The result of that approach, which gave added weight to the test score, was to disproportionately and negatively affect the academic eligibility of black student-athletes (although those who qualified contributed to a higher graduation rate among such individuals). The Presidents Commission and Council elected to support the cut-score and higher graduation rates. That was the fundamental component of Propositions 48 and 16, and the fundamental concern of Collins and the BCA. McArdle, in effect, shared that concern.

The NCAA reported this to Collins, to whom McArdle also wrote several letters supplying detailed information and volunteering to meet with her. While remaining as lead researcher, he turned over the working group chair position to James Jackson, an African-American and psychology professor at Michigan. The NCAA continued its inquiry into the Beyondism accusations. The controversy arose periodically for the next nine months. Meantime, a BCA threat to boycott men's basketball games took center stage. The threat had more to do with athletics issues than Beyondist philosophy. It became a matter of major import at the 1994 Convention.

In December, a few weeks before he took office as the Association's third executive director, Cedric Dempsey traveled to Washington, D.C., to meet with several high-profile BCA representatives. He was accompanied by the NCAA president and the chair of the Presidents Commission. The purpose was to explore the territory of conflict and confrontation, the boundaries of which seemed to be rapidly expanding. The outcome was, in the parlance of diplomacy, a frank exchange of views. But Dempsey and his colleagues came away understanding that they had much work to do to contain the conflict and avert a crisis. Later that month, the Association president attended the Heritage Bowl in Atlanta and met there with a number of HBCU presidents. The 1994 Convention was just days away. The presidents were forthcoming. Their issues needed attention at that conclave.

Progress was made at the Convention, but big trouble emerged. The Council and Presidents Commission, as mentioned in Chapter Four, decided to postpone the effective date of Proposition 16. The two groups also agreed to sponsor legislation to establish a special committee on initial eligibility to review that proposition's impact data and do additional research. The committee would have a diverse makeup. An HBCU president, William DeLauder of Delaware State, would serve as a co-chair. These steps would help answer the frequently expressed complaint that Propositions 48 and 16 had both been developed with inadequate representation from minority communities. The committee's report would be due at the 1995 Convention, and Proposition 16's expected start date was moved to 1995. This action eased some of the strain on the academic-eligibility question. However, the debate and discussion of Proposition 42, which recommended adding a 14th scholarship in Division I men's basketball, was another matter entirely. When this proposal was voted down, as Chapter Four also reported, the prospect of a BCA boycott was, in essence, voted up. The BCA made its announcement the next day.

The boycott would include both coaches and players, according to the BCA executive director, and could extend through the remainder of the season. If that happened, the postseason tournament — the source of millions of dollars for the NCAA and its members — would be adversely affected and possibly canceled. The announcement gave rise to numerous worrisome questions: Would all black coaches participate in the boycott and, if any did, how would their institutional employers respond? How would black players, most of them playing for white coaches, handle the boycott call? For that matter, how would the white coaches respond? Many of them, together with the NABC, had pushed hard but unsuccessfully for the passage of Proposition 42. Was there a role for the NABC, for the conferences and for the NCAA itself in seeking resolution to the controversy? Many questions. No clear answers.

The 33 commissioners of Division I basketball conferences set up a conference call soon after the Convention to discuss possible responses to the boycott and to consider contingency plans. The BCA was not disposed to pursue any further discussions, except one. During the week after the Convention, the organization consulted with the Congressional Black Caucus. Collins again raised the Beyondism issue, but other matters were deemed more pressing. Rep. Kweisi Mfume, Caucus chair, sought help from the executive branch, which made available the assistance of the Justice Department's mediation service. The NCAA leadership agreed to participate. So did the BCA, although it emphasized that it was delaying the boycott, not calling it off.

The two sides met first by telephone March 1. BCA participants included Temple's John Chaney; George Raveling of Southern California; Nolan Richardson of Arkansas; Georgetown's John Thompson; and BCA executive director Rudy Washington, from Drake. The NCAA

1994 (January 11) —Black Coaches Association threatens boycott of men's basketball games in response to Division I defeat of proposal to increase scholarships from 13 to 14; the boycott is averted when the NCAA and BCA agree January 14 to Justice Department arbitration.

1994 (March 17-19) —Travis Miller of the University of California, San Diego, becomes the first participant in the Division III Men's Swimming and Diving Championships to win nine career individual titles.

1994 (November 13) —Franklin Pierce College wins the first of five Division II Women's Soccer Championships during a six-year period beginning in 1994 (two under coach Mark Krikorian and three under coach Jeff Bailey).

1994 (December) —NCAA and CBS agree to $1.725 billion, eight-year television contract; ESPN agrees to expand coverage of the Division I Women's Basketball Championship.

group included Dempsey; Joseph Crowley, the organization's president; Judith Albino, Presidents Commission chair; Charles Whitcomb, the head of the Association's Minority Opportunities and Interests Committee (MOIC); and Prentice Gautt, the Oklahoma football pioneer, now NCAA secretary-treasurer. Much of the conversation focused on Beyondism; little progress was made on that or any of the other issues. The Association made available all of the correspondence with Collins, including a letter to her from McArdle. NCAA leaders had assured the congresswoman that they took her charges seriously and that the Beyondist views were repugnant to them as well. She had been told that the evidence presented thus far did not support a finding that research had been tainted or that working-group members subscribed to Beyondist beliefs. She had not been persuaded, nor were the coaches. It was agreed by the parties that the next meeting would be in person.

Anger, tense moments and the possibility of stalemate were all plentifully evident in the discussions that followed. So was an understanding that the Men's and Women's Final Fours were drawing closer. If the boycott threat was not on the table during these discussions, it was nevertheless a heavy presence in the room. But there was also a consciousness that the two sides were, after all, engaged in mediation; that they had been assembled by the U.S. Community Relations Service for that purpose; and that the assistance of this agency had been requested by the president of the United States. This too was a heavy presence. With that in mind, able help available from the mediation service and staff on both sides, and an unstated conviction that a favorable outcome was imperative, the groups reached an agreement during the third week of March. There would be no boycott. A fresh start toward the solution of some old problems was in the offing.

The agreement looked toward increased emphasis on education opportunities and greater participation "in every aspect of NCAA governance" by African-Americans and other ethnic minorities. The Association promised that the special committee to review initial-eligibility standards would have a diverse membership, including a BCA representative, and that the committee would review all elements involved in those standards. The possibility of a fourth year for partial qualifiers and nonqualifiers under Proposition 48 would again be reviewed. Several other provisions of the agreement committed the NCAA to cooperative endeavors with the BCA. Follow-up meetings with the organization would be scheduled to review progress and engage in related discussions.

The mediation agreement did not end the controversy. Collins pressed her claims on Beyondism, despite the special committee's proposal of a new approach to academic eligibility, without cutoff scores on standardized tests, based on research and recommendations from McArdle and the working group. She submitted no further evidence to sustain charges of racial bias or Beyondism adherence on the part of McArdle and his colleagues. The NCAA's inquiry determined that the material provided to Collins by McArdle's graduate student was seriously deficient and, on the whole, unconvincing. In September 1994, Collins' Black Caucus Task Force, BCA members and a study group met in Washington to discuss eligibility standards. A press conference arranged by the congresswoman was held afterward, with the standards and Beyondism on the agenda.

The special committee presented its proposal to the Knight Commission in October. This commission had already taken a strong position against the committee's recommendations. After the presentation, the Knight commissioners urged campus presidents to "stand firm on reform" and continue to support Proposition 16. The Presidents Commission again endorsed that proposition, despite concerns expressed by the Council. In January 1995, as noted earlier, the Convention delegates voted against both the special committee's recommendations and a related proposal from HBCU presidents to restore freshman ineligibility. However, the Commission also proposed legislation that would ease constraints on partial qualifiers and allow for institutional (but not athletics) aid for nonqualifers during their first year. The delegates approved these measures. A proposal to provide a fourth year for such student-athletes if they met certain academic-progress requirements came close to passage, despite opposition from a divided Presidents Commission. The effective date of Proposition 16 was postponed until 1996. The NCAA Council voted for the proposal advocated by the special committee. Some minds had been changed since the 1994 Convention. Eight years later, with a new governance structure in place, the Association retreated from the cutoff score approach that had been the backbone of Propositions 48 and 16. The decision was based in part on research accomplished in the interim showing the actual (rather than projected) impacts of the initial-eligibility

standards. The data clearly demonstrated that African-American student-athletes, as anticipated by the special committee in 1994, had been disproportionately affected. The research
was performed by the working group, which still employed John McArdle as its lead
researcher.

DIVERSITY

NEARLY 20 YEARS were required to complete the journey from approval of
Proposition 48 to the discarding of cutoff scores in 2002. For HBCU leaders, the change
was a long time coming. For women, although patience in the face of slow progress
would be needed, the governance plan approved at the 1981 Convention — two years
before the approval of No. 48 — yielded immediate results. The plan provided for four
seats on the Council and two on the Executive Committee. Among those appointed
to the Council were Judith Holland of UCLA, a former AIAW president and leading
supporter of the NCAA option; Gwendolyn Norrell of Michigan State, who would
later serve as Association vice president for Division I; P. Laverne Sweat of Hampton,
the first black female to serve in the governance structure; and Elizabeth Kruczek, athletics director, sports information director and the only full-time administrative employee in her department at Fitchburg State. Linda Estes of New Mexico, also significantly
involved in bringing women's programs into the NCAA, was chosen for a seat on the Executive
Committee, as was Mary Zimmerman. Zimmerman was associate athletics director at South
Dakota and had once served as player-coach of her high school basketball team in Poplar,
Montana.

Ten other women were appointed to the three division steering committees. Within a few
weeks of the Convention, women held 16 of the 50 Association governance positions. During
this period, letters went out to directors of athletics requesting the identity of the person to be
named as primary woman administrator (later senior woman administrator) at each institution.
This, too, was part of the plan the delegates approved. Arrangements were made to conduct all
29 women's championships for the first time in the 1981-82 academic year. Ruth Berkey had been
hired from her athletics director's position at Occidental in 1980. She now became, as Byers
described her, "the women's foremost representative" in the NCAA. She launched the women's
basketball championships and was the key person in incorporating other women's programs into
the organization.

After the fast start, women's progress in the 1980s was gradual. The number of championships grew. Women like Christine Grant of Iowa and Charlotte West of Southern Illinois, who
had earlier opposed the NCAA's incorporation of women's programs, became increasingly
involved in the work of the Association. More women were elected to governance positions,
appointed to committees and added to the Association staff. The NCAA News covered women's
teams and championships. Tens of thousands of women played college sports, their number growing yearly. Outstanding performances, past and present, were recognized at the annual Honors
Dinner. One of the Top V student-athletes each year for 1982, 1984 and 1985 was a female. The
pace picked up — a sign of things to come — in 1986, when the Top V became the Top VI and
three of the winners were women. A female was not chosen for a Silver Anniversary Award
(given each year to six student-athletes who had gained distinction on the field or court 25 years
before and in their careers since that time) until 1987. During the first 10 years of women's participation in NCAA sports, only two members of that gender received Silver recognition, the second coming in 1991. The Association's highest award — the Teddy, named for Theodore
Roosevelt — first went to a woman (Althea Gibson) that year.

Much more movement came in the 1990s. Judy Sweet, having been elected the NCAA's first
female secretary-treasurer in 1989, became its first female president in January 1991. The
Association initiated its student-athlete Woman of the Year Award the next spring. The first woman
to chair the Presidents Commission, Judith Albino of Colorado, took office in 1994, just in time to

1995 (March 25) —Middlebury
College wins the first of five straight
Division III Men's Ice Hockey
Championship titles under coach Bill
Beaney (the team added titles in
2004 and 2005).

1995 (April) —NCAA opens federal
relations office in Washington, D.C.

1995 (April 20-22)
—The University
of Kentucky's
Jenny Hansen wins
four individual titles
at the National
Collegiate
Women's Gymnas-
tics Championships
to boost her record
career total to
eight titles.

1995 (May) —
Division I
Women's
Softball Committee bans titanium
bats in 1995 championship.

1995 (May 5-6) —National Collegiate
Men's Volleyball Championship in
Springfield, Massachusetts, commemo-
rates centennial of sport.

1995 (May 21) —The University of
Maryland, College Park, wins the first
of seven straight Division I Women's
Lacrosse Championship titles under
coach Cindy Timchal.

play a principal role in handling the controversies described in this chapter. The previous year, the membership approved the athletics certification proposal, with equity as one of its four standards. That standard turned out to be the most challenging for Division I institutions to meet. The month after the 1993 Convention, Collins held a hearing on gender equity at which she said she would introduce legislation requiring reports from colleges and universities on scheduling, expenditures, scholarships, gender of coaches and coaches' salaries. (The Equity in Athletics Disclosure Act was passed by Congress the following year.)

When the long-awaited Gender-Equity Task Force Report reached the Convention floor in 1994, the membership was ready to overwhelmingly support its recommendation to add equity as a basic principle of the Association. The report made both direct and indirect references to Title IX imperatives and took note of the 1991 NCAA survey that produced evidence of continuing imbalances: Men made up nearly 70 percent of the participants in intercollegiate athletics and received approximately 70 percent of scholarship funding and 77 percent of operating budget dollars. A definition of gender equity was provided: "An athletics program can be considered gender equitable when the participants in both the men's and women's sports programs would accept as fair and equitable the overall program of the other gender." The report concluded with "a call to action" to be undertaken:

> not just by the NCAA but by what a year of deliberation clearly showed
> was critical to realizing gender equity — the commitment of individual
> institutions as represented by their chief executive officers and governing
> bodies, including state legislatures.

By 1994, this was a call that member institutions, their presidents, their trustees and — maybe, in a few instances — their legislatures had begun to answer.

Lawsuit losses helped make this happen. So did the growth of student-athlete participation and the increased television coverage of women's sports. The Division I Women's Final Four, under then-NCAA Director of Championships Tricia Bork, had become a substantial national event, with decent television ratings and full arenas. For a number of years, the annual American Honda awards banquet was held in conjunction with the Convention. The Honda-Broderick Cup, given to the outstanding female college athlete of the year, and awards to superior performers in individual sports were featured at this event. The program's governing board, while independent of the Association, included members active in NCAA affairs, and the banquet's national exposure helped the Association and its membership move forward faster on gender-equity issues and objectives.

Elsewhere on the awards front, female student-athletes were increasingly prominent participants at the yearly Honors Dinner. For the 10-year period beginning in 1986, women won nearly half of the Top V/Top VI (and as of 1995, Top VIII) Awards. During the next 10 years, to 2005, they received nearly 64 percent of these awards. Given the relative paucity of women's intercollegiate competition in earlier years, it is not surprising that few females won Silver Anniversary Award until recently. Only five were selected from 1982 through 1997. Three of them (Wilma Rudolph, 1987; Edith McGuire Duvall, 1991; and Wyonia Tyus, 1993) were from Tennessee State. During the 1960s, when competitive sports for women were still a novel idea on most college campuses, some of the HBCUs produced female track and field athletes who became stellar performers on U.S. Olympic teams. That was the case with trailblazers Rudolph, Duvall and Tyus. In the eight years after 1987, 13 women were Silver winners.

Teddy Awards for women arrived at an even slower rate. After Gibson's in 1991, more than a decade passed until Eunice Kennedy Shriver was chosen in 2002. Donna de Varona won the next year, and Sally Ride was the Teddy recipient in 2005. Alan Page played football at Notre Dame, graduating in 1967, before the Top V awards were instituted. An African-American, All-American, NFL star and Justice of the Minnesota Supreme Court, he was a Silver winner in 1992 and, in 2004, earned the Teddy. Thus, for the past four years, the NCAA's highest honor has gone to individuals whose selection represented a triumph for diversity.

In the late 1980s, two standing committees — one on women's athletics and the second on minority access — were created to give diversity a greater voice in Association policy-making. The Committee on Women's Athletics (CWA) was a logical outgrowth of the 1981 decision to bring women's programs into the NCAA. Frank and Byers started the discussion that led to the formation of the MOIC. This committee began as a task force, shortly becoming a standing committee chaired by Charles Whitcomb of San Jose State. Whitcomb served 13 years in the chair's role, working closely with his opposite numbers in the CWA. The two committees assembled a joint annual budget request, met together once a year, and collaborated on program initiation and development. Their work has covered a wide range of issues and possibilities, including student internships and scholarships, diversity training, leadership training, student-athlete health, homophobia, coaching education, diversity among officials, Native American mascots, the Confederate flag controversy, employment databases, race and gender demographics among member institutions, and other surveys. Individually and jointly, the committees established:

▶ The NCAA Fellows Leadership Development Program
▶ Leadership Institutes for Ethnic Minority Males and Females
▶ NCAA Men's and Women's Coaching Academies
▶ The Women's Minority Coaches Matching-Grant Program
▶ Ethnic Minority and Women's Enhancement Postgraduate Scholarships
▶ Diversity Training Workshops on Race, Gender and Sexual Orientation
▶ Ethnic Minority and Women's Internships
▶ Matching Grants for Advancement of Minority Women Coaches
▶ Diversity Matching Grants for Division II and III Members

The BCA and the National Association of Collegiate Women Athletic Administrators (NACWAA) have been NCAA partners in developing many of these programs. NACWAA's involvement grew through its close relationship with the CWA. Perhaps the hard-won 1994 mediation agreement helped make the BCA partnership possible. The NCAA also developed a working connection with the National Consortium for Academics and Sports (NCAS), an organization with ties to the BCA and a long history of support for diversity initiatives.

Dempsey's first year as executive director, filled as it was with controversies over race and gender, led him to place a priority on diversity during his tenure. He offered solid backing to the CWA and MOIC programs, spoke often of the need for institutional action in support of Title IX, and significantly enhanced the diverse character of the NCAA staff. When he came to the Association in 1994, 21.7 percent of the management staff members were females and 8.7 percent were African-Americans. Toward the end of his time in office, in 2002, these percentages were 36 and 20, respectively. He hired women and Blacks into senior positions, including an African-American as one of his two executive vice presidents. Dempsey wrote a dozen commentaries on major issues facing intercollegiate athletics during his final years on the job, one of them titled "The Diversity Hiring Failure." He was speaking from the bully pulpit here, and his focus in this commentary was the lack of diversity at the top: African-American and female athletics directors, black head football coaches in Division I and the hiring of women to coach women's teams. The membership, he said, fell short in all these areas. These situations persist today, the best intentions of the NCAA and institutional leadership to the contrary notwithstanding.

Dempsey's successor, Myles Brand, assumed office in 2003. He made it clear he wanted to address these matters and to avail himself generously of the pulpit opportunities his position presented. Brand launched an ambitious strategic-planning effort, a principal component thereof being an office of diversity and inclusion. He appointed Judy Sweet as a senior vice president and hired Bernard Franklin, a former HBCU president, to fill another vice presidency at that level. In 2003, Brand testified in strong support of Title IX before a U.S Department of Education commission charged with reviewing that historic legislation. When that department issued a "policy clarification" in 2005, weakening Title IX compliance requirements, he issued a press release criticizing the change the next day. Later that spring, he hired an African-American woman, Charlotte Westerhaus from the University of Iowa, to be the Association's first vice president for diversity and inclusion.

The NCAA has traveled a long road on gender equity since 1972 and a similar distance on minority issues since Frank's 1981-83 Association presidency and the passage of Proposition 48. The Association has encountered many related challenges along the way and accomplished much. Much more will be needed. Some of the data on Title IX compliance, student-athlete ethnicity, institutional hiring practices and salary differentials will be reviewed in the next chapter. They offer persuasive testimony on the distance yet to travel before the NCAA's ambitious and necessary diversity goals can be achieved. ●

Making a Splash

Swimming and diving is among the Association's oldest championships, with the men's event having been established in 1937. Each year, almost 20,000 student-athletes take part in swimming, diving and water polo.

SWIMMERS RACE IN A PRELIMINARY HEAT OF THE 100-YARD FREESTYLE DURING THE 2002
DIVISION I WOMEN'S SWIMMING AND DIVING CHAMPIONSHIPS.

AARON PEIRSOL (ABOVE) OF TEXAS COMPETES
IN THE MEN'S 200-YARD BACKSTROKE DURING
THE 2003 DIVISION I MEN'S SWIMMING AND
DIVING CHAMPIONSHIPS.

TARA KIRK (RIGHT) OF STANFORD SWIMS
IN THE 200-YARD BREASTSTROKE DURING
THE 2003 DIVISION I WOMEN'S SWIMMING AND
DIVING CHAMPIONSHIPS.

BEN HOPKINS (FAR RIGHT) OF AMHERST
PERFORMS A DIVE IN THE THREE-METER
SPRINGBOARD COMPETITION DURING THE
2003 DIVISION III MEN'S SWIMMING AND
DIVING CHAMPIONSHIPS.

PHOTO BY ERIK S. LESSER / NCAA PHOTOS

STANFORD GOALIE JACKIE FRANK SAVES A SHOT ON GOAL BY ATTACKER THALIA MUNRO
OF UCLA DURING THE 2002 NATIONAL COLLEGIATE WOMEN'S WATER POLO CHAMPIONSHIP.

CHAPTER SEVEN

THE ARENA

FOR THE NCAA, the present and future challenges look a lot like those of the past. As the Association enters its second century, protecting the principle of educational primacy remains its most fundamental mission. Amateurism, and how to define or refine it, is still on the agenda. So are the challenges of commercialism, governance, academic integrity, financial uncertainty, diversity, external intervention, the role of television and the function of enforcement. The problems associated with recruiting and subsidizing that were formidable before the NCAA was established and that have compelled attention ever since, have not gone away.

TODAY THE WORLD

HOWEVER FAMILIAR THESE challenges may be, the arena in which they must be met differs greatly from what the founders encountered 100 years ago. Then, only football and a few other sports were played, typically by a small complement of white men in a mostly Eastern American geography. The arena expanded as the numbers of sports, member institutions, participants and championships increased; women and minorities became more involved; and the rules were amplified and made more complex. It expanded with the growth of the audience, from small to huge stadiums and from an Eastern to a national perspective. It grew as improvements in transportation made access easier and as radio joined the print media in spreading the word. Television; air travel; economic, political and strategic ties; wars as well; and eventually the Internet made the world a smaller place and the arena a much bigger one. Some American sports found a home overseas, and some overseas athletes found a home on American college campuses. College athletes competed on Olympic teams, either for the U.S., another native country or another adopted homeland.

By the end of the Association's first century, the arena in which it conducted its affairs, dealt with its problems, played its games and recruited its athletes encompassed the planet. In the process, of course, the NCAA became considerably larger. The public could sense the growth, see the games, learn about the athletes and receive abundant news about the problems but still could discern only part of the picture. Much of the Association's work and many of its programs flourished almost unnoticed. This chapter provides a more expansive treatment of previously discussed subjects. The NCAA's handling of 100 years of challenges will be reviewed. Prospects will be discussed. We begin, though, with observations from others on how the Association has fared so far.

SLINGS AND ARROWS

THE NCAA HAS long been a favored subject of adverse commentary. Critics of sundry description have published or otherwise aired their views of Association governance and priorities, policies and practices, decisions, and interpretations. They have pronounced judgment in the halls of ivy and the halls of Congress; on television and radio; and in speeches, treatises, essays, columns, passing paragraphs and simple sentences. Sometimes, just a disparaging word has been sufficient. Lately, the blogisphere has joined the parade.

There are understandable reasons for all this attention. Intercollegiate athletics are a human endeavor. Those who play, coach, administer and govern are as prone to error, or even folly, as the people involved in every other walk of life. The main difference is that collegiate athletics are more visible than most endeavors and inherently more controversial than many. If one's work is both visible and controversial, critics will want to comment on it, especially if the subject's reach is broad as well. The NCAA passes muster on all three counts. Then, too, the Association makes a lot of rules ... and enforces them. People do not usually flock to worship entities — except perhaps for certain churches — whose business it is to regulate behavior and punish miscreants. Given the competitive nature of sport, the heavy emphasis on winning and the resultant urge to gain an edge on the opposition, sports-related misbehavior is more frequent than it ought to be. It's a recurrent feature of athletics his-

BRIAN WILSON OF ILLINOIS SERVES DURING THE 2003 DIVISION I MEN'S TENNIS CHAMPIONSHIPS.

"Let me quote from Shakespeare, who never knew the pleasure of sinking a 20-foot putt, scoring a touchdown, hitting a home run or doing a slam dunk. In 'Troilus and Cressida,' Pandarus says to his agitated niece, 'Be moderate. Be moderate.' These are not exactly words one might expect in issuing a clarion call for integrity in athletics, but they are good advice as we balance athletics within our institutions."
—FROM REMARKS OF FORMER GRAND VALLEY STATE PRESIDENT AREND D. LUBBERS DURING A DIVISION II CHANCELLORS AND PRESIDENTS SUMMIT, JUNE 2005

tory in America. It's almost always newsworthy. It's the reason for the rules. And it brings out the critics — those who find this type of control reprehensible and those who see enforcement as unfair. The NCAA gets its share of criticism from both groups.

Finally, there is that unique and fundamental attribute of American higher education to consider: Colleges and universities in this country have competitive intercollegiate sports programs as a significant institutional responsibility. A century after the NCAA's creation, the union of sport — especially high-profile sport — and academics remains uneasy. Faculty have expressed concern from the beginning. The greatest test of credibility for campus athletics is the strength of this partnership, the extent to which intercollegiate sport adds value (as Myles Brand has put it) to the institution's basic missions. When the link is not strong enough and the value not demonstrable, the institution is called to account, and ought to be. When the problem is of national scope, the NCAA is answerable.

The varied reasons for criticism have given rise to different kinds of critics. Sports journalists and editorialists are often first in line. The growing body of scholarly critiques attests to the significant presence of professorial commentators. Athletics administrators, coaches and supporters sometimes join the reproachful chorus, blaming the Association for rules or penalties that hurt the home institution. Legislators at state and national levels occasionally add their voices to this chorus. The periodic reform efforts of organizations such as the Carnegie Foundation, the ACE, the Knight Commission and, recently, the Mellon Foundation constitute a special category of critical discourse.

The language of criticism runs the range from specialized to general, thoughtful to hyperbolic and constructive to censorious, with slings and arrows the dominant mode. The following examples are illustrative:

PAUL GALLICO

▶ From a book review: "Sometime in the distant future a solid academic study may appear that finds something good to say about the … NCAA. It will not come anytime soon, however. … It is ironic that the more the Association's critics provide well-documented exposes of its failures, excesses and hypocrisies, the more determined this venerable organization becomes in protecting its own turf and the economic interests of its most powerful members." The review was written in support of a book that focuses on "the myth of amateurism" and portrays the Association as "the architect of a nationwide money-laundering scheme."

▶ On a somewhat related subject, the index to a highly critical volume dealing with an earlier era that "helped shape college sports" has a listing for "hypocrisy" under the NCAA entry. The listing shows 39 pages in which the subject of Association hypocrisy is mentioned. The author, a college professor, is a long-time critic of intercollegiate athletics and the organization that governs them.

▶ Another professor takes notice of a passage in the 1997-98 NCAA Manual setting forth as a principal purpose of the Association the maintenance of "intercollegiate athletics as an integral part of the educational program and the athlete as an integral part of the student body …" The author adds: "Some may wonder whom do they think they are kidding."

▶ A well-known journalist, following in the tradition of Paul Gallico, writes that the NCAA "doesn't want to change. It doesn't want to legislate itself out of existence … Everything is nice and tidy just the way it is, thank you. An ethical housecleaning would turn the whole chummy system into chaos, even if it ultimately brought integrity to the game. So let's forget about the NCAA as being anything other than an anchor against progress."

▶ An economist argues that the NCAA is best understood as a "business cartel," resting his case "on the well-established economic principle that characterizes as a cartel producers colluding to restrict output in an effort to raise prices and profits." The theory explains "the restrictions on wages paid to student-athletes" and the methods of "restricting competition and transferring income from consumers (the athletics fans) or employees (the student-athletes) to producers (the athletics departments)." The cartel concept, probably helped along by the Association's major defeats in the football television and restricted-earnings cases, has produced a cottage industry of sorts among NCAA critics. It has become fashionable to use the term as a self-evident description of Association behavior, needing no justification or theoretical framework.

▶ An alternative interpretation has a structural basis, as explained by a journalist who distributes across his recent book an adjectival portrait of the Association as a massive, mammoth, mindless, bloated, unyielding, increasingly powerful, imperial and tyrannical bureaucracy. In simpler terms, as a newspaper columnist suggests, the NCAA is the "autonomous overseer of collegiate sports, which has sometimes made the 1970s era Kremlin look like day camp at the YMCA."

◗ A university president sees the NCAA as "essentially a trade association, with the primary objective of defending the status quo of college sports as a commercial entertainment industry." He sees hope, however, in the advent of presidential dominance in NCAA policy-setting and decision-making.

The Knight Commission's 1991 report, noting that this was its "bedrock conviction," asserted that the Association must be controlled by campus presidents. This control was in place by 1997. The commission was reactivated in 2000, to examine other problems. Thomas Hearn, a veteran member who would later become commission chair, addressed these problems in a speech to the Association of Governing Boards in 2002. He spoke of the movement of intercollegiate athletics toward the "entertainment culture" characteristic of professional sports and of the threat this presents to the historic understanding that athletics programs must be subordinate to the educational mission. Many critics, including those who write of the "myth of amateurism," argue that professionalism in college sports is not a threat but a reality. These critics would likely share the "whom do they think they are kidding" sentiment of the professor who wonders about the sanctity of the marriage between athletics and education. The NCAA leadership, of which Hearn, as an influential member of the Presidents Commission, was once a part, addressed that point as it prepared for the Association's second century.

THE BIGGER PICTURE

DESPITE CLAIMS OF bureaucratic obstructionism, reluctance (or refusal) to change and opposition to progress, the NCAA has a long history of reform. The last quarter century, in particular, has been transformative. Reform has been a constant watchword. The Association arrives at its 100th birthday as a different-looking organization than the one that greeted the 1980s. The governance, programs, policies and people of 2006 are evidence of the successful implementation of the Association's ambitious agenda for change.

The 1974 Hanford report commented on the absence of campus CEOs from any significant role in the governance of intercollegiate athletics. That report, as noted earlier, observed that the presidents had failed in their responsibility to assure "the ethical conduct of college sports." Ten years later, the Presidents Commission had a major presence in the NCAA structure. By 1997, the presidents controlled the Association and each of its divisions, and ethical conduct was much on their minds. Women's sports, excluded from NCAA coverage for 75 years, were brought into the fold in 1981. During the next decades, women gained Association governance and top-level national office staff positions in increasing numbers. The first female president was elected in 1991; the first female chair of the Presidents Commission in 1994. Women have chaired divisional presidents' bodies and the NCAA Executive Committee since the new structure's establishment in 1997. Women's championships now outnumber men's. The Association advanced from staunch opposition to Title IX interpretations in the 1970s and '80s to the adoption of a positive gender-equity report in 1994, then to strong support for Title IX by the turn of the 21st century. Similarly, in governance and hiring processes, policy development and strategic planning, the NCAA has given high priority to the broader goals of diversity and inclusion. Student-athletic well-being, as discussed later, has taken center stage. Academic reforms have been a dominant concern since 1983 and, even at their most controversial, have given both symbolic and substantive recognition to the importance of the educational mission.

Problems remain in all of these areas. Progress in resolving them will be among the transformed NCAA's future principal challenges. The changes of the last 25 years present a record of remarkable accomplishment, especially when measured against the size, complexity, large geography, customary inertia and capacity for conflict that help determine what is possible in the Association's decision-making process. As has been the case with other elements of the organization, this process is often not well understood.

Division I has been the focus of much of the critical literature on the NCAA, with an occa-

NCAA PHOTOS

1995 (May 21) —The University of Maryland, College Park, wins the first of seven straight Division I Women's Lacrosse Championship titles under coach Cindy Timchal.

1995 (May 24) —Federal court judge in Kansas City, Kansas, rules that compensation limits on restricted-earnings basketball coaches are illegal.

1996 (February 13-15) —NCAA Football Rules Committee approves tie-breaker format for regular-season games.

1996 (March 29-April 1) — Pennsylvania State University's Olga Kalinovskaya becomes the only woman to win four straight titles in one event (foil) at the National Collegiate Fencing Championships.

1996 (May 14-18) —Methodist College wins the first of eight women's golf championships team titles (three in combined Divisions II and III competition, and five in Division III competition), including seven straight titles beginning in 1998.

sional nod to the other two divisions. Specifically, it's Division I football and men's basketball that command the interest of commentators. That is where the entertainment culture is most evident and where the primacy of the educational mission gets its sternest test. But this absorption with two sports played at the highest level leaves much of the story untold. Apart from NCAA publications, the bigger picture is mostly missing from news columns and evaluative commentaries. For example, the general public is probably unaware of these important statistics: The number of active members rose to 1,028 in 2004. Division I-A members, which dominate the news, numbered 117 that year. The rest of the Association — the remainder of Division I plus 281 in Division II and 421 in Division III — accounted for nearly 90 percent of the active members. That is part of the bigger picture.

The NCAA sponsored its first championship (track and field) in 1921. During 2003-04, the Association administered 88 championships in 23 sports and three divisions (44 women, 41 men and three coed), at a cost of $61.2 million. There were 48,847 participants, almost evenly divided between men and women. Sixty-six institutions brought home championship trophies. During the year, approximately 360,000 student-athletes took part in intercollegiate competition. These numbers, too, are a component of the bigger picture.

Words often do not adhere over time to their original meaning. Such is the case with the term "student-athlete," which was invented in the 1950s when the possibility arose that college football players could be determined to be institutional employees by courts and other state agencies. Byers said that, as a consequence, the expression "was embedded in all NCAA rules as a mandated substitute for such words as players and athletes." Critics, taking note of the term's less-than-immaculate conception, view continued use by the Association and its members with a cynical eye. However, within the NCAA and on the campuses, the student-athlete label has progressed well beyond its origins. It is not generally understood as a way around the employee designation. It simply has a practical application, and it helps protect the indispensable link between athletics and education. Critics have performed a useful service in citing many cases where this tie has been loosened to the point at which exploitation better describes the relationship.

Numerous initiatives have been launched in the last decade and a half to strengthen the position of student-athletes on the campuses and in the governance of the Association. In the late 1980s, Richard Schultz helped establish Student-Athlete Advisory Committees (SAACs) for each NCAA division. SAAC members soon were appointed — eventually as voting members — to other Association committees and won the right to speak on the Convention floor (and used it). The SAAC idea also took root on individual campuses where, among their other responsibilities, members served on athletics certification committees and were interviewed by visiting evaluation teams. A standard on student-athlete welfare was included in the certification legislation passed in 1993.

Cedric Dempsey made clear from the start of his tenure as the NCAA's chief executive officer that student-athletes were his first priority. His State of the Association Addresses frequently emphasized this point. A greatly expanded Principle of Student-Athlete Welfare was set forth in the NCAA constitution one year after his appointment. Student-athletes were given significant coverage in his 2002 Will to Act series of position papers on the key issues confronting the organization. Dempsey believed, and often stated, that "student-athletes are at the heart of our decision-making." But he was not naïve about the difficulty of pursuing what he called this "unassailable" priority. "Striking a balance … between academic success and athletics access," he said, "is a formidable exercise." His consistent advocacy had an impact on campuses. Institutional CEOs cited student-athlete welfare as the principal issue facing the NCAA in polling connected with a major Association research project between 1999 and 2002. Dempsey's successor has continued the commitment. "Student-athletes come first," Brand said during his initial year as Association president. "The NCAA has to be focused on student-athletes, focused on the conditions under which they play, but also on education." He observed in his first State of the Association address that, "In the end, it is all about the student-athlete."

The enhanced standing of student-athletes is also a part, for critics a largely unremarked part, of the bigger picture. Rhetoric alone does not suffice to validate this claim. The creation of various programs bolsters the case, as do financial allocations. The catastrophic-insurance initiative, for example, was instituted in 1992, covers all student-athletes at active member institutions and provides up to $20 million in lifetime benefits. The NCAA pays an annual premium of approximately $10 million. Each year, a significant share of the Association dollars expended through the conferences is earmarked for programs for student-athletes. During 2003-04, the figure was more than $30 million. The Student-Athlete Opportunity Fund, which is available to families as well, is another case in point. In its first year, $17 million was available in this fund, which is scheduled to increase at a rate of 13 percent annually. The Special Assistance Fund, initiated in 1994-95, helps student-athletes with demonstrated financial need. During the first 10 years of its existence, it provided $84 million of aid to more than 200,000 recipients. The NCAA assisted nearly 26,000 student-athletes under this program during 2003-04 alone. The Association allocated $17.5 million that year for academic-support services at the institutional level. Among the several other benefit programs (including internships, postgraduate scholarships, and the previously mentioned ethnic minority and women's enhancement awards) is degree-completion funding for those who have exhausted their athletics eligibility and are within one year of finishing their academic work. Through 2004-05, the Division I program expended more than $11 million in a 18-year period to assist more than 1,800 recipients. Their graduation rate was 95 percent. Every spring since 1997, the NCAA has invited more than 300 student-athletes to attend a national leadership conference. These men and women are ethnically diverse, represent all three divisions, and compete in a variety of sports. Thus far, nearly 3,000 athletes have been involved. All of these programs and activities are part of the substantial effort undertaken in recent years, both on campuses and in conference offices, as well as by the NCAA, to make student-athletes the Association's highest priority. It's a story that needs telling. It's the biggest part of the bigger picture.

There is one more component of that picture to discuss here. It's another function whose focus is on student-athletes and, in a measure, it is 100 years old. The NCAA was born out of a growing concern about the deaths and severe injuries attributed to football. Rules changes eliminated the flying wedge and its mass-play cousins. As noted previously, this concern was serious enough that for a decade after the first Convention the Association issued an annual report on football fatalities. The 1920s push for mandatory physical education programs in colleges and high schools was partially a product of concern for the health and safety of those who played the game. But, apart from making rules and occasional pronouncements, the NCAA could not do much because it had no staff and little money until the 1950s. It is instructive that late in that decade (1958), the Committee on Competitive Safeguards and Medical Aspects of Sports (CSMAS) was formed, but nearly two decades passed before a full-time staff person was hired. The position was assigned responsibility then for research in general, to be carried out through small grants to faculty researchers at the member campuses. Many of these grants covered health and safety — catastrophic and fatal injuries; equipment standards; and a comprehensive, well-developed illness/injury reporting system that became an important source of information and assistance to the campuses. The Association published its first Sports-Medicine Handbook in 1977. Substance abuse and drug-testing were major items of concern in the early 1980s. NCAA drug-testing became mandatory in 1986. Health and safety became a significant element of a broader research program.

The controversy that followed the passage of Proposition 48 added an important component to the program. The angry response to this legislation — specifically its reliance on standardized tests and cutoff scores — led the Council to form the Special Committee on Academic Research to study the academic preparation of student-athletes. This research, which demonstrated Proposition 48's decidedly adverse impact on Blacks, caused the Council and Presidents Commission to delay full implementation until 1988. With the legislation in effect at that point, and Ursula Walsh installed as the Association's first director of research in 1985, Professor John McArdle was recruited as the leader of a team of outside researchers. The importance of this group's longitudinal analysis was underscored by the contentious passage and implementation of Proposition 16 in 1996. As noted in Chapter Six, the work of this team resulted in a decision to eliminate the controversial cutoff score provision — the heart of the matter with both propositions — in 2002. The Division I Board of Directors then initiated a new approach to academic

1997 (January 13) —Membership restructuring is approved; new governance structure implemented in August. The new structure provides a more federated means of governance, along a greater leadership role for chief executive officers.

1997 (May 30-June 1) —The **University of Washington** wins the first Division I Women's Rowing Championships.

1998 (March 19-21) —Richard Quick coaches a team to the Division I Women's Swimming and Diving Championships title for the 12th time (five times at the University of Texas at Austin, then seven times at Stanford University).

1998 (March 21) —Washington University of St. Louis wins the first of four straight Division III Women's Basketball Championship titles under coach **Nancy Fahey**.

1998 (May 4) —Federal court judge awards $67 million to plaintiffs in restricted-earnings case; NCAA and plaintiffs subsequently announce $54 million settlement.

Building Skills

The NCAA Leadership Conference provides student-athletes with a forum to openly discuss issues that may affect them on their campuses and in their communities while also providing them with the opportunity to enhance their leadership, communication, decision-making and problem-solving skills. The attendees represent Divisions I, II and III and fall, winter and spring sports.

NCAA PHOTOS

1998 (June 6) —Sixty-eight records are broken or tied as the **University of Southern California** defeats Arizona State University, 21-14, in the Division I Baseball Championship title game.

1999 (March 12-13) —Wheaton College (Massachusetts) wins the first of five straight Division III Women's Indoor Track Championships team titles under coach Paul Souza.

1999 (March 20) —The University of North Dakota wins its third straight Division II Women's Basketball Championship title, making it the seventh straight year a team from the same state won the championship (North Dakota State won four straight times beginning in 1993).

1999 (May 17) —Brigham Young University, Hawaii, wins the first of five Division II Women's Tennis Championships team titles between 1999 and 2004 under coach Dave Porter.

eligibility, described later in this chapter, and turned to the research staff and McArdle's team to develop the analysis that would undergird this approach.

With the academic-eligibility studies supplying some of the basic building material and the health and safety element achieving high-priority standing, the NCAA's research program has become a substantial enterprise. A wealth of data has been generated during the last two decades on academic performance, graduation rates, substance use and abuse, revenues and expenses of athletics departments, race demographics, progress toward equity, and student-athlete gambling behavior. Policy decisions often rely heavily on these data. Sports-medicine research now covers a multitude of subjects. The Committee on Competitive Safeguards and Medical Aspects of Sports is responsible for studies of HIV, eating disorders, nutrition, nutritional supplements, wrestling, weight-loss regimes, concussions, depression, anterior cruciate ligament injuries and baseball bat characteristics. This committee also deals with matters such as equitable medical treatment for male and female student-athletes, health insurance, coach and athlete education programs, spring football practice injury rates, and lightning safety as a component of event management. Plans and legislation are developed from the research on health and safety issues. Recently, the Association embarked on a longitudinal examination of the lifelong impact of participating in athletics, possibly the most ambitious project yet undertaken by the research division. Research has a high priority in the NCAA. It, too, is a significant part of the bigger picture.

THREE-PART HARMONY

WHEN THE ISSUE of federation came before the Special Convention of 1973, the Association had 664 active members. Serious concern had arisen about disparate institutional size, decreasing commonality of mission, equitability of access to championships and the old problem of maintaining a level playing field. Unhappiness over the distribution of television wealth, addressed earlier, was also a factor and would soon become a larger one. The earlier effort to reorder the membership into two divisions had failed because two was a number insufficient to meet a growing need. This spawned the Association's first Special Convention in 67 years, which gave added significance to the demand for federation. Three divisions resulted from this Convention. In the succeeding decades, many have wondered whether three were enough.

The basic differences among the three were clear. Division I programs featured substantial sports sponsorship and scholarship numbers, national as well as regional recruitment and competition, an intra-division scheduling emphasis, attendance considerations, and a presumption of reliance on self-generated financial support. Division II institutions had a regional focus, fewer sports, major institutional funding and significant numbers of local or in-state student-athletes paying for a large share of the costs of their education. In Division III, the governing philosophy owed much to precepts cherished by the NCAA's founders: no athletics grants-in-aid, no distinctions between student-athletes and other students, and sports programs conducted not for the general public but for the competitors and the campus community. These broad divisional operating principles have provided a structure within which the NCAA has been able to grow in both membership and complexity. However, challenges within and between the divisions have tested this structure's viability. Periodic adjustments have been made. The fundamental question of handling these challenges while retaining a commitment to Association welfare has been put forward on more than one occasion.

When it became apparent in the late 1970s that, at least for Division I, further structural change was necessary, subdivision was the answer. Football (and its television dollars) was the driving force, and I-A and I-AA were the result. The I-AA label was applied solely to distinguish between levels of football participation. The institutions within Division I that did not sponsor football needed their own subdivisional designation. The creation of I-AAA was a response to that need. The subdivision boundary lines, particularly between I-A and I-AA have been revisited periodically. The I-A schools have wanted to protect against increases in the number of their I-AA compatriots moving up. Members of I-AA have been concerned about the incorrect public perception that the double-A designation extends beyond football to other sports, in that way consigning the subdivision to a lower overall standing. An effort by a Division I football study committee in 2001-02 to tighten I-A membership criteria also produced some I-AA enhancements. It soon became clear that the stricter criteria, especially for attendance, would likely force a number of I-A institutions out of the subdivision. The Division I Board of Directors softened the standards in 2005 and provided a significant scheduling benefit for I-AA. In addition, the Board discussed whether the subdivision labels needed to be abandoned in favor of an unqualified Division I classification. The membership criteria and postseason championship provisions differentiating I-A from I-AA would be retained, but not the separate designations. The I-AAA terminology would also disappear, though again the regulations applicable to non-football-playing institutions would remain. The nomenclature changes were under study at the time of publication.

Just as Division I has struggled with classification issues, Division III periodically has considered subdivision arrangements. Division II faced the prospect of losing members to Division I, where those reclassifying (or thinking about the possibility) often presumed that both higher status and additional dollars awaited. And the more highly federated NCAA established under the 1997 restructuring legislation, while working reasonably well, had other issues with which to contend.

When the three divisions were created in 1973, 237 institutions elected Division I membership, 194 opted for II and 233 for III. The numbers in 2004 were 326, 281 and 421, respectively. Of the Association's 1,028 members that year, 41 percent were in Division III. There had been a steady increase in all divisions over three decades, but Division III, at 83 percent, was the clear leader. Although other factors were involved, growth brought problems to this division. Size of enrollment, diversity of mission and numbers of sports created a range of differences that made consistent interpretation and applications of the Division III philosophy more challenging. An enhanced interest in championship competition complicated matters in a variety of ways: A greater emphasis on winning developed, to improve chances of selection for postseason games. Commitment to the concept of treating athletes the same as other students weakened. Conference membership grew in some instances not on the basis of shared philosophy or geographic proximity but because regular-season champions in most cases automatically qualified for postseason play. Issues associated with Division I, such as redshirting and longer playing and practice seasons, became priority concerns for Division III. Increasingly, questions have been raised about financial aid practices. The division philosophy has been the membership cornerstone from the beginning. The principle of awarding no financial assistance based on athletics ability is a central component of that philosophy. Growth in all its forms puts all of the division's principles at risk. Finding ways to reduce the risk and reaffirm the principles became a major reform objective.

In 2001, the Andrew W. Mellon Foundation entered the reform picture. William Bowen, the foundation's president and former CEO of Princeton, co-authored a book ("The Game of Life: College Sports and Educational Values") with James Shulman based on a historical study of undergraduate students at 30 academically selective institutions. Study subjects included Division I-AA public and private universities, along with four Ivy Group I-AA schools and a number of Division III institutions. The authors found a wide and growing divide between the "intense athletics enterprise" and the "core teaching-research function" of selective institutions. A second volume, with Bowen and Sarah Levin as principal authors, appeared in 2003 ("Reclaiming the Game: College Sports and Educational Values"). This book is based on a "data-driven" study of students from 33 schools, 25 of them selective Division III colleges and universities. The other eight are Ivy members. The subjects — nearly 28,000 of them — represented both athletics and the general student population. Recruited athletes were compared with all others. The study revealed major differences across a range of measures, including recruitment itself. This practice has become more intensive everywhere, the authors reported, and "there is no counterpart, outside of athletics, to the time and resources devoted to recruiting athletes." The extensive evidence gathered for this study suggests that student-athletes at the nation's most academically prestigious institutions are not representative of the overall student body. Their classroom performance is alleged to be poorer, and an athletics "culture" is thought to separate them from fellow students. This divide, like the related separation of academic and athletics functions in general, is said to be growing. While many commentators dispute the books' methodologies and conclusions, no one denies that the issues they raise are real ones.

WILLIAM BOWEN

PHOTO COURTESY MELLON FOUNDATION

1999 (July 27) —NCAA relocates national office to Indianapolis.

1999 (November 18) —NCAA and CBS agree to $6 billion, 11-year contract for rights to Division I Men's Basketball Championship and other championships, including marketing opportunities.

1999 (December 11) —Northwest Missouri State wins its second straight Division II Football Championship title with a four-overtime, 58-52 victory in the final against Carson-Newman College in Florence, Alabama.

2000 (May 31-June 3) —Seilala Sua of the University of California, Los Angeles, becomes the first six-time career individual titlist at the Division I Women's Outdoor Track and Field Championships with victories in the discus and shot put.

2000 (October 27) —A new "blue disc" NCAA logo featuring a modern typeface is created to provide a "greater feeling of action and movement."

2001 (March 17) —Iowa State University's Cael Sanderson (a three-time winner at 184 pounds before capping his career with a victory at 197 pounds) joins Oklahoma State University's Pat Smith as the only four-time individual champions at the Division I Wrestling Championships.

The College Sports Project (CSP), established in 2003 with Mellon support, grew from findings of the two studies co-authored by Bowen. Its objectives are to assure that athletes "are first and foremost students" and that "athletics administrators and coaches … embrace their roles as educators." Toward these inter-related ends — "representation" and "integration" in shorthand form — the CSP has held a series of meetings with college and university presidents and expressed strong interest in making Division III the focus of major reform. The NCAA has been represented at these meetings, and the Mellon efforts have helped advance the reform agenda initiated by the Division III Presidents Council in 2002. This agenda, called the Future of Division III, was developed with widespread participation by members and strong leadership from institutional CEOs. Although some of the changes proposed were similar to those sought by the CSP, complications abounded in adapting ideas suited to highly selective institutions to a constellation of 400-plus colleges and universities representing a considerable range of selectivity and great variety in size, scope and athletics ambition.

In its first set of proposals, put before the 2004 Convention, the Presidents Council looked toward bringing certain policies and practices into closer alignment with Division III philosophy. After extensive discussion, and with a large number of presidents participating, Convention voters adopted seven of the Council's nine recommended reforms. The voters also created a financial aid reporting system, implemented in 2005, to ensure that grants awarded to student-athletes are consistent with those awarded to the general student body. Failure to submit the required report can result in a denial of access to both championship participation and the Division III grants program. If after review an institution does not adequately justify its financial aid practices and the problem is a persistent one, the matter can be reported to NCAA enforcement services. In addition to the new reporting (and compliance) system, the delegates in 2004 decided to eliminate redshirting and shorten playing and practice seasons. Further proposals for change would come at the Centennial Convention, based again on substantial discussion during the intervening two years. The second round of reform, preceded by a survey of member views, dealt with growth management, championship access, conference affiliation, and, to some extent, the representation and integration questions emphasized by the CSP. The growth of the division has placed championship issues near the top of the agenda because Division III is so large that tournaments may become too long, causing participants to miss more class time, or include too many games. The long-standing argument over the appropriateness of a national championship emphasis will receive attention, as will the alternative of giving primacy to in-season competition and conference championships. Relatedly, the division is searching for ways to inhibit growth — either through a cap on membership or less rigid means — in hopes of heading off new movement toward subdivision. The subdivision question has been debated for years, but, again, growth and its challenges threaten to bring it to the fore. Survey findings suggest reasonably strong opposition to subdivision, but also a significant minority in favor. A group of liberal arts colleges, influenced by the Bowen studies and CSP initiatives, has indicated that a "legitimate" Division III could be achieved by 100 to 150 such institutions. Remaining current members would choose between Divisions I and II, or perhaps at some point even a fourth division.

A greatly reduced Division III membership seems unlikely but, coincidentally, Division II has reached a point at which it would welcome new members. Not long ago, as The NCAA News reported, that division considered itself "filled to overflowing." It had initiated "an aggressive examination of how to manage potentially explosive — and perhaps harmful — membership growth." When Division III approved an increased sports- sponsorship requirement, it proved difficult for a number of institutions to meet. Division II, with a less demanding sponsorship rule, seemed an attractive alternative. A larger concern was membership attrition from the National Association of Intercollegiate Athletics. The NAIA had lost

40 percent of its members since the mid-1970s, many joining the NCAA. Division II became a desirable destination, a trend that showed signs of continuing and perhaps accelerating. The NCAA received more than 30 requests for provisional membership in 2000, and 35 other schools were already in the provisional qualification process. Serious funding issues were in the offing. And, since some Division II institutions sponsored nonscholarship football, it seemed possible that enough Division III members could join them that Division II might be forced to create football subdivisions.

The anticipated growth crisis did not materialize. The NCAA declared a two-year moratorium on accepting new members and established a project team to study growth. Strengthened sports-sponsorship, financial aid and provisional-membership requirements were enacted. No large-scale Division III migration occurred. The NAIA attrition problem stabilized. Between 2000 and 2004, Division II added 17 active members (institutions, mostly, that had already been in provisional status when the moratorium was established). In four years, the division grew 6.4 percent, slightly more than the total Association rate. It had begun a strategic planning effort in 1999 and assembled an updated version in 2004. Membership was among the priority components. Division II has worked hard to define its identity. Six years after it reached a critical point in handling the prospect of rapid growth, its chief concern at this juncture is losing members. Many institutions are moving, or thinking about moving, to Division I. Some of these institutions have long-standing ties to Division II and have helped shape an understanding of the division's place in the NCAA. Some are in regions where other institutions not interested in leaving are forced to consider the option anyway. The stability of certain Division II conferences has been shaken by the loss of key members. Division I-AA and I-AAA conferences have come looking to add to their own memberships. Division II has lost 10 members during the last few years. Although the total number for the division has not yet been adversely affected, it is clear that could happen.

Money, as noted earlier, is a major concern in these decisions. Through their conferences, Division I-A members receive much greater dollar allocations than other members. Additional enticements include enhanced visibility and the sense that a Division I classification adds to institutional prestige. A perception that improved academic standing comes with a move to Division I also plays a role and further whets the appetites of fans, governing board members and political leaders for a change of divisional scenery. At the other end of the Division II spectrum, members concerned about strained finances proposed a reduction in the number of permitted football equivalencies from 36 to 24. If approved, this reduction almost certainly would have caused further attrition by wealthier members to Division I. The proposal was defeated at the 2005 Convention, but the financial challenges remain for the institutions that sponsored it. The possibility of subdividing has therefore re-entered the discourse.

In 2005, the Division II leadership commissioned a study to determine, in part, whether the likely result of reclassification to Division I is a greater reliance on institutional, nonathletics funding to cover the increased expenses. The study also examined other financial questions. Research results were reported to the first Division II Chancellors and Presidents Summit in June. The report found that the average Division II program with football has annual revenue of approximately $2.6 million and expenses of $2.7 million. These averages are nearly $5 million less than the relevant figures for Division I-AA. The percentage of total institutional spending (2.6 percent) in Division II is less than that in I-AA (3.6 percent). The study examined 20 institutions that had moved from Division II to I-AA during the period 1994-2002. Perhaps the most important findings were that increases in football spending by those institutions did not equate to an increase in winning records or in additional football revenues. At the bottom line, the study revealed no economic benefits in moving up, given an average increase in spending ($3.7 million) compared with a $2.5 million jump in revenue. About 80 percent of the revenue growth came in the form of institutional support, state support and student fees. These data, one expects, will become part of the analysis institutions undertake as they consider the possibility of joining Division I. It will also be important for these institutions to bear in mind that, as some former Division II schools have learned, finding a conference home in Division I can be a daunting task.

Dealing with the growth and migration facing all three NCAA divisions has been further complicated by a basic rule of federation: Each division sets its own membership criteria. Beyond a threat to this or that division is the overall question of whether the Association itself is placed in jeopardy. Division II believes this possibility may be at hand and has relayed that concern to the Executive Committee. President Brand has taken the position that "the primary issue … is the effect each division's identity search — and the resulting migration from one division to another — has on the NCAA." He noted that the identity matter is not confined to athletics, that aspirations change for institutions in general and that the desire to "rise up" may seem irresistible. However, it can be ill-advised. The will to excel is worthy, he said, but moving up a perceived hierarchy does not automatically raise the status of an institution. Rather, Brand advised, institutional mission should determine athletics affiliation. Member colleges and universities should "strive to excel within that context."

From a governance perspective, the Association clearly works best when its three divisions work together. Altering the basic rule of federation may be impossible, but the Executive Committee, whose focus is on the welfare of the entire Association, might be able to lend a hand in applying Brand's counsel to determining who belongs where in the NCAA divisional scheme, and why. That would be a proper exercise in achieving three-part harmony.

CALLS FOR REFORM

THE DIVISIONAL IDENTITY issues, and the difficulties of growth and migration, are another part of the NCAA story that commands relatively little public interest. These matters are not the stuff of headlines. Discussions of them do not usually appear above the fold in the sports sections of daily newspapers or as lead items on the sports segments of television news shows. Much of the information about Divisions II and III is limited to either NCAA publications or the hometown/home-state media of the member institutions. Division I is where the public's attention is, and much of it is focused on I-A, where visibility is greatest, stakes highest and temptations strongest. It houses the six conferences that dominate football rankings and the BCS, and the institutions that have long enjoyed ascendancy in postseason basketball. The temptations are also the hardest to resist in I-A. During the 27 years from the beginning of subdivisions (1978) through 2004, the Association levied penalties in 340 enforcement cases. Division I-A institutions were involved in 194 (57 percent). Division I, including all three subdivisions, accounted for 295 (87 percent). Division II colleges and universities were involved in 35, or 10 percent. In Division III, over all those years, only 10 infractions cases reached the penalty stage. One I-A institution was punished seven times. A second had six violations and two others had five. Seven universities from I-A had four cases and 18 had three. The seriousness of the infractions and the severity of the penalties varied widely; however, probation was among the sanctions in 87 percent of the I-A cases.

Painful front-page stories often lay behind these statistics. Coaches, players, administrators, boosters, trustees and presidents have been implicated. Viewed from another perspective, these were old stories — restatements in effect of tales told for a century. Cheating scandals have always helped fuel reform in intercollegiate athletics. Other factors usually have provided momentum, too: concerns about exploitation of student-athletes, for example, or a desire to return to the ideals of an earlier era. In the first years of the 21st century, the scandals have been joined with — perhaps even overshadowed by — a host of troublesome developments that have energized reformist impulses. Reform agendas abound, though their priorities and directions may differ. Some see change as coming necessarily from outside the NCAA. The target, for most, is Division I, particularly I-A. Explicitly or implicitly, the over-riding emphasis is on the academics-athletics relationship. One view is that this relationship has been lost, perhaps beyond recovery. Another is that it is under threat, as it has always been. A third is that the collegiate model, in which education is the linchpin, is at a crossroads. During 2003, and in the months immediately before and after that year, a series of painful occurrences spotlighted the nether side of college sports.

In October 2002, following a faculty no-confidence vote, the president of Gardner-Webb resigned. Two years earlier — acting, he said, on the basis of what was fair for the student-athlete involved — he ordered that an F be removed from the transcript of a star men's basketball player. In March 2003, the president of Fresno State decided to withhold his regular-season conference champion men's basketball team from postseason competition because of allegations of academic fraud against players and staff from previous years. That same month, St. Bonaventure made the same decision and forfeited six regular-season games for using an ineligible player. Shortly thereafter, the institution's CEO resigned when it was divulged that he had ruled eligible a basketball player who had a certificate in welding, but no required associate's degree, from a community college he previously attended. Later, in an apparently related incident, the chair of the university's Board of Trustees committed suicide.

Also in March, Georgia fired an assistant men's basketball coach, suspended his father (the head coach) and removed the team from postseason play. The head coach resigned amid charges of academic fraud, payments to players and other infractions. The men's basketball coach at Baylor and the school's athletics director resigned in August, after the disappearance and death of a player and assertions of rule-breaking. Within a week, a newspaper published the contents of tape transcripts of the coach requesting his players and assistants to tell investigators that the murdered player had been a drug dealer whose death was related to that crime, which was false. In September, the Baylor faculty voted no-confidence in the institution's president. The next month, a booster charged with paying a high school coach $150,000 to direct one of his players to Alabama was indicted by a federal grand jury. He was eventually convicted of bribing a public servant, sentenced to six months in prison and ordered to pay $96,100 in restitution for structuring bank withdrawals to hide a crime. It was revealed in November that Auburn's president, accompanied by two members of his governing board, traveled secretly to Louisville to offer the head football coach there the Auburn position. Neither Louisville officials nor the Auburn head coach, who had not been fired (and subsequently remained in the job), were aware of the trip or the offer.

Shortly after the New Year, a football recruiting scandal at Colorado — involving the use of sex and alcohol to attract players to the university — became a major national news story. After an inquiry by the Colorado Board of Regents and the implementation of a new policy on recruiting, both the president and the director of athletics resigned. The head football coach, initially placed on administrative leave, was allowed to continue in his position. An independent commission determined that while players had participated in the recruitment practices, no coach or administrator had approved them.

Numerous other problems surfaced in 2003 regarding the behavior of players and coaches and covering a multitude of illegal or otherwise inappropriate actions and demeanors. This also was the year when the long-expected falling of the membership dominoes from one conference to another to another finally happened. The Atlantic Coast Conference took three members of the Big East, which in turn recruited five institutions from Conference USA. C-USA then added four Western Athletic Conference (WAC) universities and one from the Mid-American Conference. The WAC brought in three members of the Sun Belt Conference. Nearly 14 percent of the I-A membership changed conference affiliation. Whatever the rationale(s) for all the changes — money, stature, television exposure, survival — media reaction was generally negative. The NCAA, of course, had no involvement in any of the changes and no authority to intervene. But the Association does play the lightning-rod role, as Byers maintained, when college sports are under attack. Fairly or not, with all of the transgressions and controversial transactions of this period, the Association had to deal with some of the public expressions of dismay. When reform took wing in the early years of the 21st century, it was therefore logical that the NCAA would help lead the effort.

Although the Mellon/Bowen books are mainly about the challenge of maintaining educational primacy at selective Division III institutions, their findings are an admonition to Division I as well. If the collegiate bond is fraying at these schools, where athletics scholarships are prohibited, the challenge to maintain that tie is likely to be much greater where heavy stress is placed on public exposure, big dollars and big victories. In light of that challenge, the Knight Commission, reactivated in 2000, observed in its 2001 report that the situation had reached a critical point. While changes in the NCAA — presidential control, academic and fiscal integrity, and certification of Division I athletics programs — had been helpful, the problems, the report suggested, could no longer be resolved within the organization. These changes, though embraced by the Knight Commission in previous years, were now characterized as modest. More was needed, and to provide it, the commission proposed the creation of a Coalition of Presidents, financially independent of the NCAA and the major I-A conferences. This group would deal with education reform, "arms race" spending and the excesses of commercialism. A number of other targets for reform,

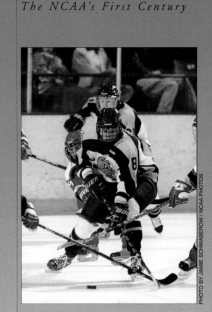

2001 (March 25) —First National Collegiate Women's Ice Hockey Championship is played in Minneapolis, where the **University of Minnesota, Duluth**, wins the first of three straight championships under coach Shannon Miller.

2001 (May 13) —The University of California, Los Angeles, wins the first National Collegiate Women's Water Polo Championship title.

2001 (May 24-26) —Rhondale Jones of Lincoln University (Pennsylvania) wins three events at the Division III Women's Outdoor Track and Field Championships to finish her career with a record nine titles in outdoor competition.

2002 (March 9) —First Division III Women's Ice Hockey Championship is played at Elmira, New York, where Elmira College wins the first of two consecutive championships.

2002 (May 28) —Eastern Connecticut State University becomes the first team to win four Division III Baseball Championship titles, all under coach Bill Holowaty.

2003 (January 1) —Myles Brand of Indiana University, Bloomington, becomes fourth NCAA president, succeeding Dempsey. He is the first institutional CEO to serve in the position.

2004 (January 12) —Division III delegates approve most of a landmark "Future of Division III" legislative package, including measures to create an electronic financial aid reporting process and eliminate the practice of "redshirting."

2004 (February 4) —The NCAA announces an agreement with the Indiana Sports Corporation making Indianapolis the permanent "backup site" for the Men's and Women's Final Fours in case of an emergency that requires those events to be relocated, and ensuring that the city frequently will host the Association's high-profile championships and Convention.

2004 (April 5-6) —The University of Connecticut becomes the first Division I institution to win men's and women's basketball titles in the same year. It is the third consecutive title for the women's team.

including coaches' compensation, scholarship reductions, advertising limitations and the length of sports seasons, also were proposed. The participation of other entities — the NCAA, ACE and AGB, for example — was encouraged. As for the Association, the commission reported that "time has demonstrated … (that) the NCAA … cannot independently do what needs to be done." It has "a near-irreconcilable conflict" between its responsibilities to enforce the rules and to generate large revenues for the membership.

In the early 1990s, the Knight recommendations received a positive public reception, and — though just who provided the principal impetus for reform may be disputable — the commission's proposed changes were implemented by the NCAA. In 2001, however, the new proposals led to a less-than-enthusiastic response. The ACE indicated it would help the suggested coalition get started. The Association of Governing Boards (AGB) appointed a committee to study the matter and 18 months later chose a different road to reform. The head of the American Association of State Colleges and Universities (Constantine Curris) criticized both the commission and its recommendations. "Simply stated," he wrote, "there is not much here." He viewed the fundamental problem as the "extraordinary infusion of dollars" into intercollegiate athletics, with "little benefit to student-athletes and virtually no financial benefit to the academic enterprise." Besides, he added, the NCAA is still "the primary and perhaps only vehicle to effect reform" and its effectiveness would be undercut by the proposed Coalition of Presidents. A group of campus CEOs from the six major I-A conferences met with the Knight leaders but did not endorse any of the report's suggestions. The Division I Board of Directors, meeting six weeks later, rejected the coalition proposal. The chair, William Kirwan of Ohio State, said "the Board is the appropriate body to drive the reform efforts."

Robert Atwell, former ACE president and a long-time supporter of athletics reform, complimented the Knight Commission's exposition of the issues but was skeptical of its recommendations. "Isn't it time for would-be reformers of big-time intercollegiate athletics," he wrote, "to admit defeat, fold their tents, go home and concentrate on the real business of education?" There is just too much standing in the way:

> It is hopeless to imagine that big-time college sports will ever return to the amateur student-athlete model for which we are so nostalgic. The commercial interests are too powerful and the booster fanaticism is too overwhelming for any lonely band of university presidents — usually unsupported by their boards or faculty and opposed by alumni and other fans — to overcome them.

Atwell proposed an option whereby the revenue-producing sports in Division I (football and men's basketball in most cases) would be separated from the other sports, their players hired, paid a market wage and enrolled as students only if they wished. In this way, he concluded, "it would finally be acknowledged that, when it comes to big-time sports, many higher education institutions are in the entertainment, not the education, business."

Dempsey appeared before the Knight Commission shortly after it resumed operations. He was a member now, as his predecessor had been (and still was). He provided a "scorecard" showing the NCAA's progress in meeting the goals and principles the commission had set forth in its 1991 report. Dempsey expressed concern regarding speculation that the commission was back in business because the NCAA had "failed to adequately address the issues the original group identified." As the scorecard demonstrated, he said, "that was not the case." Later, he described the commission's "A Call to Action" report as having painted an "overly broad and dark … picture of intercollegiate athletics …" He noted, though, that "the truest stroke" of the report might be the challenge it issued: "The search now is for the will to act." Accordingly, Dempsey, in his waning months as Association president, titled his comprehensive message of reform to the membership "The Will to Act Project." Despite his disagreement with at least some of the Knight conclusions and recommendations, he took a firm line in introducing the 13 essays:

> *Although there will be disagreements over the details, it is clear that college*
> *presidents at NCAA member institutions are frustrated and even embarrassed*
> *by too large a number of highly publicized issues that at best advertise a*
> *a blatant hypocrisy and at worst represent negligent contempt for the mission*
> *and good name of higher education. Low graduation rates among high-profile*
> *athletes, escalating salaries for the most elite of football and basketball*
> *coaches, the tension between the amateur status of student-athletes and the*
> *drive for commercial dollars are among the concerns that the public, media*
> *and university administrators all note when they describe the failure of*
> *intercollegiate athletics to live up to its values. All agree that serious attention*
> *to meaningful reform in a number of areas is required.*

In October 1999, faculty members, journalists and others from around the country met in Des Moines, Iowa, to discuss the abolition of corruption in intercollegiate athletics. The participants decided on a name: the Drake Group (formally, the National Alliance for Collegiate Athletics Reform, or NAFCAR). The organization gained a certain national standing, in part perhaps because of some provocative ideas proposed by its members or other meeting participants: One was establishing a super conference of 30 to 35 institutions exempt from academic regulations and prepared to pursue athletics as a professional enterprise. Another was reconstituting the NCAA as an organization of faculty, academic deans and provosts, becoming to the extant NCAA "what anti-matter is to matter." A third was retiring the term "student-athlete" and replacing it with "student." Eventually, the group's priorities included more familiar proposals such as a 2.000 GPA requirement for continuing eligibility; a one-year no-participation mandate for freshmen and transfers; and the elimination of one-year renewable scholarships in favor of need-based financial aid. Even so, the Drake Group, which is still active, retains its image as being well disposed to reforms advanced by the Association's harshest critics.

Other faculty organizations looked toward different solutions to what all involved seemed to agree were serious problems. The Faculty Athletics Representatives Association, speaking through members of its executive committee, expressed concern about the Knight Commission's 2001 recommendations. The Knight focus on Division I-A, the FARA members wrote, failed "to recognize the positive experiences and academic achievements of the vast majority of students who play sports in all three divisions …" Moreover, the commission entrusted "primary responsibility for reform in the very hands under which the problems intensified." Faculty, FARA said, "must be at the center of reform because academics are the center of their existence, and they are the group with the most liberty to act independently." Galvanizing higher education behind the agenda for reform means that presidents (and others) must recognize "how much the independence and academic focus of faculty are critical to the project."

The FARA leaders' statement was evidence of a significant stirring in the ranks of faculty groups as the issues highlighted by Dempsey, the Knight Commission and the critical literature gained (or regained) national prominence. Within six months of each other in 2001, faculty senate groups in the Pacific-10 and Big Ten Conferences announced their support for major reforms. In May 2003, the Association of Southeastern Conference Faculty Leaders was formed, with changes in mind and a substantial faculty role envisioned. Earlier that year, the American Association of University Professors (AAUP) issued a revised statement on the place of faculty in the governance of college sport, calling for greater involvement in several areas and stronger action in furthering the reform agenda. In 2002, the Coalition on Intercollegiate Athletics (COIA) started as an e-mail network of faculty members from institutions in the BCS conferences, expanding the next year to become a coalition of faculty senates from all interested Division I-A universities. The coalition's purpose is "to promote serious and comprehensive reform … so as to preserve and enhance the contributions athletics can make to academic life by addressing long-standing problems … that undermine those contributions." In the meantime, the AGB aligned itself with reform-oriented faculty leaders to develop standards for governing boards in carrying out their intercollegiate athletics responsibilities.

In August 2003, the COIA, AGB and NCAA formed the Alliance for Intercollegiate Athletics Reform to

2004 (May) —Syracuse University wins its ninth Division I Men's Lacrosse Championship, more than any other school, before a record crowd of 43,898 fans at Baltimore's M&T Bank Stadium.

2004 (November 20) —Wartburg College's **Missy Buttry** becomes the first woman in any NCAA division to win three individual cross country titles.

2005 (January 10) —The Division I Board of Directors adopts an Academic Progress Rate, subjecting teams that fail to meet established minimum scores to possible penalties ranging from loss of scholarships to postseason bans and membership restrictions.

2005 (March 11-12) —The University of Wisconsin, La Crosse, wins its 12th team title at the Division III Men's Indoor Track Championships, extending its record.

2005 (June 24-26) —Division II brings together presidents and chancellors in Orlando, Florida, to discuss issues important to the future of the division. It is the first such summit in Association history.

2006 —Association celebrates its 100th anniversary.

PHOTO BY JEFF THOMPSON / NCAA PHOTOS

get collaborative efforts off the ground. The heads of the three organizations signed a letter to institutional CEOs noting their agreement on "the importance of presidential authority over athletics" and their conviction "that the success of reform requires broad-based support from boards and faculties." The Alliance partners also signaled their intention to participate actively in the AAUP's annual governance conference, scheduled for October 2003 in Indianapolis. The year of troubles was also turning out to be a year of cooperative endeavor on behalf of urgent change for college sports.

Myles Brand addressed the AAUP conference two months later. The theme of his speech was intercollegiate athletics at a crossroads. He minced no words, referring to "scandals on a major scale over the last several months." He said "coaches have been acting badly in ways that damage not only the integrity of their own profession but the credibility of college sports and, indeed, all of higher education." Further, "charges of academic fraud among student-athletes continue to plague some of the best institutions in the country." Brand returned often to the critical importance of the collegiate model and the threat to this model that was abroad in the land. The model, he stressed, "is firmly grounded in the education of students who participate in athletics. This is our target and should guide how we conduct intercollegiate athletics. If we fail at this, we fail at the notion that athletics should be associated with the academy at all … I am unbendable on this point." Brand went on to describe some positive features of the current college sports landscape, other problems that will need attention and some thoughts about what lies ahead. These were, taken together, an outline of at least some elements of a reform agenda.

THE AGENDA

THE SPECIFIC ISSUES are familiar. Some of them have challenged the Association for a long time. The context within which the NCAA is called upon to deal with them, however, changes regularly. Current realities dictate that old challenges be handled in new ways. Much of the work is already in progress. But there is a lot yet to be done as the Association begins its second century. Despite the progressive changes of recent years, governance remains a fit subject for fresh thinking. Amateurism concerns were present at the NCAA's creation, and though they differ now from those that confronted the founders and later generations of Association leaders, they are still contentious. Enforcement issues, especially recruitment and subsidization, were readily apparent before the Association got started and are as daunting as ever. Questions regarding finances, commercialism and broadcasting also have deep roots, plus increasingly consequential interrelationships. The challenge of diversity is relatively new for the NCAA, which has energetically addressed it in recent years. But there are promises to keep and miles to travel before this job is satisfactorily done. All of these issues are among the major items on the reform agenda for 2006 and beyond and warrant further discussion here. And there is one more item, in a sense the most important of all. If primacy of the educational mission is where the NCAA is to make its most basic case, as it must, then academic reform must head the agenda.

Academics. The Association began to link eligibility with academic performance with the 1.600 rule in 1965. That rule, which was more complex than the numbers suggested, fell victim to misunderstanding, home rule and the emergence of certain social forces. As we have seen, 1.600 was abandoned in favor of a simple, undemanding 2.000 GPA requirement in 1973. At about that time, as explained previously, George Hanford wrote his review for the ACE, noting the absence of campus CEOs from significant involvement with college sports. A decade later, the ACE, with a push from the College Football Association, became a prime mover of Proposition 48 (and followed up the next year with a proposal for presidential control of the NCAA that helped propel a more moderate approach to presidential participation, the Presidents Commission, into the spotlight). The initial-eligibility focus of Proposition 48, noted for its cut-score and attendant controversy, was an effort to reestablish the academic underpinning of athletics programs. Proposition 48 gave birth to an heir in

1992 when the membership gave initial approval to Proposition 16, with refinements still to come. More intense debate followed, aimed at the discriminatory character of the cut-score.

Meanwhile, the NCAA had begun to look at continuing academic eligibility as a way of shoring up educational primacy. When the research findings of the early 21st century demonstrated beyond argument that cut-scores produced problematic consequences, the Association, led by the Division I Board of Directors, abandoned that approach. The Board determined that the sliding scale should slide all the way, enabling low standardized-test scores to balance with high GPAs and satisfactory performance in an increasing number of high school core courses. That approach addressed initial eligibility, but the Board also decided that a better measure of academic potential is how student-athletes performed in class *after* they get to college.

This approach was initiated in 2002. The next year, the Association proposed a new method for calculating graduation rates whereby student-athletes who leave institutions before graduation and in good standing do not adversely affect the rates, and transfers who enter in good standing can be included.

This method, known as the "Graduation-Success Rate" (GSR), corrected serious problems in the required federal rate methodology. The Association began collecting graduation-rate data for all divisions, using the federal methodology with the 1984 entering class. The Division I data have attracted significant public interest, despite the survey's noted shortcomings. Generally, the annual reports have shown student-athletes graduating at a higher percentage than the overall student body and females performing at a higher academic rate than males. The rates of black student-athletes in Division I men's basketball and I-A football (sports in which general academic performance has often been substandard) have received substantial public and Association attention. They have typically been lower, and in some years much lower, than rates for white males in the two sports and for white and black male and female student-athletes in the all-sports calculations. The rates for black basketball and football players have exceeded the percentages for the overall black student body population, but that has been small comfort.

The GSR legislation was approved in 2003, with the understanding that its rates would be published annually, along with the mandated federal graduation rates. The NCAA also strengthened continuing-eligibility standards so that student-athletes (including junior college transfers) would have to complete 40 percent of their graduation requirements by the start of their third year, 60 percent by the fourth year and 80 percent by the fifth. The Division I Board of Directors then turned its attention to a "real-time" measure of academic progress developed through a complex data collection process each semester. Each team in the division — approximately 6,000 of them — is then assigned an Academic Progress Rate (APR) figure based on the data. Retaining academic eligibility and remaining at the institution are key factors in calculating the APR. The formula establishes a cutoff score that equates statistically with a 50 percent graduation rate. Teams falling below this rate can be subject to "contemporaneous penalties" if a player who is academically ineligible leaves the team. That player's vacated scholarship could not be filled unless an exceptions rule is met. Historical penalties, eventually using GSR standards, begin for institutions that continue to have teams falling below the cutoff score. They proceed from a warning, through scholarship and recruiting restrictions and postseason competition bans, to restricted membership. The Association is developing a rewards system for teams that consistently perform well on their APRs.

The first round of data collection took place in 2003-04 when information was gathered on 6,002 teams. Of that number, 363 (six percent) fell below the cutoff score. The figure for men's sports was 280 (10 percent) and for women's, 83 (2.6 percent). Football had the highest number of teams (61) and percentage (26) below the APR cutoff. Sixty-one baseball teams (21.5 percent) and 60 men's basketball teams (18.4 percent) also failed to meet the mark. On the women's side, basketball had the highest number (15) and percentage (4.6) below the cutoff. No contemporaneous penalties will be assessed until two years of data are available. Rolling four-year periods will be used to determine historical penalties.

APR legislation, coupled with more demanding continuing-eligibility standards, opens a new and promising chapter in academic reform. The clear intent is to materially strengthen the academics-athletics tie. When the 1.600 rule, the first effort to establish that connection, was eliminated, Byers described the decision as "a terrible day for college athletics." Institutional presidents were not much in evidence that day. Thirty-three years later, the presidents themselves have created much more demanding academic requirements than 1.600 and substantial penalties for teams and institutions that fail to meet them. Doubters have expressed reservations about this approach. But the change is a bold stroke — "the most sweeping academic overhaul in NCAA history," as one writer described it —

with a basis in solid research. It is the kind of action required if the collegiate model is to survive and prosper.

Amateurism. The first NCAA constitution contained a statement of the "Principles of Amateur Sport." The statement forbade:

> *Proselytizing, the offering of inducements to players to enter colleges or*
> *universities because of their athletics abilities and of supporting or maintaining*
> *players while students on account of their athletics abilities, either by athletics*
> *organizations, individual alumni, or otherwise, indirectly or directly; singling*
> *out prominent athletic students of preparatory schools and endeavoring to*
> *influence them to enter a particular college or university; the playing of those*
> *ineligible as amateurs; the playing of those who are not bona fide students in*
> *good and regular standing; and improper and unsportsmanlike conduct of any*
> *sort whatsoever, either on the part of the contestants, the coaches, their*
> *assistants or the student body.*

The language was attuned to its times, and while not specifically registering the elitist inclinations of the British leisure class, Britain was nevertheless its ancestral home. Most of the forbidden practices described here eventually were sanctioned by the Association, though not without a struggle. For nearly 50 years, the dominance of home rule meant that compliance with such principles was voluntary. In 1916, a definition of amateurism (amended in 1922) was set forth in NCAA bylaws. Its emphasis on the physical, mental and social benefits of athletics and on participation as "an avocation" has survived a history of abuse and adjustment. "Amateurism" has weathered the constant challenge of summer baseball in the early years, the later acceptance of recruiting and the approval of athletics scholarships in 1956. The concept has served as the foundation for a continuing assault on such scholarships as "play for pay" and therefore an abandonment of amateur principles. (The rationale for scholarships, however, is in part educational and in part based on the assistance they provide in assuring competitive equity.) The NCAA's fundamental commitment to amateurism saw it through a lengthy battle with the AAU — and along the way, the U.S. Olympic Committee — over the control of athletics competition in which college students were involved. The outlines of that often bitter contest were visible at the beginning. Government intervention, at the behest of U.S. presidents, sometimes was required to restore the peace. The Association stayed the course, and, with Congressional passage of the Amateur Sports Act in 1978, its place as the predominant power in amateur athletics was secured. The problems within the NCAA, however, gradually grew more complicated.

As the number of sanctioned sports increased — each with its own rules — bylaw provisions multiplied. The inconsistencies between them, and the divisions sponsoring them, became more evident. The spread of recruiting to foreign countries added to the confusion about eligibility and competitive equity. Exceptions and waiver-request policies differed from sport to sport. The Division I Amateurism and Agents Subcommittee was asked in 1997 to examine the growing problem. The subcommittee chair, Christine Grant of Iowa, explained its dimensions in a 2000 interview:

> *What emerges from an analysis of the current state of amateurism is an*
> *exceedingly complex series of problems because we … are attempting to*
> *collect accurate data in order to treat in a uniform fashion all prospective*
> *student-athletes in the world … These prospective student-athletes (national and*
> *international) belong to a vast array of sporting organizations, each of*
> *which has a different set of rules pertaining to amateurism and most of*
> *which cannot provide accurate records of financial transactions between*
> *the athlete and the organization.*

Most of the subcommittee's analysis focused on athletes' experiences before enrolling. Resulting recommendations were based on extensive research and a commitment to enhancing student-athlete welfare while assuring competitive equity. The subcommittee concluded that prospects should be permitted, before enrollment, to keep prize money from place finishes in competition. Research suggested that competitive advantage came from the level of competition and the length of time of an athlete's involvement, not from the acceptance of prize money. In addition, the subcommittee recommended that pre-enrollment student-athletes be allowed to enter the professional draft and be drafted, sign a contract to participate and accept compensation for participating with professionals. Any issue of competitive equity could be addressed through a research-based rule that would require a prospect to forfeit a season of competition for every year of participation as a professional. Also, one academic year in residence, without eligibility to play, would be required upon initial full-time enrollment. A few adjustments to the regulations covering post-enrollment issues were also proposed.

Some elements of Division I strongly opposed the subcommittee's recommendations. After a lengthy review, Divisions II and III approved some of the proposed changes. Both divisions accepted the post-enrollment recommendations. Division II passed legislation allowing prospects to enter the professional draft, sign a contract, play and receive compensation for doing so. The prospects have college sports eligibility after a year of residency and would lose a year for every year of organized professional competition. Division III agreed to the same changes except that prospective student-athletes could not be paid for professional work. Division I rejected all the suggested reforms even though that is where the greatest challenge to a credible 21st century commitment to amateur principles resides. Division I is the source of many requests for waivers of the amateur rules. Further, most of the difficulties over international competitors occur at this level.

To help ease the pressure, the NCAA plans to create and administer an amateurism clearinghouse that will certify international and domestic prospects and transfers in Divisions I and II. The two divisions will have to agree on some of the particulars for this arrangement to be effective. The clearinghouse could be operational by fall 2006, which would help, but major problems must be resolved beforehand. Still, a day of reckoning may yet arrive as intercollegiate athletics continues to deal with the expansion of the arena around the world.

Finances. In his Will to Act essay on what he termed "The Funding Dilemma," Dempsey discussed the misperception that Division I sports programs yield "vast amounts of profits … through gate, television and other revenue streams." The dollar figures do seem high, he said, with perhaps $4 billion in annual revenues coming into athletics department treasuries. The problem is that expenditures exceed $5 billion. He noted that the number of I-A members showing income higher than expenses had fallen from 48 to 40 in the last two years. That was in 2002. Dempsey's successor observed in 2004 that the number making a profit was two or three dozen at the most. Later, Myles Brand reduced the figure to 12, indicating that estimate might be on the high side. The dollar amounts are much lower in the other two divisions, but deficits are still present. From the perspective of divisional philosophy, the big difference is that Division I is dedicated to the "principle of self-sufficiency," meaning that support revenues should come exclusively from external sources.

With Division I institutions spending at a faster rate than can be balanced by new income sources, athletics departments frequently turn to corporations for help. That practice leads to accusations from critics that commercialism is on the rise and threatening to undermine the collegiate model. Outsized coaching salaries feed the passions here, and a marketplace logic can take over. These salaries are driven higher, either to retain coaches or hire them away. Success equates with winning. Winning generally means more gate receipts and television exposure. The perceived need for bigger, better facilities may enter the picture and add to the debt. Winning is important to help pay the bills. An arms-race psychology develops, and the need to win both that race and the games themselves can lead to rule-breaking. In this situation, educational primacy becomes ever harder to preserve.

That's the argument, and sometimes the financial dilemma pushes athletics programs deeper into the logic. The risk, in any event, is serious. However, some of the assumptions require careful analysis. In seeking corporate assistance, athletics departments behave very much like the universities that house them. Corporate citizenry in modern America is tied to philanthropy, and the result does not have to be excessive commercialization. Institutions are in the controlling position. As President Brand pointed out, the central question is not the source of revenues but their use. That is the case for both institutions and their athletics programs. There is nothing wrong with commercial revenue, Brand has said, if it is used to "provide opportunities for young men and women to receive scholarships and to participate in sports." The NCAA operates a successful corporate relations program on its own terms, supporting essential Association values and bringing in millions of dollars that assist the membership. It is a model the members can follow as well.

Recent studies suggest that much of the conventional wisdom regarding the compulsion to spend more is not borne out by the data. The studies examined a number of hypotheses, among them whether there is a correlation between athletics expenditures and success, and between revenues and success. The data showed no such correlations. Put simply, an investment of $1 produces a return of ... $1, and maybe less. Further, the evidence demonstrated no correlation between alumni giving and success, or between successful performance on the field or court and an institution's ability to attract better students. More students may enroll as a result, but they are likely to be much like the students a school already has. Limitations on the availability of data, it should be noted, mean that the absence of correlations in these areas could be demonstrated only for a medium term. Even so, the studies can have great value in helping Association members deal with the very real financial problems confronting them. They provide an insight also into a part of the arms-race question, concluding, for football and basketball, that it cannot be proven that increased expenses at one institution "are associated with increases at other schools." Even when it comes to expenditures on football stadiums, such a correlation is weak and appears to have significance only within conferences.

It is now a root assumption in the NCAA that growth in both revenues and expenditures in not sustainable and that the deficit situation is likely to worsen in the absence of a strategy to resolve it. Certainly, major Division I athletics department revenue increases in recent years — from television income, including the Division I Men's Final Four and the major postseason bowl games — have been substantial. But that growth rate seems unlikely to continue and doesn't extend to much of Division I or to Divisions II and III. Viewing audiences for the Men's Final Four, though they fluctuate significantly from year to year, are not increasing from a long-term perspective. For example, the audience in 1997 was 103,729,500, and for 2005, it was 99,921,060. In between, viewership dipped as low as 72,930,000. Annual men's basketball average attendance across all divisions shows little or no growth. The average in Division I in 2004, was exactly the same as in 1988 and has gone down during 10 of the last 13 years. It has decreased 13 of the last 15 years in Division II and 15 of 20 in Division III. The Division I men's postseason tournament attendance averages show no meaningful growth since 1998.

In football, I-A total attendance has enjoyed a 26 percent increase since 1991, although the annual average figure for 2004 is only 8 percent above the 1991 number. Total attendance in I-AA and Divisions II and III has been largely stable since 1978, but down in terms of the average between that year and 2004. Televised Division I football now fills nearly every possible time slot from Tuesday evening through Saturday night. Some weekend games start at 9 a.m. in one time zone or another and continue until midnight and beyond. Daytime games on weekdays, competing with NFL television on Sundays and Monday nights, or continuing to add to the number of allowable regular-season games appear to be the options left for expansion. With so many other entertainment choices such as the Internet and 100-plus TV channels splitting audiences, even expanding to these options may add little if any value. It is worth remembering that 28 years ago, shortly before the NCAA lost control over football television and just ahead of the emergence of ESPN, viewers had three network choices (ABC, CBS, NBC). The major bowls remain sources of big returns for the BCS schools, but growth in that limited market is unlikely to offset stable or declining sources of revenue elsewhere. Recall, too, what happened to football television after the Association was no longer in charge. Almost immediately, the buyers controlled a market the seller had previously owned, and the dollars going to campus athletics departments took a nosedive.

No source for the funding needed to match the rate of college sports' growth — for Division I in particular — seems apparent, given the current expenditure patterns and deficits. Self-sufficiency for most members has become a goal out of reach. This further complicates the reform agenda. Brand's view is that additional institutional funds to help balance budgets are defensible only "to the extent that athletics does in fact complement or directly provide part of the educational mission," and that "decisions about funding should go through normal university channels." One way or another, the revenue challenge must be resolved if the collegiate model is to govern college sports. Brand has appointed a panel of presidents, with representation also from institutional governing boards, to plan a future in which the financial challenges will be handled and the collegiate model will hold the line.

Diversity. Despite the advances described in Chapter Six, major challenges confront the Association and its member institutions in meeting their diversity obligations. In some areas, progress has stalled for years. Although the responsibility lies principally with the campuses, the NCAA, as the collectivity of those campuses, has a supportive role to play — in planning, priority setting, program development, resource assistance and, to a degree, in serving as a model for the members. The goals can be simply stated: (1) substantial growth in opportunities for women and minorities to advance to key positions and (2) improved results in meeting the mandates of Title IX. Regarding the latter objective, as previously noted and further explained here, a recent U.S. Department of Education policy clarification has changed the rules and, in fact, produced in the process more clouds than clarity.

For minorities, perhaps the most frustrating statistics are the number and percentage of African-Americans in Division I-A head football coach positions. According to the NCAA's 2003-04 race and gender demographics survey, there were then four black head coaches in the subdivision (2.9 percent of all such positions in I-A football that year, down from 5.6 percent in 1995-96 when six African-Americans had head coaching jobs in the subdivision). Black student-athletes playing I-A football in 2004, on the other hand, represented 45.1 percent of the total. At one point, after the end of the season that year, only two black head coaches remained in I-A. For the 2005 season, the number was up to four again. However, across all sports and divisions, the figures for black head coaches showed a 22.8 percent increase during the eight-year period. Division I also saw a significant gain in both the number and percentage of black assistant coaches in football. The head coach position in Division I men's basketball is another growth category, with Blacks holding 61 such positions (23.2 percent) in 2003-04, up from 50 (17.4 percent) in 1995-96. Overall, however, there was little growth as Division II showed no increase in number and Division III registered a decrease in both number and percentage. All of these figures are exclusive of HBCUs.

The administrative picture in the 2003-04 report — again, without including the HBCUs — is similar. African-Americans held 26 athletics director positions in the Association that year, an increase of two since 1995-96. Divisions I and II lost ground slightly during the period; the Division III number increased from eight to 12. Notably, though, the Association-wide number climbed to 33 by summer 2005. Until recently, little attention has been given to building a pool of qualified minority applicants, a shortcoming that NCAA-sponsored leadership institutes and coaching academies are intended to address. And, perhaps signaling an improved future trend, there has been a large increase over the years in the number of Blacks and other minorities serving as associate athletics directors, particularly in Division I.

DIVER LAURYN MCCALLEY OF THE UNIVERSITY OF TENNESSEE, KNOXVILLE, IS NAMED THE 2005 WOMAN OF THE YEAR.

Slow growth, if any, has been the story for women in key administrative positions among the member institutions. With all divisions included, the 2003-04 survey reported that there were 18 more female athletics directors than there had been eight years earlier. Of the 168 individuals serving in the position in 2003-04, only 22 in Division I were women, the same number as in 1995-96. Five of the 22 were in I-A. At the beginning of the 2005-06 academic year, that number again was five. The principal growth was in Division II, where a gain of 12 female athletics directors — to 43 — was realized. Division III continued to house most of the women in the position (103 in the recent survey). The latest data revealed that, across the Association, 18.3 percent of the athletics directors (7.9 percent in Division I) were females. Considerable growth occurred at the next level down. Between 1995-96 and 2003-04, the number of women in associate director positions increased from 228 to 397. The overall number of associate positions had a parallel growth, however, so in percentage terms there was little change in any of the divisions since 1995-96.

From the time women's intercollegiate competition began to flourish, the movement of men into the coaching ranks of women's teams has been a major concern. The salient point is a gradual but consequential decline in the percentage of females in head coach positions. In 1995-96, 56 percent of the women's teams at NCAA member campuses were coached by males. By 2003-04, the figure increased to 59 percent (as compared with 46 percent in 1984). There was no material change in Division I. The other divisions were down, 1 percent in Division II and 4 percent in Division III. On the positive side, there was a 10-plus percent growth in the number of women's teams, including increases in all three divisions.

A 1988-89 NCAA study of the subject concluded that, since the 1972 passage of Title IX, there had

MYLES BRAND SPEAKS AT THE 2005 WOMEN'S FINAL FOUR CHAMPIONSHIP BRUNCH IN INDIANAPOLIS.

been a "precipitous" decline in "the proportion of women serving in leadership positions (administration/coaching)." While the rate of decline has slowed since then, the problem remains unresolved. Salary differentials, limited opportunities for advancement and infringement on family life have been among the reasons cited for the lack of progress at the leadership level. From a broader perspective, the relatively slow growth in funding allotted to women's programs may be a factor. The NCAA's 2002-03 Gender-Equity Report noted that in "most measured categories women's athletics did not make any gains on their male counterparts" since the previous year. Changes in these categories, the report observed, "have not happened quickly over the past 12 years." More money was being spent on women's programs, and in some areas such as scholarships, funding increases for women's teams were greater than for men's teams. But proportionately, with funds for men's programs also growing, there were "no notable increases" in overall financial support for women's athletics since the 2001-02 report. Over the long term, female participation was certainly a substantial growth area, along with scholarship spending, but the same could not be said for expenditures in areas such as operating budgets and recruiting.

Participation rates, scholarships, recruiting and operating dollars are among the elements of Title IX with regard to which progress for women's athletics must be measured. There is a three-part test for participation. An institution is compliant if it can demonstrate that it satisfies one part (or "prong") of this test. In March 2005, the U.S. Department of Education's Office for Civil Rights, with neither notice nor opportunity for public input, issued an "additional clarification" of the third prong: Institutions can now use Internet-based surveys of their female students to demonstrate that they are accommodating the athletics interests and abilities of those students and thus meeting the third-prong requirement. In addition, OCR said women students who do not return the surveys can be counted as not interested in athletics participation. The idea of using student surveys, along with other measures, for passing this part of the test has been around for years. Relying on them as the exclusive determinant of accommodation has previously been considered an inadequate approach, now made more so by OCR's curious acceptance of non-returned surveys as no votes.

The Association responded quickly. President Brand, as mentioned in Chapter Six, offered an immediate criticism of OCR's surprising decision. A month later, the Executive Committee unanimously approved a resolution describing the clarification's likely adverse impact on women's intercollegiate athletics and urging the Department of Education to rescind it. The resolution noted the department's 2003 commitment, after a lengthy and controversial series of hearings by a commission it had assembled, to "strongly enforce the standards of long-standing Title IX" policies, that commitment being the reason this additional clarification was so surprising. Finally, the Executive Committee called upon member institutions to decline to use the newly authorized procedure. NCAA Senior Vice President and Senior Woman Administrator Judy Sweet concluded that if "we had such a piece of legislation in place in 1972, or in 1982, we would not be where we are today with increased opportunities and participation."

It seems possible, if not probable, that the designation of senior woman administrator, in the Association and on the campuses, might never have been created had there been no Title IX. It is part of a history of significant steps forward for women's athletics since 1981 when the NCAA began sponsoring women's programs. It is true, as we have seen, that the Association and its members resisted some of those steps and that there is a great distance yet to travel. It is of interest, even so, that on this occasion, taking issue as it has before with a policy clarification by OCR, the Association embraced the kind of expansive understanding of the goals of Title IX it had once resolutely opposed.

Governance. The new structure, approved by the 1996 and 1997 Conventions, was a product of two years of study, debate and accommodation. It represented a major change, and it created uncertainty on several points: Would there be too much federation and too little consideration of the common good? Would the presidents really take the time to accept the responsibility now provided them to be in charge of every division as well as the Association itself? Would Division I, and particularly the I-A equity conferences, take advantage of its superior position in the new structure to push its interests at the expense of others? Would the new process of rules-making work well? Would the annual Convention, having lost its key legislative function in Division I, continue to be a vehicle for enhancing communication and building relationships across the boundaries of division, position and geography? Given that the momentum for restructuring and much of its legislative detail had been provided by the equity-conference commissioners, would that group — as some believed — now be the true wielders of NCAA authority?

Since the starting point for restructuring was the white paper proposing that virtually every key decision in the Association be placed in the hands of the equity conferences, there was a reasonable fear that working for the common good would disappear while what became the major BCS entities ran the show. However, the good-faith negotiations that followed the white paper's release, the evolution of the Executive Committee toward a position of consequence, the leadership provided by presidential bodies and notably the approach to decision-making in the Division I Management Council and Board of Directors eased this concern. Compromises are sought, and often found, among the contending parties. Although all three subdivisions are represented on the Board of Directors, with I-A having a majority, the Board formed an advisory group of other I-AA and I-AAA presidents to help ensure that all sides are properly heard. The recent deliberations and final decision by the Board on I-A membership standards is a good indication of how the presidents have pursued a strategy of accommodation to good effect.

Still, restructuring has produced a changing of the guard in several ways. For one, the presidents are in charge. Conference offices in Division I are a much more important component in policy making. Athletics

Halftime at a major college basketball game in December 2003: A telecommunications company "staged a free-throw shooting promotion, giving away 100 free wireless minutes for each free throw made. A recording by Sly and the Family Stone filled [the arena], and to healthy applause from the crowd, a fan sank six free throws. Next, cheerleaders lofted T-shirts into the stands to promote a health club. … Later in the half, a boy played basketball against a giant inflatable milk carton promoting a dairy, and the Pepsivision scoreboard became an optician's 'eye cam', panning the crowd for the 'most beautiful eyes' in attendance." The home team band was mostly silent.
—FROM A STORY BY DENNIS K. BERMAN IN THE WALL STREET JOURNAL

administrators and faculty athletics representatives — major players in the prior structure — often feel far removed from the central business of Division I. In 2003, The NCAA News published columns by a FARA spokesman and an athletics director making that point and offering strong criticisms of the new governance arrangement. Quarterly rules-making received poor reviews from the start. Many people, presidents included, felt shut out of the system because of its burdens and complications. Later decisions made the process semiannual, and then annual. These changes have helped. The Convention certainly is not what it used to be. Divisions II and III still legislate there — each institution, as in the old days, having one vote — but Division I, with its representative approach, does not. The unfortunate result is that relatively few Division I delegates participate. At the 1997 Convention, the last one before restructuring took effect, 2,685 individuals attended. In 2003, the number was 1,603. Most eligible Division I delegates simply stayed away. CEOs from that division, who were sometimes out in force during the 1980s and '90s, are infrequent participants. Efforts to make the Convention meaningful for Division I continue but face a tough challenge. Another objective is finding ways to involve those who see themselves as out of touch with NCAA processes. The attrition, migration and division membership standards issues need major attention. The haves and have-nots situation in I-A is a governance problem, in part. If this gap becomes a chasm, as some think is inevitable, the Association will need to find an answer. And keeping in the forefront the obligation to retain and maybe strengthen the sense of common identity that makes the NCAA an association … that, too, is part of the governance challenge.

The presidents have had a long journey from the era when it was generally assumed they were either disinterested in NCAA affairs, or looked the other way, or both. They made the Presidents Commission work when a legion of skeptics thought it couldn't. They enhanced their position during the short but eventful life of the Joint Policy Board in the early 1990s. They managed restructuring during the middle of that decade. Now, the Association responsibility is theirs. The NCAA is controlled by college and university presidents and chancellors. One of their own is the organization's president. The challenges of governance are indisputably theirs to handle.

STAYING THE COURSE

IN THE EARLY 1990s, the NCAA negotiated a contract with CBS covering rights fees for postseason Division I men's basketball from 2003 through 2013. Under this agreement, the fees would increase year by year from $300 million at the outset to $764 million in the final year. Total income to be derived from the contract is $6 billion. In dollar terms at least, the Association has come a long way since the 1939 tournament — the first one — that left the organization $2,500 in arrears.

The $6 billion figure can be seen as a tribute to the drawing power of college sports. A second agreement, under which the NCAA receives rights fees from ESPN, provides another kind of testimony. This agreement began at $10 million for 2002-03 and will nearly double to $19 million-plus by 2012-13. It will bring $163 million in rights fees into the Association treasury over the life of the contract. ESPN's obligation is focused on Division I women's postseason basketball — a growth enterprise in itself. However, 13 other sports, from baseball to wrestling, receive coverage. Several involve both men's and women's competitions, and all three divisions are represented. It's not just the money in this case. It's the broad coverage, which exemplifies the attention given to sports of all sorts by today's media. A single ESPN has not been equal to the task of satisfying the public demand. Now there are several derivatives of the original network.

Elsewhere, fans can purchase packages that allow them to watch large numbers of college games in addition to those on regular network schedules. Skateboarders, cycle riders, Little Leaguers, log rollers, kick boxers, pool shooters, poker players, extreme skiers, iron-man (and woman) triathletes, dogs competing on obstacle courses and humans competing in games created for reality shows — all these and many more are virtually standard fare in the modern sports televison marketplace. Institutions provide live game feeds via computer as well as through local telecasts. Sundry pundits pronounce judgment on a surfeit of television and radio shows, call-in versions notably included. Newspapers offer columns on fantasy leagues. Other columnists regularly grade the performances of coaches and players. Children can watch make-believe contests on hand-held devices. Viewers of all ages can play video college football games replete with playbooks, mascots, fight songs, injuries and weather. It's all entertainment, and it is within this seemingly sports-saturated environment that the NCAA will launch its second century.

Concerns about intercollegiate athletics as commercial diversions are hardly new. Recall Professor

McKenzie's speech to the 1910 Convention pointing out that, after 1,200 years, sports in ancient Greece had reached a concluding era in which they took on the character of professional entertainment. He asserted that the college game in America had evolved into something close to that final stage. The stress on winning, construction of ever bigger stadiums, charging admissions and setting athletes apart (and often above) other students lent support in those days to McKenzie's claim. He had plenty of company at the time, and over the course of nine intervening decades, a legion of critics inside and outside the NCAA membership has sounded similar alarms. The entertainment emphasis arises with at least equal force now. When overdone, it presents a serious threat to the Association's commitment to education as the pre-eminent value of college sports.

Persistent and familiar themes, as we have seen, tell so much of the NCAA's story. There is, of course, more to that story than dealing with the entertainment challenge. Amateurism principles have had to be adjusted to suit changing times and circumstances. The standards established to guide institutional behavior have passed through a period when the 10-point code of 1922, the seven-part code of "unjustifiable practices" of the early 1930s, the Executive Committee's 1940 adoption of investigative and interpretive powers, and the Sanity Code of 1948 failed to make much of a dent in the doctrine of home-rule dominance. Standards came out the other side of that era to gradually fill rulebooks requiring nearly 1,200 pages of definition by century's end. The enforcement of codes and rules survived the age of home-rule failure to become — as Walter Byers described it — a bedrock NCAA function. The problems related to wagering on college sports that antedated the pari-mutuel betting on an 1876 intercollegiate regatta have never gone away. Association leaders complained of them often in the early years. Byers got his first tough assignment in finding a way to handle a significant piece of the basketball gambling scandals of the late 1940s. Assorted surveys have reported a persistent willingness of student-athletes to wager on college sports, the latest showing golf, lacrosse, football and basketball as the most likely to be bet on and, surprisingly, Division III student-athletes as the most likely bettors. The NCAA eventually created an office to highlight the gambling problems and ways for members to address them.

There are other themes that, though they may not stretch back across a century or more, have required frequent attention in recent decades. Federation is one such theme. Financing is a second. Academic eligibility is a third. Litigation has lately joined the list. Health and safety may be said to have given birth to the NCAA and to have led to passing interest for a while thereafter. But, apart from a periodic rhetorical nod, this theme became a consistent focus only in the last 40 years. And finally there is the question, regularly asked and differently answered since 1906, of who's in charge.

It started with students, well before the Association was established. As was noted in Chapter One, they did the hiring and fundraising, managed the programs, and sometimes even coached the teams. They were joined later by alumni, a development that ultimately both enriched alma mater and gave her cause to wonder on occasion whether the resultant pressure to win was worth the price. Faculty came into the picture when the student/alumni model proved unequal to the increasingly complicated task. They were the major force in bringing the NCAA into existence and in leading it through its first half-century of operation. Their influence waned as athletics administrators took on a greater role in governance and as the locus of coaching appointments moved out of physical education departments and into separate campus jurisdictions (a change with implications as well, especially in Division I, for the preservation of educational primacy). Then, as observed earlier in this chapter, along came the presidents. With that, the "who's-in-charge" issue presumably now has been settled. But there are other leadership roles, certainly, and related questions about who should be involved.

Leadership in the modern NCAA has to do in part with the need to balance interests and to bring meaningfully into the process those who speak for those interests. Restructuring has made this a more complex under-

Formal Opening of N. C. A. A. Headquarters Set Wednesday

Walter Byers, a Graduate of Westport High, the Executive Director, and Assistant Duke Wayne Tackle Problems of the Large Organization.

By Bob Busby.
(A Member of The Star's Sports Staff.)

KANSAS CITY, long a center of collegiate sport enthusiasts now quite

proper perspective within the bounds of the basic purposes of the higher educational system.

Origin in East.

THE KANSAS CITY STAR ANNOUNCES THE OPENING OF THE NEW NCAA OFFICE AND TRANSPOSES WAYNE DUKE'S NAME IN THE PROCESS.

FROM NCAA FILES

taking. The challenge in Division I to keep key campus constituents involved has been made more difficult by a regimen that now filters much input and many decisions through conference offices. Cedric Dempsey, who became the Association's CEO as the restructuring discussions got underway, has said that the biggest weakness of the new structure is the loss of direct contact between the NCAA and its member institutions in Division I. "The big picture became clouded by the conference office perspective," he observed, and giving up Convention decision-making resulted in the loss of a national dialogue. In such a context, he argued, parochial interests tend to dominate. A 2002 NCAA survey reported on other issues related to restructuring, one being, as noted earlier, the paradoxical situation whereby presidents firmly control Division I governance while the general involvement of CEOs from the division's membership has significantly declined. Focus groups used as part of the survey expressed strong concern that — despite Divisions II and III respondents' "especially enthusiastic" embrace of the new structure — as "division autonomy grows, the Association as a whole is diminished."

The need to balance competing interests, assure a proper voice and connectivity to groups like Division I athletics directors and faculty representatives, and strengthen the ties that bind NCAA members into an Association is not a subject of great debate. But there is disagreement about a component of the intercollegiate athletics mosaic over which the NCAA exercises no control — championship competition in I-A football. Irony is at work here. The sport that gave life to the Association and consumed so much of its energies over so long a time is now governed, at the top level, for postseason championship purposes, by an entity outside the NCAA's jurisdiction.

The Bowl Championship Series is principally the property of the equity conferences that led the way to Association restructuring. The other I-A conferences have a measure of access, recently provided. The NCAA itself has none, and those who govern the BCS seem convinced that none is necessary. In Dempsey's view, there is "perhaps nothing more representative of our basic problems than the BCS. It does not stand for what is in the best interests of the whole for football." Richard Schultz — commenting on what he saw as a kind of pyramid scheme through which substantial new facilities are built, ever higher salaries are paid to power coaches and significant debt is accrued by institutions in the major BCS conferences — has suggested that sooner or later "one block or another of the pyramid will crumble." A possible answer, he said, one that would bring the NCAA back into the I-A football championship picture (and probably produce significant additional revenue), would be playoffs configured as an add-on to the bowls. Equity-conference presidents have firmly opposed such proposals. Pursuing this kind of change would be a tall order for the Association's leadership.

Organizations, like the people who inhabit them, generally need time to absorb and operationalize major changes. Refinements are often necessary. Midcourse corrections often occur. Leaders have the responsibility of monitoring the pace of change and maintaining a protective balance between reform and organizational stability. Hard choices have to be made in the process. Tall orders may take a while. It is fair to suggest that the NCAA has provided from the beginning a forum for candid discussions of the need for intercollegiate athletics reform. If Palmer Pierce's "League of Educated Gentlemen" idea enjoyed a long emblematic reign, the language of annual Conventions and numerous ad hoc committees during that era was nevertheless often passionate, provocative and full of recognition that stern measures were needed to confront serious problems. Still, 45 years were required to move the Association from debate and occasional experimentation to a recognition that the problems could not be resolved without staff, budget and enforcement authority.

Despite protestations to the contrary from critics, the NCAA has proved itself receptive to consequential changes since 1951. When Byers opened the organization for business that year from a hotel room in Chicago and hired Marjorie Fieber as his secretary and Wayne Duke as his assistant, reform was at the top of the agenda. When Arthur Bergstrom joined the staff a few years later, enforcement became the face of reform. The growth of the Association was partially a response to the need for and implementation of substantial changes. The last quarter-century has been at once a period of transformation and restoration as the NCAA has taken steps to reassert itself as an entity founded on and committed to the predominance of educational values.

Change has been an almost constant companion in recent years. The Association moved its offices from Kansas City to Indianapolis, losing many key staff members and much institutional memory in the process but acquiring as well new ideas and fresh perspectives from their replacements. The responsibility to serve the membership, firmly anchored during Byers' tenure as CEO, has been expanded to include a "reasonableness" approach to handling cases where particular needs of student-athletes run counter to precedents established in interpreting the rules. Staff members have been empowered to inject their own judgment, based on the facts of the case, to ensure fair treatment. Discussions of additional staff empowerment have gone forward. In the absence of the national dialogue the Convention once provided, President Brand has moved — through speeches, broadcasts, op-ed pieces and, in general, a bigger bully pulpit — to engage a wider audience in a conversation about intercollegiate athletics and its problems and prospects. A new strategic plan that recommits the Association to the collegiate model of athletics informs this conversation. The plan insists on an understanding of "the supportive role that intercollegiate athletics plays in the higher education mission and in enhancing the sense of community and strengthening the identity of member institutions."

The plan is ambitious, as Brand has acknowledged. The collegiate model, he has said, is at risk. He told the delegates to the 2004 Convention that he wanted "to go on record in calling attention to this potential disaster." There is a drift toward the professional model, he said, and if the trend continues, the college game "as we know it will disappear and, with it, the educational value to student-athletes and the institutional good will and support from alumni and fans." To counter the threat, the pace of change, which has been rapid of late, may have to accelerate even more. Tall orders may need to be contemplated. Hard choices may be at hand. It will be necessary, as Brand has observed and as the implementation of the strategic plan will require, "to reconnect athletics programmatically and financially with the rest of the university." The entertainment emphasis will need to be kept in its proper place in the overall equation.

The NCAA's second century begins with this challenge. Help is available. Divisions II and III, as noted, are seriously addressing the substantial issues confronting them, with strong presidential leadership. Brand has formed a task force of Division I presidents, and its chair (Peter Likens of Arizona) has declared that "we see the trends of recent years as not sustainable." The group will examine mission and values, fiscal responsibility, student-athlete well-being, and presidential leadership. The Coalition for Intercollegiate Athletics, the organization that looks toward reform through an alliance of faculty senates in Division I-A institutions, has grown significantly. The COIA, which believes in the discipline and values of athletics and their contribution to community and institutional loyalty, proposes to work with presidents and others in strengthening academic accountability and establishing a program of automatic renewal of athletics grants-in-aid for a five-year period. The NCAA's branding initiative has helped change public perceptions of the organization from a decidedly low standing in 1998 to a more positive view — including a stronger sense of the Association's link with higher education — in 2005.

The NCAA has seen hard times and large challenges in its first 100 years. It has known failure and encountered dark hours. In its early years, it saw faculty harshly criticizing one another at its annual meetings, and presidents sometimes doing the same. It came through the "race of armaments" and "contest in dreadnoughts" after World War I and the excesses that followed in the Roaring Twenties. It has borne heavy criticism from a series of commissions, from Carnegie to Knight, and attacks from a long line of media and professorial commentators. It has experienced the comings and goings of a hundred (or more) special committees. It has absorbed major losses in courtrooms and withering recriminations in legislative hearings across the land. It has been inaccurately portrayed by the media and often enough by its own members as a kind of third party, peculiarly unrelated to the institutions that make its rules and are in fact its masters.

But the Association has also often answered the call, understood the challenges, made the changes, contributed to the successes, learned from the failures, punished the cheaters large and small, articulated the values, and dutifully and plentifully served its members. It has governed an enterprise that, for all its faults, has often been a place where difficult social problems like race relations and gender discrimination are seriously confronted. The old values of sport — discipline, teamwork, persistence and sportsmanship among them — can still command respect. The case that Dartmouth's Ernest Hopkins made in 1925 — that sports contribute greatly to a college's community life — can still be made. Intercollegiate athletics yet today, as William Howard Taft observed 90 years ago, can add to those "memories and associations" that help cement for alumni and alumnae lifelong ties to alma mater.

When those 28 delegates gathered at New York's Murray Hill Hotel 100 years ago for the first Convention of what soon became the NCAA, there was ample reason for grave concern about the future of the college game. The previous fall, football had known a season of discontent, and there had been others earlier. There were reasons to expect a short life for the new organization. But the founders persevered, as did their successors. They stayed together, and they stayed the course. For the National Collegiate Athletic Association, as it begins its second century, that option remains open. It is still the best option for college sports. ●

"Sports through their popular and ceremonial appeal to alumni could serve — and do still — as a core of identity and remembrance, their stadiums and coliseums bearing names and symbolic decorations of past triumphs that consecrate both field and court in ways impossible of application to classrooms or laboratories."
—WILFORD S. BAILEY AND TAYLOR D. LITTLETON, "ATHLETICS AND ACADEME"

THE UNIVERSITY OF DENVER ATTACKS THE NET AGAINST NORTH DAKOTA
UNIVERSITY DURING THE 2005 DIVISION I MEN'S ICE HOCKEY CHAMPIONSHIP.

Index

WISCONSIN'S PASCAL DOBERT LEADS THE PACK DOWN THE BACK STRAIGHTAWAY EN
ROUTE TO HIS VICTORY IN THE 3,000-METER STEEPLECHASE DURING THE 1997 MEN'S
DIVISION I TRACK AND FIELD CHAMPIONSHIPS AT INDIANA.